Newcastle
City Council

Newcastle Libraries and Information Service

☎ **0191 277 4100**

Please return this item to any of Newcastle's Libraries by the last date
shown above. If not requested by another customer the loan can
be renewed, you can do this by phone, post or in person.
Charges may be made for late returns.

HITLER'S PARATROOPER

HITLER'S PARATROOPER

The Life and Battles of Rudolf Witzig

Gilberto Villahermosa

Frontline Books
London

Hitler's Paratrooper

This edition published in 2010 by Frontline Books,
an imprint of Pen & Sword Books Ltd,
47 Church Street, Barnsley, S. Yorkshire, S70 2AS
www.frontline-books.com

Copyright © Gilberto Villahermosa, 2010

ISBN: 978-1-84832-559-3

CIP data records for this title are available
from the British Library

All illustrations courtesy of the Rudolf Witzig Collection
Maps created by Alex Swanston, Pen and Sword mapping department

For more information on our books, please visit
www.frontline-books.com, email info@frontline-books.com
or write to us at the above address.

Printed in Great Britain by CPI Antony Rowe

Frontispiece: *Postcard of Rudolf Witzig produced shortly after the fall of Eben Emael. Witzig autographed a postcard like this one for his future wife, Hanna, at a dance.*

CONTENTS

	Acknowledgements	vii
	List of Illustrations and Maps	ix
	Maps	xii
	Introduction	xvii
Prologue	Glory or Death	xxi
Chapter 1	A Child of War	1
Chapter 2	Fallschirmjäger	14
Chapter 3	Eben Emael	34
Chapter 4	Crete	74
Chapter 5	The Spearhead Shattered	98
Chapter 6	North Africa: First Battles	115
Chapter 7	North Africa: To the Last Man	137
Chapter 8	From Partisans to the Red Army	161
Chapter 9	Holland: 'No Longer War'	177
Chapter 10	Holland: Last Battles	202
Chapter 11	The New German Army and Retirement	220
	Notes	238
	Bibliography	253
	Index	262

ACKNOWLEDGEMENTS

In 2005, while assigned to NATO's northern region headquarters at Brunssum in the Netherlands, I was approached by a Belgian colleague who was aware that I was writing an article on the great Belgian fort Eben Emael and its conquest by a small group of elite German paratroopers in the Second World War. 'Gil,' my friend asked, 'do you know who led the assault on Eben Emael?' 'Of course,' I answered confidently, 'Rudolf Witzig.' 'Correct', responded the Belgian Army colonel, adding with a smile: 'His son is downstairs in the cafeteria.' And so I rushed quickly rushed downstairs and introduced myself to German Army Engineer Colonel Jürgen Witzig, then commander of the multi-national Civil Military Cooperation Group North. Jürgen and I quickly struck up a friendship, and when I told him I was working on an article on Eben Emael and needed information on his father, he quickly agreed to assist me.

Within a short period of time Colonel Witzig made available all his father's personal papers and photo albums for my use. It was an historian's treasure-trove, containing large segments of the Luftwaffe 7th Fliegerdivision's official War Diary, Witzig's personal diary from the war, notes, files and maps on the operation to seize Eben Emael, after-action reports on his battalion's participation in the North African campaign, the draft of an unpublished book Rudolf Witzig had written outlining the history of his parachute engineer battalion and regiment in the war and its battles in Belgium, North Africa, France, Lithuania and East Prussia, and a detailed family history, just to name the most important. In addition, there were numerous other magazine and newspaper articles and documents on Eben Emael and Crete. Finally, there were numerous Second World War history books with annotations in the margins made by his father.

Jürgen Witzig made all these available to me without any reservations whatsoever, explaining that he was preparing to deposit the bulk of this collection in the German Bundesarchiv and that it might not be available to researchers for some time as it had first to be properly organised. He also agreed to a number of interviews and patiently answered all my other enquiries via email. And he arranged for my wife and I to visit him and his mother, Hanna, in Mainz and to interview her as well. Finally, he put in me in touch with members of the German Patratroopers' Association, including some who had served with his father in North Africa, France and Lithuania. Like Jürgen, these veterans welcomed me and my project, which had now grown into a full biography of Rudolf Witzig, inviting me to their 2005 reunion, where I interviewed a number of them. They too proved warm and generous, providing me with photographs and documents and patiently answered all my questions. As a result, 'my cup runneth over' and I have amassed a wealth of information on Rudolf Witzig, his parachute engineers, and the German airborne forces in the Second World War. The result of that generosity is this book, a biography of the most famous German parachute engineer of the Second World War.

In the course of my research and writing, I have received support from many individuals and organizations. I am deeply indebted to the staffs of the National Archives and Records Administration in College Park, Maryland and the U.S. Army Military History Institute at Carlisle, Pennsylvania for their diligence in finding and reproducing the German interrogation reports so critical to this story.

I would like to thank my wife Natalie and our sons Alexander, Nicholas and Michael for their support, understanding and assistance during the several years it took to create this volume. All proved to be valuable proofreaders. Nicholas, a gifted writer, also edited the manuscript, while Michael, a talented photographer, spent several precious months working on the photographs. I am also deeply indebted to U.S. Army Historian, published author, and close friend, Lieutenant Colonel (Retired) Mark J. Reardon, who was involved in every aspect of the book's development. Mrs Barbara Sieber proved instrumental in translating many of the Witzig Collection documents from German into English and has also earned my gratitude. Finally, I would like to thank my editor, Deborah Hercun and the team at Frontline Books for turning a sow's ear into something better resembling a silk purse. Finally I would like to thank Michael Leventhal for his support and friendship. This book would have been impossible without both.

ILLUSTRATIONS AND MAPS

Illustrations

Postcard of Rudolf Witzig — Frontispiece

Witzig with fellow soldiers from 16th Engineer Battalion — page 2

Witzig on parade in 1935 — 3

One of Witzig's comrades from 16th Engineer Battalion — 4

Machine-gun training with the 16th Engineer Battalion — 5

An artist's representation of Höxter — 6

Commanders of the 31st and 57th Engineer Battalions in 1937 — 7

Witzig and classmates at the War School — 7

War School Cadet Witzig on horseback — 8

Witzig (left) and a fellow War School cadet — 9

16th Engineer Battalion on parade in 1937 — 10

A pontoon bridge built by Witzig's battalion during an exercise — 11

2nd Company, 16th Engineer Battalion, on parade in 1937 — 12

Fallschirmjäger troopers practicing parachute landings — 15

Parachute training, Airborne School, Stendal, 1938 — 16

A German paratrooper in the spread-eagle position — 16

General Kurt Student — 22

General Milch inspecting paratroopers — 25

Paratroopers at their base in 1938 — 26

1st Parachute Battalion during a ceremony at Stendal, 1938 — 27

The Fallschirmjäger emblem — 28

Parachute Battalion passes in review, 1938 — 31

An aerial view of Fort Eben Emael — 35

Model used to plan the assault on Eben Emael — 36

Aerial photograph of Eben Emael — 37

Eben Emael, a retractable armoured cupola — 39

One of Eben Emael's massive forts — 40

Drawing of the explosion of a shaped charge — 50

The effect of a shaped charge on an armoured cupola — 52

German experiment with shaped charges — 53

Battle damage at Eben Emael   54

Veldwezelt Bridge   57

Vroenhoven Bridge   58 & 59

A German soldier in front of one of Eben Emael's fortifications   61

Adolf Hitler with the CO of 51st Engineer Battalion   63

Lieutenant Gustav Altmann   64

Return of the heroes of Eben Emael   67

Commanders of Sturmabteilung Koch   70

Captain Koch being pinned with the Knight's Cross   71

Hitler shakes hands with Captain Koch   72

Witzig at Göring's Karinhall   75

General Milch decorating a Luftwaffe officer   76

General Milch at Karinhall   78

Hermann Göring and General Hans Jeschonnek   79

Göring with Koch and Witzig, May 1940.   82

Göring greets Luftwaffe recipients of the Knight's Cross   85

Göring with Milch and Witzig   86

Göring and recipients of the Knight's Cross   88

A Ju-52 en route to Crete   92

German wounded during the battle of Crete   95

Grave of Major Scherber on Crete   96

Witzig reporting to Milch after a parachute jump   99

A German paratrooper descends to the ground   100

Paratroopers at the German Airborne School, Stendal   101

Witzig during training prior to the battle of Crete   104

Generalmajor Meindl   105

Witzig recovering from his wounds at the Berlin Hansa Clinic   111

Witzig relaxing with friends in Berlin prior to the battle of Crete 113

Witzig receiving orders from Colonel von Broich   127

Witzig with one of his parachute-engineers in Tunisia   129

A street scene in Tunis   132

Witzig presenting medals to his men in Tunisia   138

Witzig giving orders in North Africa   141

Knocked-out British tanks in February 1943   146

Witzig as commander of the 18th Parachute Regiment   207

Witzig and Generalleutnant Hermann Plocher   211

Witzig with fellow officers after the war   228

Lieutenant-Colonel Rudolf Witzig of the Bundeswehr   229

Witzig and two other veterans visit Eben Emael   230

Witzig visiting Eben Emael after the war 231

German war memorial on Crete 235

Plates

(between pages 170 and 171)

Plate 1: Rudolf Witzig, the Eagle of Eben Emael

Plate 2: Witzig in a 16th Engineer Battalion sports competition

Witzig and comrades training in 1935

Plate 3: Witzig and friends off duty in 1936

Cadet Rudolf Witzig at the Kreigsschule in Dresden

Plate 4: Two views of practice jumps from a Ju-52

Plate 5: Rudolf Witzig with one of his soldiers in the field

Plate 6: Aerial view of Fort Eben Emael

Hitler with the conquerors of Eben Emael

Plate 7: Witzig briefing Hermann Göring in May 1940

Schmundt and Below, Hitler's aides, with Koch and Witzig

Plate 8: Göring with Witzig

Göring with Milch and Witzig

Plate 9: Hitler walking with Göring

Witzig with Göring's chief aide, Erich Gritzbach

Plate 10: Witzig asleep in Göring's Ju-52

Plate 11: Witzig relaxing outside Göring's train, August 1940

Witzig with Gritzbach

Plate 12: Witzig in front of one of the fortifications at Eben Emael

Witzig in Düsseldorf after the attack on Eben Emael

Plate 13: Witzig briefing a group of students in March 1941

Plate 14: Witzig's engineers at work near Jefna

Witzig at Jefna during the North Africa campaign

Plate 15: Propaganda image of paratroopers in action

Plate 16: Witzig and one of his lieutenants in North Africa

Maps

Europe under German Rule, 1941–42 xii

Fort Eben Emael xiii

Battle for Crete xiv

Belgium and the Netherlands, 1944–45 xv

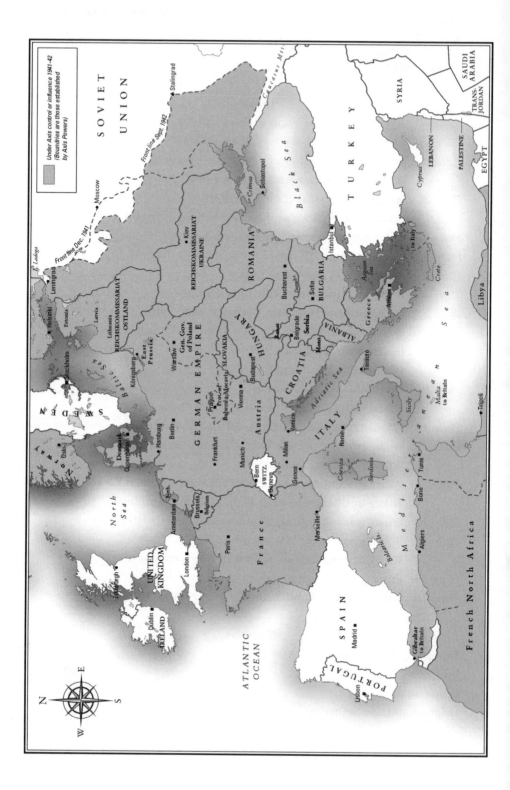

Under Axis control or influence 1941-42
(Boundries are those established by Axis Powers)

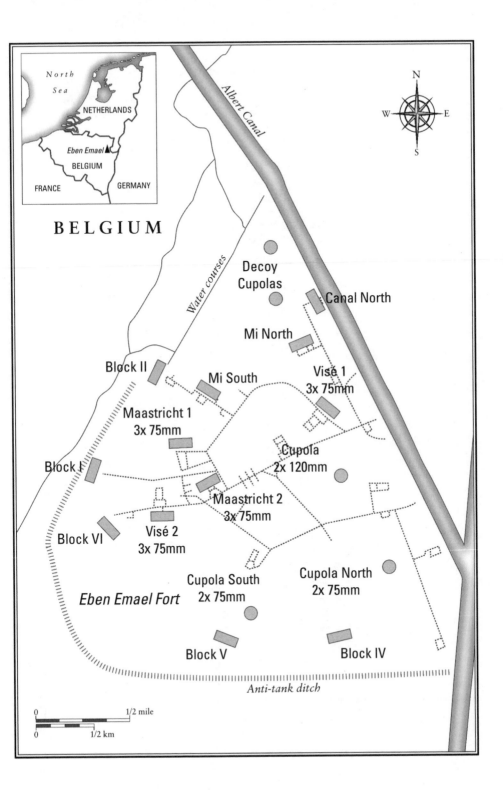

North
Sea

NETHERLANDS

Eben Emael ▲

BELGIUM

FRANCE   GERMANY

BELGIUM

Albert Canal

Water courses

Decoy
Cupolas

Canal North

Mi North

Block II

Mi South

Visé 1
3x 75mm

Maastricht 1
3x 75mm

Cupola
2x 120mm

Block I

Maastricht 2
3x 75mm

Block VI

Visé 2
3x 75mm

Eben Emael Fort

Cupola South
2x 75mm

Cupola North
2x 75mm

Block V

Block IV

Anti-tank ditch

0   1/2 mile

0   1/2 km

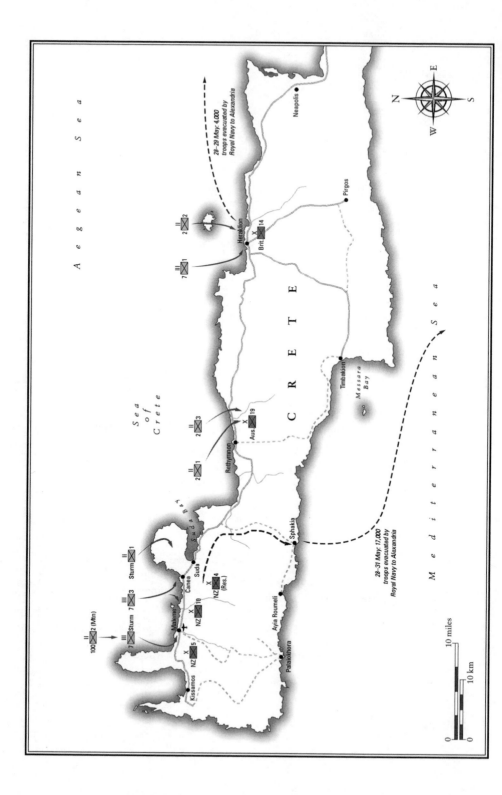

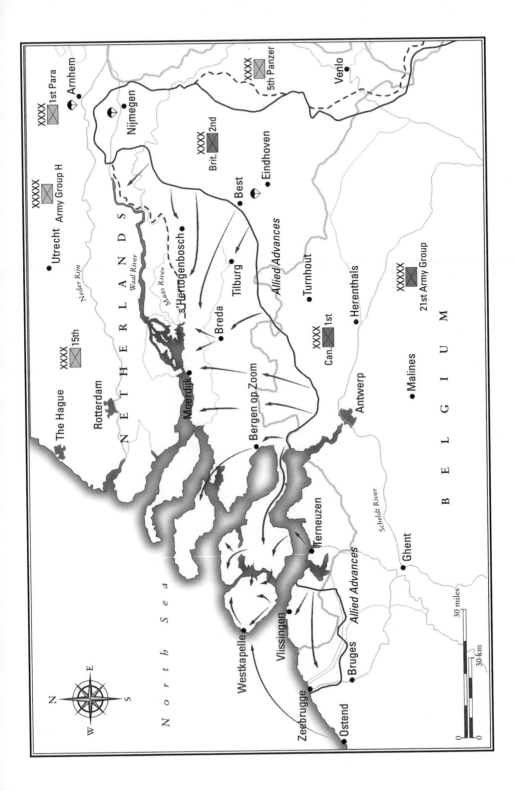

INTRODUCTION

Why another book on another German paratrooper? Hasn't enough already been written lauding and perhaps even mythologising these elite troops of the Luftwaffe, the German Air Force, in the Second World War? Certainly the more we know of the individuals who made up and led the Wehrmacht, the German armed forces, and especially Hitler's elite forces, his Fallschirmjäger or paratroopers, in the Second World War, the greater will be our comprehension of the conflict and the military organisations that managed successfully to overrun so much of Central and Eastern Europe, Scandinavia, North Africa, the Balkans, the Mediterranean and the Soviet Union so quickly. But almost as quickly as the tide of Nazi aggression inundated so much of the free world, it began to recede as it encountered stubborn resistance: first, against Winston Churchill and Great Britain's Royal Navy and Royal Air Force; and then against Stalin and the Soviet Union's Red Army. Britain's prolonged stand ensured that, as in an earlier world war, the United States would have to become involved, thus ensuring the final defeat of Nazi Germany. And Hitler's invasion of the Soviet Union, meant the destruction of the Wehrmacht and, within six months of Barbarossa being launched, the beginning of the end of the Third Reich. Thus, in a very short period of time, the soldiers of Hitler's Wehrmacht experienced the euphoria of victory and the sting of an agonising and prolonged defeat. One of those soldiers was Rudolf Witzig.

When I started this book I was struck by how little was available in either English or German on Rudolf Witzig, a German paratrooper of great distinction. This is in stark contrast to many histories and accounts of the Fallschirmjäger and individual German paratroopers in the Second World War. Yet even well-known English-language accounts of the capture of Eben Emael, Witzig's greatest triumph, provide only cursory information on the young lieutenant responsible not only for planning the operation that led to the capture of a multi-billion pound fortress (if built today), the last word in steel and ballistic concrete of its day, but also pioneering the tactics, techniques and procedures for the loading and combat use of gliders and shaped charges. It is as though the conquest of Eben Emael somehow had no connection with the man and the men who conquered it. Rudolf Witzig was the quintessential first-generation Fallschirmjäger. He was an elite soldier within an elite and extremely tight-knit brotherhood, and the only German parachute-engineer to win the prestigious Knight's Cross with Oak Leaves during the Second World War. In all, Hitler awarded that decoration to only fifteen German paratroopers. And Rudolf Witzig was also one of only sixty-nine 'Hunters from the Sky' to win the prestigious German Cross in Gold.

Witzig also has the unique distinction of being one of very few junior officers of any army in the Second World War, Allied or Axis, to be singled out in the official histories of so many of the participating countries, including the United States, the United Kingdom, New Zealand, and Germany. He was a lieutenant at Eben Emael in May 1940, where Hitler's paratroopers were used for the first time in conjunction with gliders and shaped charges to effect operational level results. He was a captain on Crete, where Germany's Fallschirmjäger played the major role in the unprecedented capture of a fortified island from an opponent more numerous than the invaders. Once again Hitler's paratroopers achieved strategic results. Witzig was a major at the time of the Allied landings in North Africa in November 1942, where he and his parachute-engineer battalion, rushed to the scene, played a crucial role in preventing the British and Americans from reaching Tunis and Bizerta and achieving an early end to the campaign. He and his paratroopers thus doomed the Allies to a long and debilitating attritional campaign. It was, however, a war that proved every bit as debilitating to Witzig and the Germans as it did to the Allies. The Allied invasion of Normandy in June 1944 found Witzig commanding another airborne engineer battalion, this time in France, and engaged in a frustrating struggle against French partisans. But, as the Allies streamed ashore in Normandy and prepared to break out of the constricting *bocage*, Witzig's battalion was rushed to the Baltic states in a hopeless attempt by Hitler to stem the tide of the Red Army's onslaught into the territories of the Third Reich. For the third time in as many years, his entire battalion was wiped out. Yet a short time later he found himself commanding a parachute regiment as a lieutenant-colonel in the Netherlands in the last battles of the war. There he experienced some of the most fierce and brutal fighting of the war. Long afterwards, he remained reluctant to revisit his experiences in Holland. Thus, despite his relatively humble rank, Rudolf Witzig's accomplishments on the battlefield brought him unparalleled recognition from his opponents.

Like his Fallschirmjäger and Wehrmacht comrades, Rudolf Witzig was very much a product of his time. He was born during the most bitter years of the First World War and saw the political and economic turmoil and upheavals of the Weimar Republic. He experienced the occupation of the Ruhr by French and Belgian troops and their shooting of a German citizen. Fortunate to have been born into a loving and economically viable family with a father, he lost that father at a young age and, like millions of other young German boys and girls at the time, was courted by the Hitler Youth and later the Wehrmacht. He volunteered to serve first in the Germany Army and then in the Fallschirmjäger at a time when the vast majority of young German men were being conscripted. He experienced the war from its first triumphant days, as the Wehrmacht swept across Poland, France, the Soviet Union, and North Africa, through to its last agonising weeks, as some 200 Allied divisions converged on the shattered remnants of Hitler's Third Reich. He had marched and fought across the breadth and depth of the war, from Poland to Crete and from North Africa to Lithuania and witnessed the decimation or complete destruction of three of his much-loved battalions. And yet he never broke faith with his oath to Hitler and Third Reich, defending tenaciously and counter-attacking fiercely until the very last days of the war. But when the time came to form a new German Army, Rudolf Witzig set out to prove that he was every bit as dedicated to the new Federal Republic of Germany as he had been to the Third Reich.

At the same time, though he was an ardent paratrooper and an extremely capable commander and soldier, Rudolf Witzig was never a member of the Nazi Party; nor was he ever required to have a political officer in any of his units – a benefit of being personally decorated by the Führer of the Third Reich while still a young lieutenant. Nor is there any evidence that Witzig ever internalised the teachings of the Nazi Party, despite his upbringing as a Hitler Youth. Indeed, when provided by the German Army with some eighty Jews from Tunis to dig defensive positions for his soldiers in November 1942, he recorded that they arrived without supplies of any type, including food and blankets, and returned them to Tunis unharmed, an act that sets him apart from most of his paratrooper and Wehrmacht contemporaries. Thus, by getting to know Rudolf Witzig and his Fallschirmjäger comrades better, we gain greater insight into the political and military organisations they were a part of, and a better understanding of the reasons for Nazi Germany's military victories and final defeat.

We are fortunate to have a treasure-trove of documents and unpublished interviews available to reconstruct Rudolf Witzig's life. The bulk of these come from his own collection in the possession of his son, Germany Army Colonel Jürgen Witzig. This collection includes Rudolf Witzig's personal photo album as well as two videotaped interviews. Where possible I have tried to let Rudolf Witzig speak in his own words, using his reports, documents or interviews. I have also conducted interviews with his wife, Hanna, and son, Jürgen, as well as with veterans who served with Witzig in the Second World War. A fifty-page interview, conducted by officers of the U.S. Army's Center of Military History in 1988 and covering Witzig's participation in the assault on the Belgian fort Eben Emael, provided new insights into that event. I have also made extensive use of the Headquarters United States Army Europe Historical Division's Foreign Military Studies Branch interrogation reports, first to set the scene for each phase of the war and then to provide the German perspective on the strategic situation as well as the situation on the ground at the time. Where Rudolf Witzig's own words were not available, and this is especially true of the fighting in Holland in the last six months of the war, I have used the words of other participants, most notably his army, corps, and division commanders. Copies of the relevant interrogation reports have been obtained from the National Archives and Records Administration in College Park, Maryland and the U.S. Army Military History Institute at Carlisle, Pennsylvania. I have also made extensive use of the Canadian Army Headquarters reports for the Second World War, published by the General Staff's Historical Section. The reports serve as the basis for the four-volume official history of the Canadian Army in the Second World War. And I have used the official histories of the key nations involved to place Rudolf Witzig's battles in their strategic context.

The result is the life and battle history of a single and unique German soldier who changed the course of the war several times over.

Prologue

GLORY OR DEATH

The German paratroopers sat silent and tense, crowded together in the wooden and fabric gliders bouncing them to their destination. Any attempt at conversation was drowned out by the roaring engines of their tow planes as the fleet of Ju-52s tugging the gliders sliced its way through the early morning darkness. No one dared to smoke, for the paratroopers were surrounded by thousands of pounds of high-explosive. Each man pondered silently the seemingly impossible task facing them. The mission they were about to undertake had never before been attempted. This small handful of elite soldiers would face more than ten times their number ensconced behind and beneath stone ramparts. Still, the German paratroopers radiated confidence, for they were young and had trained relentlessly for this moment. They were prepared for any contingency and were bringing into play two secret weapons never used before in combat. They were the elite vanguard of a mighty army, the likes of which the world had never seen. Some 136 infantry and armoured divisions, 2,500 tanks and armoured vehicles, and 2,000 bombers and some 1,800 fighters stood poised along the length of the German border, from the North Sea to Switzerland, waiting to sweep across the breadth of Western Europe, from the Low Countries, through France, and all the way to the English Channel.

But first that army, numbering more than two million men, desperately needed the bridges spanning the Maas River which separated Germany and Belgium. Jealously guarding those crossings were a series of ultra-modern forts, the last word in their day of ballistic concrete and steel defence. The queen of those forts and the key to victory was Eben Emael, a behemoth bristling with searchlights, anti-tank guns, and artillery pieces and occupied by more than a thousand Belgian soldiers.

The success of the entire German Army depended on these eighty-five Fallschirmpionieren, German airborne engineers, a new breed of soldier, led by a new breed of leader – a young and supremely confident lieutenant. His name was Rudolf Witzig and he and his men were headed for Fort Eben Emael. Witzig was immensely proud of his paratroopers. Each was a volunteer, a high-quality soldier of excellent morale. He had personally trained them and had himself developed the loading plans for the gliders they were riding into battle, as well as the tactics, techniques and procedures that would decide its outcome in the coming hours. Their success, and that of the whole German Army, depended on surprise, speed and audacity. This would be, for many, their first major combat action. Ahead lay glory or death . . .

Chapter 1

A CHILD OF WAR

Rudolf Witzig was born on 14 August 1916 in Röhlinghausen Westphalia, Germany to Rudolf Friedrich Witzig and Amanda Henriette Adolfine Ziehn. He was the third of four children. His parents had been married four years earlier in Kiel, his mother's home town. Rudolf Friedrich, who was from Magdeburg, had served briefly as a soldier in a German artillery regiment from October 1898 to August 1899, before sustaining an injury to his hand, which ended his military career. 'His conduct in terms of morale and duty was good,' recorded the younger Rudolf proudly in a family history many years later, when his own military career, spanning almost forty years, had ended.[1] The elder Rudolf then attended the Neustadt technological college near Mecklenburg, where he earned high marks. Afterwards he worked as a manager in the civil engineering field in Kiel and elsewhere. During the First World War he ran a machine factory in Röhlinghausen, which employed a large number of women and produced artillery shell fuses. After the war, he founded a large electrical company 'Witzig and Winter' in Gelsenkirchen, which dealt with large-scale manufacturing projects.

The younger Rudolf was born during extremely hard times. Germany was in its third year of the First World War, a war which had become 'total' for the home front. The food supply had become horrendous and civil war appeared in the offing. Ration cards were required to procure almost all foodstuffs, clothing, and even soap. Malnutrition was beginning to exert a terrible toll on the German population and mortality rates for women and children under the age of five rose by more than half as the national birthrate dropped by half.[2] Food shortages brought renewed and intensified labour unrest and increasing public protests, riots, and the plundering of grocery stores, mostly by women and youths. A wave of strikes by factory workers and coal miners, critical to sustaining the war effort, swept the country as food prices continued to soar, while incomes sank. 'Sacrifice, privation,

Rudolf Witzig (on the left) with a group of fellow soldiers from the 16th Engineer Battalion, III Motorised Corps, in Höxter in 1935.

death, on a huge scale, left Germans of all political hues bitterly searching for the reason why', writes historian Richard Evans, in the first volume of his monumental new account of Hitler's Germany. Young Rudolf was fortunate indeed to have been born into an economically viable family with a strong father present, especially a loving one. In the midst of widespread hunger, illness, and death, the Witzig family's existence appears to have been a comfortable middle-class one.

It is clear, from the family history written by the younger Rudolf long after the Second World War, that his childhood was a happy one and his relationship with his father, a close one. 'My father often went hiking with his children', he remembered. 'We learned to know our surroundings. He always had things to tell us, both funny and serious, and jokes and games were part of his nature. As soon as it was possible, my father took me along on excursions with my mother.'[3] The Witzig home was often filled with friends and music. 'My father loved company. Therefore, my parents often had guests in their house.'[4] Rudolf's childhood memories were thus positive ones. 'I associate the most beautiful childhood memories with our house', he recalled.[5] From his father, Rudolf learned a love of sailing, swimming, hiking, travelling, and even photography. 'My father took a lot of photographs, which he

Witzig (on the left) with fellow soldiers from the 16th Engineer Battalion, III Motorised Corps, in Höxter in 1935.

developed in his darkroom in the attic. Prints were produced in the daylight and sunlight in special wood frames under glass sheets.'[6] During a seaside holiday in 1924, the family watched a fire consume much of the town of Norddorf and young Rudolf witnessed his father rescuing his two sisters from drowning. Thus, by the time he was eight, Rudolf had learned the importance of family and friends, self-sufficiency, courage and camaraderie.

Rudolf recalled the harshness of life in Germany after the war, remembering the billeting of the Reichswehr, the Weimar Republic's army, in the area. He also recalled the expulsion of the Communist government council from Essen, and the French and Belgian occupation of the Ruhr in January 1923. 'There were captive balloons over the mines and metal factories', he wrote. 'Everywhere there were barbed-wire roadblocks and checkpoints at bridges and gates. Once, French guards shot a citizen dead. I can still see the endless funeral cortege, in top hats and umbrellas.' The impressions these scenes left on the young boy were 'unforgettable' and 'bad'.[7]

In 1923 the German economy reached a state of hyperinflation. By June the price of a single egg reached 300 marks and a pound of coffee cost 30,000 marks. By November the mark, which had been trading at

One of Witzig's comrades from the 16th Engineer Battalion wearing the German First World War steel helmet.

4.2 to the dollar in July 1914, was trading at 4.2 trillion to the dollar. The disastrous results of the runaway inflation left many children feeling frightened and dreading real or potential impoverishment, a feeling exacerbated by the high unemployment and wage cuts during the Great Depression, which rocked the country from 1929. Unemployment rocketed to 30 per cent and the catastrophic economic situation resulted ultimately in the fall of the Weimar Republic.

Rudolf Friedrich Witzig died of heart disease when Rudolf was barely eleven years old and his siblings only four, twelve, and fifteen. The loss must have been particularly devastating for the young boy, who adored his father. 'From that time, my mother carried the entire burden', he remembered.[8] The family moved to Kiel, Amanda's home town. There they were surrounded by her four sisters and their husbands. 'They were all pretty fond of us children,' remembered Rudolf, 'and the relationship among them – especially the sisters – was very close.'[9] It is perhaps significant that Rudolf records that the husband of Amanda's sister Ilse was an officer in the Kriegsmarine, the German Navy, for he does not mention any of his other uncles. Perhaps it is this uncle who provided the young and impressionable boy with the father figure and male role-model he needed after the loss of his father. And the fact that both his much-loved father and his uncle had been or were military men no doubt influenced Rudolf greatly in his choice of future career, for he was living at a time when German military men were being held up as national heroes. Indeed, Rudolf's younger brother George would follow in his uncle's footsteps and join the Kriegsmarine for U-boat duty.

Amanda rented a partially furnished house in Kiel and lived off the interest of devalued war bonds and a small rental income from Rudolf

Friedrich's business premises in Gelsenkirchen. 'We lived very thriftily without suffering from it,' Rudolf wrote later:

> She raised her children in this way, while allowing us sufficient freedom. She worked hard. She grew vegetables in the garden and did all our laundry by hand, sewed all the children's clothes herself and knitted and darned socks and took care of the rented rooms. And she did all of this without help from others.[10]

Still, she always seemed to have time for her children. 'One of my best memories is of my mother singing [Hermann] Löwe ballads and playing them on piano', he remembered. 'Even today I know the melodies and words.'[11] Amanda Witzig never remarried.

Rudolf's peaceful childhood days, however, were quickly coming to an end. On 30 January 1933, shortly after he turned sixteen, German President Paul von Hindenburg, appointed Adolf Hitler Chancellor. Two months later the Reichstag, the German Parliament, passed an Enabling Act, granting Hitler's National Socialist Party dictatorial powers. Hitler and the Nazis had come to power despite the fact that the majority of Germans – 56 per cent – had not voted for them.[12] Still, between 13 February 1919 and 30 January 1933 the Weimar Government had gone through no fewer than twenty different

Machine-gun training with the 16th Engineer Battalion in 1935.

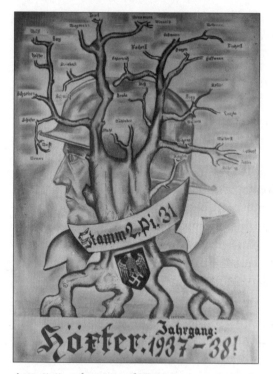

An artistic schematic of Höxter, a town in eastern North Rhine Westphalia on the left bank of the Weser River, from Rudolph Witzig's photo album. Hoxter was Witzig's first military home.

cabinets.[13] The German people were no doubt hoping for greater stability. Many sought strong leadership and a ruthless and even uncompromising willingness to strike down the enemies of the nation without compunction. They were not to be disappointed. The Nazi Party quickly assumed complete control over Germany's national life and future. A dictatorship was created and opposition was brutally suppressed. An extensive armaments programme, expansion of the small armed forces permitted the Reich under the Treaty of Versailles, and large public construction programmes brought the country a measure of economic recovery and improved its military posture. Germany soon regained a semblance of the position it had held as a European power before its defeat in 1918.[14]

To raise the Reich to what he considered its rightful place among the nations of the world and, more importantly, to accomplish his aggressive and expansionist foreign policy aims, especially the conquering of new *Lebensraum* ('living space') in the east and the protection of these lands through relentless Germanisation, Hitler needed large and well-equipped armed forces and the war industry to support them. Planning had already been prepared for a larger wartime force based on the peacetime Reichswehr. Hitler decided to apply these expansion plans in peacetime instead. The Army was to be increased from 10 small divisions (7 infantry and 3 cavalry) totalling 100,000 men to 21 divisions with a strength of 300,000 men. During his first summer in power Hitler also put an end to military and industrial collaboration with the Soviet Union, which had proven so beneficial to both sides. And later in the year his government withdrew from the disarmament conference then in progress and from the League of Nations.

Commanders of the 31st and 57th Engineer Battalions on parade in 1937.

Rudolf Witzig (front row, third from the right) and classmates at the War School in Dresden in 1936.

War School Cadet Rudolf Witzig on horseback, 1936.

Henceforth, Germany would follow a more independent path in foreign affairs, not allowing itself to be bound by such restrictions as the Treaty of Versailles, which the country had already violated repeatedly.[15] Hitler introduced universal military conscription in March 1935, ignoring protests from Britain, France, Italy, and the League of Nations, and had already begun the expansion of his armed forces.

In the meantime, Rudolf attended high school in Kiel, where he studied Latin and French, tutored by his mother. Already the Nazi regime was making itself felt throughout the German education system. 'With the Nazis' arrival in government, the entire teaching process in schools was subjected to many changes, the curriculum of history received very special attention and was altered drastically', remembered Henry Metelmann, one of Rudolf Witzig's contemporaries.

> I think it took less than a year before we were issued with much revised history books which showed a very strong underlying emphasis on the need for German *Lebensraum*. Those Kaisers, kings and military leaders who since the early Middle Ages had battled to find it in the east, were described as wise and forward-looking and given historic prominence . . . We were taught that German lands, having reached as far as the Black Sea and into what was now the heart of Russia, had through neglect been settled over many centuries by lower-raced Slavic people who had come from behind the Urals, from Asia. Much history was explained in terms of battles, wars, kings and great leaders, as if it were a process almost ordained by God.[16]

German youth were never allowed to forget the Treaty of Versailles. 'Though of course already strong on the curriculum during the Weimar days, Nazi teaching used it to explain almost everything that had gone wrong in Germany,' recalled Metelmann. 'Hitler in his many speeches simply called it *der Schandvertrag* ('treaty of shame') or *das Diktat*. It set the tone of so much in our young psyches to be directed towards revenge.'[17] According to Metelmann, the direct pressure on teachers to teach the line of Nazi ideology in almost every sphere showed itself outwardly in a gradual replacement of history books and methodical intro-duction of portraits of Hitler and paintings of battle scenes. 'Schools,' continued Metelmann, 'became little more than Nazi training institutes, where German youth were prepared for their eventual role in the ensuing world war.'[18]

Witzig (left) and a fellow War School cadet on an outing.

The 16th Engineer Battalion on parade in Höxter in 1937. Lieutenant Witzig served in and later commanded the 2nd Company of the battalion.

After the move to Kiel, Rudolf also joined the Deutscher Pfad-finderbund, the German Boy Scout Association. 'We spent wonderful days in our countryside hostel, an ancient thatched farm house in Schierensee, situated 15 kilometres south-east of Kiel,' he remembered, 'and on excursions to the surrounding area. These holiday trips brought us often to North Schleswig and Denmark.'[19] The Scouts were associated with the Bündischen Jugend, the German Youth Association, an umbrella organisation for youth groups not associated with any specific political party or religious organisation. Although many of the groups involved were right-wing (and even anti-Semitic), they were dissolved by the Nazi regime in 1933 and replaced by the Hitler Youth.[20]

After some time with the Scouts, Rudolf joind the Deutsches Jungvolk, the arm of the Hitlerjugend (Hitler Youth) for boys between the ages of ten and fourteen.[21] The Hitler Youth movement undertook both political indoctrination and military training for male and female members and sought to create a Nazi generation loyal only to Adolf Hitler. By the time Hitler had come to power there were more than two million members and three years later membership would reach more than five million, providing the Führer with the allegiance of 60 per cent of Germany's youth.[22]

The Hitler Youth held many attractions for Germany's young people. First was the figure of the omniscient and omnipotent father, Adolf Hitler, who provided immense guarantees of safety at a time shaken by continued economic depression and recurrent fears of war. Then there was the wearing of military-like uniforms, fitness training, military education and training, and a strong sense of community with like-minded youth. Young officers from the Wehrmacht (armed forces) often

A pontoon bridge built by Rudolf Witzig's engineer battalion during a field exercise in 1937.

The 2nd Company, 16th Engineer Battalion on parade in Höxter on 20 April 1937. Lieutenant Rudolf Witzig marches with the sword in the front row.

visited Hitler Youth camps, to inspire its members and arouse their interest in the military and the technology of war. This indoctrination and training helped reduce the time required to transform members of the Hitler Youth into German soldiers, sailors and airmen. Young German boys and girls of the Hitler Youth were also heavily subjected to racist teaching both at school and in the Hitler Youth camps. What Rudolf made of all of this is unknown. However, the Allied Second World War experience in Europe fighting fanatical German boys, especially during the last months of the war, shows that by the war's end there were many young Germans who accepted such teachings.

There is little to suggest that Rudolf was coerced into joining the Hitler Youth. On the contrary, like millions of young, patriotic German boys at the time, without a father and seeking to take part in the rebuilding of the Reich, he probably did so willingly. His father's own Army service, brief as it was, and his uncle's service in the Navy no doubt motivated him to emulate these male role-models. Military service was in his future and the Hitler Youth offered Rudolf an early entry into an organisation that prepared him to join his country's armed forces. Furthermore, in light of the instability racking the country, his mother was no doubt happy to have Rudolf in a secure and structured environment dominated by strong and positive male figures.

Once in the Hitler Youth, he quickly displayed considerable leadership talents, rising first to the post of Fähnleinführer, or patrol leader, and command of 90 youths, and then Stammführer, or company commander, and leadership of almost 300.[23] It is unlikely that Rudolf would have achieved this level of success without full commitment to the values and objectives of the organisation and it was his responsibility to inculcate those values in his subordinates.

Demographically speaking Rudolf Witzig was a prime candidate for membership in the Nazi Party, which was more successful in attracting middle-class voters than working-class voters, Protestants than Catholics, men than women, Germans who lived in the countryside and small towns, more than those who lived in the big cities, and Germans who lived in the north and east more than those in the south and west. And the Nazi Party had a particular appear for the young.[24] According to Michael Kater, half of the entire German student body had joined the Nazis by 1930.[25] Born and raised into a middle-class Protestant family living in a small town in northern Germany, Witzig could thus have been a poster boy for the Nazi Party. Still, both his wife, Hanna, and son, Jürgen, insist that Rudolf Witzig was never a member of the Nazi Party. Interviews with soldiers who served with Witzig during the war as well as a check of Nazi Party membership bear this out.[26]

By the time he was eighteen years old, Rudolf Witzig had matured into a serious and quiet young man. He possessed a good sense of humour, liked to laugh, and very much appreciated the German humourist, Victor von Bulow. He also appreciated a good play on words. Although he was 'strict' and 'straight', especially when it came to women and alcohol, he loved sweets (especially chocolate) and music and enjoyed singing. A sportsman, he loved the outdoors, from the mountains to the seas, and appreciated physical challenges of every kind. Frugal in every sense, he could encapsulate any argument or attempt at persuasion into a few words. He was meticulous in manner and had established a reputation as a detailed planner. Finally, though not stubborn, he was tenacious in his beliefs. In short, while he possessed many of those characteristics typical of the northern German, he was also his father's son in every sense and had a much more, easy-going and positive outlook on life and events than the typical northern German.[27]

Chapter 2

FALLSCHIRMJÄGER

In 1935 Witzig received his high school diploma and joined the Heer (German Army), as a Fahnenjunker, or officer candidate. He was nineteen years old. The same year service in the German armed forces became compulsory for all males. Thus, as a volunteer, Rudolf was unusual in that the majority of the almost eighteen million soldiers who served in the Third Reich's armed forces during the Second World War were conscripts. Only relatively few men, between one and two million, were career soldiers and volunteers.[1] Hitler's Wehrmacht enjoyed a much higher status than its counterparts in the West during the interwar period. From the time Hitler came to power in 1933, the Army was seen, and viewed itself, as an integral part of state and society in the Third Reich, and formed the second pillar of the Third Reich, alongside the Nazi Party. Especially after the introduction of conscription, the Army was also considered an essential part of the education system. 'Conditioning young German minds was one of the Nazi regime's priorities', notes Second World War historian Matthew Parker, 'great care being taken at various stages – when joining the Jungvolk at ten, the Hitler Youth at fourteen, and the Wehrmacht or Arbeitsdienst (Labour Service) at eighteen.'[2]

Witzig joined the German armed forces at a time of great political and military turmoil and upheaval. On 16 March 1935, Adolf Hitler once more publicly denounced the Treaty of Versailles and announced the introduction of conscription, increasing the size of the peacetime army to 36 divisions and 12 corps. A subsequent law, of 21 May 1935, brought the Luftwaffe, Germany's new air force, into the open and established it as a separate service. The law of 21 May also set the period of training for conscripts to one year. This was necessitated by a lack of trained cadre personnel. Fifteen months later the expansion of the armed forces would permit the extension of the period of service to two years. By October 1937 the active Army would have 500,000–

600,000 men under arms and consist of 4 group commands, 14 corps, and 39 divisions, including 4 motorised infantry and 3 Panzer (armoured) divisions. Twenty-nine reserve divisions would also be available to be called into service on mobilisation. The number of reserve divisions would grow as men were released from the active Army upon completion of their compulsory training.[3]

German Airborne School, Stendal, 1938. Fallschirmjäger troopers practicing their parachute landing falls.

At his induction, Rudolf Witzig, like every German soldier, was compelled to begin his legally established military obligation with the following oath: 'I swear by God this holy oath: I vow that I will render unconditional obedience to the Führer of Germany and its people, Adolf Hitler, the Supreme Commander of the Armed Forces, and that, as a brave soldier, I will be prepared to stake my life for this oath at any time.' If, because of an oversight, this oath had not been administered to a soldier, he was held to be in the same position as though he had sworn it. The oath was regarded as the affirmation of an inherent legal duty.[4] Even when it became clear, much later in the war, that Germany could not win, the vast bulk of its soldiers, sailors and airmen fought on, bound by their oath to Adolf Hitler and Germany to continue the struggle and sacrifice their lives.

German Airborne School, Stendal, 1938. A German paratrooper falling through the sky in the spread-eagle position.

German Airborne School, Stendal, 1938. German paratroopers in the air. Note the leather gloves to protect their hands.

One of the changes Rudolf would benefit directly from was the extensive building programme begun in 1935 to house the growing number of active Army formations. As a result, a large number of barracks, made of brick or stone and designed to house a battalion or regiment, were constructed over the next two years. Workshops and indoor training facilities were excellent and firing ranges for small arms, as well as open fields and wooded areas for limited field exercises, were usually located within a few kilometres of the barracks. Accommodation at the large training areas was also improved and expanded.[5] Photographs of the period show Witzig reading in a comfortable but spartan barracks room.

At the time that he entered the German Army there were three ways of becoming an officer. In the first, untrained volunteers, such as Witzig, usually at the age of sixteen or seventeen, enrolled for an unlimited period and entered the Army as officer applicants after a preliminary examination by a selection centre for future Army officers and non-commissioned officers (NCOs). A second route was one taken by conscripts already serving, who were under twenty-eight years of age and who applied for an officer career. These were first appointed reserve officer applicants, or if they had already attained NCO rank reserve officer candidates, by their regimental or independent battalion commanders. A note was added to their records indicating that they intended to become career officers. These were accepted as active officers upon graduating from one of the officer candidate courses, but first they had to attend a reserve officer applicant course if they had already attained NCO rank. Finally, professional NCOs could, after at least two months of service in the field, be appointed officer candidates and sent to an officer candidate course.[6] Witzig's route towards becoming an officer was a tried and tested one in the German armed forces and one followed by the majority of career officers. The demands of the rapidly expanding German armed forces necessitated a large influx of new officers and NCOs to lead the new formations. The 4,000 regular officers of 1933 would grow to 24,000 by 1939, and the number of reserve commissions would increase proportionately.[7]

The first phase of Witzig's training as a future officer lasted ten months and was oriented towards new volunteer officer applicants. It was divided into two periods: four months of basic training followed by six months of NCO training in an officer applicant school. The first part took place in a training unit, the second at an Army NCOs' school.

Witzig appears to have done both his basic and NCO training with the 16th Engineer Battalion of the III Motorised Corps in Höxter. As in most armies, initial military training was long, arduous, and realistic. Unlike in some armies, however, basic training in the German armed forces sought to replicate combat conditions as closely as possible. Recruits like Witzig trained day and night, rain or shine. Basic training was dangerous as live-fire exercises were routine in order to simulate combat conditions as realistically as possible. Often, soldiers were killed or wounded and the German military accepted a one per cent fatality rate as the necessary price for saving more lives later on the battlefield. Training was forward-looking and thorough and every soldier was taught to be able to perform not only his own job but that of his superior as well. Food was plentiful, if not always tasty, and most soldiers quickly put on weight and muscle. Personal hygiene and cleanliness were stressed and discipline was rigorously enforced. By the time basic training was over, soldiers like Rudolf Witzig had bonded with their comrades, developed a sense of group identity, and felt that they belonged to a mighty army indeed.[8] Witzig's photographs show him performing physical exercises with other soldiers, marching with full combat equipment, training with rifle, machine gun, explosives, and flamethrower, riding horses and motorcycles, and building bridges. A good many of the photos, especially those with friends, show him smiling.

All training in the German Army stressed individual leadership, initiative and mission-oriented tactics. Commanders were expected to give their subordinates broad orders and to leave the implementation of those orders to the discretion and experience of those subordinates. Such an approach provided maximum flexibility and initiative. 'Junior officers did not simply learn "school" solutions to the problems they might encounter, but were instead taught to think for themselves,' note Stephen and Russell Hart and Matthew Hughes, 'to apply their military knowledge and expertise, to have confidence in their own decisions, and to act upon them.'[9] The system worked well in the early years of the war but proved less effective in later years, after the Wehrmacht suffered enormous casualties and the quality of leadership and training declined.

Witzig's basic training was followed by six months of NCO training, during which he would have been trained as a squad leader and then promoted to NCO rank. Upon conclusion of these two phases of training, he would have been transferred to a field unit, for a period of not longer than three months, in order to demonstrate his leadership abilities in the field. Upon the successful conclusion of this part of his training he would have been appointed an officer candidate and sent to an officer candidate course.[10]

In March 1936, Hitler ordered German troops into the demilitarised zone on the left bank of the Rhine in clear defiance of the Versailles Treaty. It was one of the Third Reich's first steps towards renewed self-assertion in the international arena. The move was, in many respects, a bluff as German troops were under orders to retreat if they encountered any resistance and Göring's Luftwaffe was considerably smaller and weaker than the Western powers believed. Still, the Western powers' passive acceptance signalled to Hitler their military impotence and unwillingness to become involved in another European war.[11]

That same year Witzig attended the Kriegsschule in Dresden. 'War schools' such as these were equivalent to Officer Candidate Schools (OCS) in the United States. The officer candidate course was three to four months in duration and attended not only by those personnel who had passed the officer applicant training period, but also by conscripts and professional NCOs who had been appointed reserve officer candidates by their regimental or independent battalion commanders. This would have provided Witzig with exposure to a wide range of officer candidates with various levels of experience from all the various combat and support arms as well as from all over Germany. Towards the middle of the course, he, along with all the other candidates, was promoted to officer candidate staff sergeant. Upon graduation he was promoted to Oberfähnrich, or advanced officer candidate. After graduating, he attended an advanced officer candidate course lasting another three months. These courses were usually conducted at the specialist service schools and Witzig would have attended one of the engineer schools, to learn the basics of his role and responsibilities of a combat engineer officer. Upon graduation from this course, he was promoted (rather than commissioned) to Leutnant, or second lieutenant in the Heer.[12] His photos from the period show a smiling and slender, but well-built and muscular, young man with light hair and light complexion surrounded by close friends.

In March 1938, following the exertion of considerable pressure on the Austrian government, Austria was annexed by German troops, who crossed the border and were met by the almost universal acclaim of the

Austrian people. With this *Anschluss*, the unification of Germany and Austria, Hitler had created the Greater German Reich. Rudolf spent that summer cruising aboard the *Gorch Fock*, a large sailing ship of the German Navy, a reward for his outstanding performance during officer training. Witzig would retain a love for sailing all his life and was already showing talent as a photographer, meticulously recording each phase of his life in photographs. Later that year, Witzig returned to Höxter and was posted to the 2nd Company of the 16th Engineer Battalion. It was there, while taking dance lessons, that he met Gerda Remmers and her younger sister Hanna, who would later become such an important part of his life. The two sisters, the daughters of a local doctor, had enjoyed a relatively carefree and joyful upbringing in 'a nice big house and garden' in Höxter. The death of their ten-year-old sister Liesel, five years earlier, had, however, cast a veil of sadness over the Remmers household, especially for fourteen-year-old Hanna, who had been very close to her older sister.[13]

Still later in 1938, Witzig volunteered for duty with the new Fallschirmjäger or paratroop force, which had been formed only two years earlier. He was no doubt motivated by his drive to excel and to be a part of this new and elite force which accepted only the best. The Fallschirmjäger were part of Hermann Göring's Luftwaffe, the youngest and most 'Nazified' of the three services, and many paratroopers considered themselves 'true Nazis'. During the Second World War, the Fallschirmjäger would gain a well-earned reputation for boldness and determination in the attack and dedication bordering on fanaticism in defence, leading many Allied commanders to conclude that they were ideologically motivated. However, for the majority of Hitler's paratroopers, it was their training as elite troops and commitment to each other which was the primary factor that caused them to fight as well as they did. 'From the very earliest days of their formation Germany's would-be paratroopers had to demonstrate exceptional levels of physical and mental stamina, as well as the strength of personality needed to form part of a cohesive, confident and motivated body of men', writes one historian of Germany's airborne arm.[14]

The seed for the creation of the Third Reich's parachute forces had been sown five years earlier, in 1933, when Hermann Göring, in his capacity as Prussian Minister of Police, had formed a special force of the Prussian State Police, which used aircraft and paratroop detachments, to fight the German Communist Party's Red Front Fighters' League.

This force was so successful that it was expanded into a regiment called the *General Göring* Prussian State Police Regiment. When the Luftwaffe was formed in 1935, the regiment became a key component of the new service and Göring used this disciplined force as the foundation for Germany's first parachute battalion. Commanded by Major Bruno Oswald Bräuer, the unit was renamed the 1st Jäger Battalion, *General Göring* Regiment. Bräuer had won the Iron Cross First and Second Class during the First World War as an infantryman. After the war he was accepted into the Reichswehr and soon afterwards became a lieutenant. In January 1920 he joined the police and as a police major and then a lieutenant-colonel he led the *General Göring* Regiment's 1st Battalion. On 23 November 1938 he would become commander of the 1st Parachute Regiment.[15]

The Fallschirmschule, or Parachute Training School, was established in 1936 at the Stendal-Borstel airfield and the autumn manoeuvres at Bückeburg the following year witnessed an airborne assault by an entire parachute battalion. By the spring of 1937 the German Army had authorised the establishment of its own parachute infantry company, consisting of three parachute infantry platoons, along with a heavy-machine-gun and mortar platoon. Soon afterwards an independent airborne engineer platoon was formed. The following year this expanded into a battalion. 'At this point, it was not yet clear whether Fallschirm-jägertruppe [Parachute Forces] would be established and, [if so], if they would be attached to the Heer or the Luftwaffe', remembered Witzig. 'This is why there were two parallel battalions existing at the beginning.'[16] Because it lacked its own parachute school, the Army was forced to share the Luftwaffe's school at Stendal. Army paratroopers took the same course as their Luftwaffe comrades, under the latter service's supervision, before receiving the Fallschirmschützen-abzeichen, their qualification badge. Later all of Germany's airborne forces would be merged under the command of Göring.

On 1 July 1938 Generalmajor Kurt Student, a Luftwaffe officer, was appointed commander of Germany's fledgling airborne forces. As a deception measure, Student's new command was officially designated the 7th Fliegerdivision. Its mission was to capture terrain by parachute jumps and landing troop-carrier gliders. In addition, an Army unit, the 22nd Infantry Division, was trained and equipped for transport by air and designated as an air-landing division.[17] As he had recently completed an appointment as head of the Flying School Inspectorate

Student was already familiar with the Parachute School at Stendal and the conceptual arguments surrounding the development and employment of the new parachute arm. Hitler had ordered the 7th Fliegerdivision to be combat-ready by 15 September 1939 and Student had to resolve arguments concerning the employment of his new command. Student is rightly considered the father of Germany's airborne forces.

A unique soldier, Student's military career spanned three entirely different forms of government: the German Empire, the Weimar Republic, and then the Third Reich. He was and remained a monarchist at heart and both Hitler and Göring knew and respected this. Born in Neumark on 12 May 1890, Student had been commissioned as a lieutenant in 1909 and reported for pilot training four years later. He was one of the veteran 'old eagles' by the end of 1914. After the war he entered the Reichswehr. After several staff and troop postings he was promoted to Generalmajor and made commander of the 3rd Air Division. By this time he had already established contact with the Stendal Parachute School.[18] Student, who directed special attention to

General Kurt Student, Commander of the Luftwaffe's 7th Airborne Division, greeting officers at a German airfield.

the training and equipping of the division with air-landed artillery, flak, and anti-tank guns, believed the key to their success in battle lay in the fact that they were all volunteers and in their training.

> The first thing to do is to instil regimental spirit – to make a man proud of belonging to the parachute corps. This pride must stem from a comradeship which is wider and deeper than that of any other regiment or corps. Training must be based not on formal discipline based on fear and blind obedience but on the principle of mutual confidence.[19]

Several views were current among Germany's growing cadre of airborne commanders at the time as to the best way of employing airborne forces. One method, called 'oil spot tactics' consisted in creating a number of small airheads in the area to be attacked – at first without any definite point of main effort – and then expanding those airheads with continuous reinforcements until finally they ran together. Another consisted of committing airborne troops as a main effort to build up a strongpoint from the very beginning.[20] Student spent time considering the various options for the deployment of parachute forces and came to his own conclusions:

> In my view airborne troops could become a battle-winning factor of prime importance. Airborne forces made third-dimensional warfare possible in land operations. An adversary could never be sure of a stable front because paratroopers could simply jump over it and attack from the rear where and when they decided. There was nothing new about attacking from behind of course – such tactics have been practised since the beginning of time and proved both demoralising and effective. But airborne troops provided a new means of exploitation and so their potential in such operations was of incalculable importance. The element of surprise was an added consideration; the more paratroopers dropped, the greater the surprise. On the other hand there is always the danger that dropping a large number of men in close proximity to an alert and responsive enemy can produce an unpleasant surprise for the paratroopers. I have considered all these important questions very carefully.[21]

Success, however, would depend as much, if not more, on the quality of the individual Fallschirmjäger as on the doctrine pursued.

Recruitment in the German airborne forces was highly selective with recruiters on the look-out for particularly physically and mentally fit individuals weighing less than 85kg. Recruits came from many different sources, attracted by the possibilities of a new and more exciting branch of the armed forces. In the Luftwaffe many volunteers came from the ranks of those with more menial duties. In the Heer, group recruitment from existing infantry formations was common and it was in this way that the first Fallschirm-Pioniere Kompanie, or Parachute Engineer Company, in which Rudolf Witzig would later serve, was formed. The prewar period saw no shortage of recruits and eagerness to join the new formation only increased as paratroopers started to gain their wartime reputation, with the German propaganda magazine *Signal* featuring extensive coverage and photo-essays of the Fallschirmjäger in Holland, Belgium, Norway and Crete in 1940 and 1941.

Witzig attended the parachute school in Stendal in 1938. By this time it had been expanded to accommodate 12 training companies and 180 parachute instructors. The output of the school was 4,000 parachutists a year in peacetime, but later three branch schools were formed, which by war's end were capable of training 57,000 paratroopers annually.[22] The bulk of new recruits were eighteen-year-old volunteers. 'Any of three various motives had induced these young fellows, who were scarcely more than boys, to volunteer for the parachutists: idealism, ambition, or adventure,' remembered Friedrich August Freiherr von der Heydte, who would later command an airborne battalion during the bitter battle for Crete in May 1941. 'The idealist were by far the most difficult to handle', he recalled. 'Quite a few of them, who had been in the Hitler Youth and were saturated with national slogans, failed when they came to recognise that a soldier's trade is rough and that in time of war enthusiasm has value only when paired with knowledge, endurance, toughness, and self-control.'[23] It was these values that the parachute school sought to instil in its recruits. Heydte went on to note that the ambitious also presented their superiors with many problems as 'they were a latent danger to the feeling of comradeship and, therefore, to the morale of the troops'.[24] He concluded: 'I liked the adventurers best. They had jumped easily into life and they found it worth living, whatever it brought along, provided that it did not become monotonous. Their heads were filled with nonsensical pranks, but also with good ideas. They were born parachutists.'[25] This description fits Rudolf Witzig well and, based on his background and later performance

General Milch inspecting paratroopers of the Engineer Platoon, 1st Parachute Battalion, 1st Parachute Regiment, 7th Airborne Division in May 1939.

in the Second World War, suggests that he was a large part adventurer with a bit of the idealist thrown in as well.

Training lasted eight weeks and was evenly divided into four weeks of basic and four weeks of parachute training. Basic training consisted of an intensified version of standard infantry instruction, each recruit being taught the fundamental combat skills – including use of weaponry, demolitions, and tactical deployment – along with marching and parade-ground skills. This phase of the training was particularly strenuous and severe, with 30-km forced marches being common. The recruits were made particularly aware of the gulf of seniority between them and their qualified counterparts and instructors. Discipline, however, was not as severe as in other Army units, with as great an emphasis being placed on instilling the right attitude and self-belief system in order to enable the soldier to undertake some of the most demanding missions and combat duties in the German armed forces.[26]

All paratroopers remember this part of training as extremely tough. Martin Pöppel, a first-generation German paratrooper, assessed it as 'unbelievably hard, but basically fair'.[27] The weak were ruthlessly weeded out and the failure rate was high. Training began at six o'clock in the morning and often continued until late at night. Conditioning

Paratroopers of the Parachute Battalion march in formation at their base in Stendal in 1938.

included physical training, battle runs, and thorough familiarisation with the parachute and harness, accompanied by training in long-jumping, leap-frogging, falling, and rolling on the ground. Use was made of trampolines, towers, and stripped-down Ju-52 transport aircraft. 'You did not want to go on because you were absolutely shattered after days of training like that', remembers Robert Frett Loehr, another German paratrooper.[28] 'There were people who were so worn out and tired that they couldn't crawl to their beds', recalled Joseph Klein. 'They were so exhausted that they slept on the floor. We had three-tier beds and they couldn't make it up to the top.'[29]

If the recruit made it through the first four weeks then he was allowed to proceed to the part of training which would distinguish him as a member of an airborne regiment. Parachute training lasted for a further month. Jump training began on the ground and in the gymnasium, for the recruits had to master the basic body dynamics of jumping and landing, and also learn the theory of airborne deployment. After practising ground rolls until they came naturally, the recruits would jump from a mock aircraft door set at a height of three metres, leaping initially into sand. Then they would practise techniques of gaining their feet when being dragged across the ground by an open parachute, the 'wind' source being provided by the powerful propellers of ground-mounted aircraft engines. After all these skills had been mastered the new recruit proceeded to his first parachute jump.[30]

Only when his instructors felt he was fully ready was the recruit taken up in a transport, and only after a flight without jumping (to condition him to the sensation of flying, a novel experience before the age of mass air travel) was he permitted to attempt his first jump, made from an altitude of 180 metres from a Ju-52 transport. 'The first jump would be a nerve-racking experience', and there are many first-hand

Paratroopers of the 1st Parachute Battalion during a ceremony at their base in Stendal, 1938.

The Fallschirmjäger emblem.

accounts of recruits being utterly debilitated by fear', writes Chris McNab. 'The vast majority, however, did climb aboard the aircraft, entering with parachute static lines clamped between their teeth so as to free both hands for pulling them through the aircraft hatch.'[31] Succeeding jumps followed, consisting of varying groups of men at different times of the day and night and at progressively lower altitudes. The final jump, involving three twelve-man sticks in three aircraft flying at less than 120 metres was followed by a tactical exercise on the ground. Injuries were frequent and fatalities not uncommon. Between each jump parachutes had to be carefully washed, aired, and dried before being repacked – by the recruits themselves – for the next jump. Yearly repetition of the sequences was required to retain the Jump Badge. Every attempt was made to include jumps from the Heinkel He-111 (which required jumping from a centre hatch in the fuselage) and the Dornier Do-23. Only after he had successfully completed six parachute jumps would the recruit be awarded his jump badge and the title of Fallschirmjäger. The qualification insignia, the Fallschirmschützenabzeichen, featured a gilt diving eagle clutching a black swastika framed by a silver oval wreath (sometimes blackened) with laurel leaves on the left and oak leaves on the right. The badge was presented in a blue box with a certificate of achievement and its award, usually during a formal parade, meant the end of training. Fallschirmjäger training produced a superbly professional paratrooper. It was, however, both time- and resource-intensive and it later proved impossible to sustain under wartime conditions. This set the first generation of Germany's airborne arm apart from its wartime successors in terms of excellence. And it also meant that every first-generation paratrooper lost in Belgium, Holland or Crete proved virtually impossible to replace.[32]

A qualified paratrooper, the young and fit Witzig would later cut a striking figure in his standard dark blue Luftwaffe uniform with the distinctive 'Storming Eagle' badge on his left breast, which he wore in and out of the barracks. He would have worn the same yellow patches as other Luftwaffe troops on the collars of his jacket, but had his regimental title – dark green for the 7th Fliegerdivision – embroidered on his uniform cuff. In the field he wore the field blue side cap with the Luftwaffe grey eagle and national cockade. For battle he would don the field-grey paratrooper's helmet without a brim (to prevent the parachute lines from snagging in the helmet), thickly padded with foam to absorb the shock of a landing and marked with a forward-facing Luftwaffe eagle on the left side. The kid leather chinstrap was attached on both sides of the helmet and at the back, ensuring it remained on the paratrooper's head through the turbulence and shock of the parachute jump and landing. Over his equipment he would don the long, distinctive paratrooper jump smock, which opened in the front and was secured from neck to crutch by either buttons or a heavy-duty brass zip and which gathered and fastened around the top of each leg. Olive green in colour, it came down to the mid-thigh and had four pockets – two on the chest and two horizontal ones on the thighs. The national emblem was displayed on the upper right breast, while his rank badge was sewn on both upper arms of the smock. Field-grey in colour and made of wool or cotton twill, Witzig's paratrooper trousers had two side and two hip pockets and were normally tucked into his boots. His paratroopers' utility knife (also known as a gravity knife), which was intended to be opened with one hand to cut tangled parachute lines, was kept in his right-hand side pocket above the knee. He also had a boot dagger with a clip on the back, which could be carried on a belt, in a lapel, or down one of his boots. On his feet he wore special high-sided leather jump boots, which laced up the side. Black leather gauntlet gloves were also issued to protect hands from rope burns and lacerations. Other protective gear included early-pattern knee protectors, worn inside the trousers, or later-pattern knee pads, also worn on the outside, and elbow pads. A special ammunition bandolier, with twelve compartments each holding ten rounds of rifle ammunition and which had to be looped around the neck, ran down to the waistband, where it was tucked into the trousers. Getting ready for battle was complicated. Once the paratrooper landed, he was expected to remove his jump smock and then all his equipment and then to put his kit, including a water bottle, special-issue gas mask, spare magazines and hand grenades, back on again over the smock, a time-consuming endeavour in the midst of combat.[33]

Following airborne school Witzig was posted to the Fallschirm-Infanterie Bataillon, or Parachute Infantry Battalion. The battalion was first based at Stendal but would later move to Braunschweig. It was commanded by Major Richard Heidrich, a First World War veteran and winner of the Iron Cross First Class. Heidrich, who had served in the Reichswehr as an infantry officer, had formed the battalion as a major. In 1938 he was placed in command.[34] 'At first I served on the staff of the Parachute-Infantry Battalion', remembered Witzig, 'and in the late autumn of 1938 I took over the engineer platoon of the battalion.'[35] From 1938 to 1940 Witzig served as the commander of the airborne engineer platoon of what was now the Parachute Battalion, 1st Parachute Regiment. On 1 August 1939 he was promoted to Oberleutnant, or lieutenant.

During this period he was also exposed to the senior leaders of the Nazi Party and the German Army and Luftwaffe as his platoon participated in airborne demonstrations for the leadership. One photo shows Witzig reporting to General Milch and a host of other senior officers after having completed a parachute jump. Milch, who had overseen the development of the Luftwaffe in the prewar years as part of the rearmament of Germany, would later attain the rank of field marshal and, despite his Jewish origins (prompting Hermann Göring to declare: 'I decide who is a Jew!'), would be put in charge of combat aircraft development and production. His many mistakes would contribute to the Luftwaffe's loss of air superiority over Germany during the war.

It was also at Stendal that Witzig first became acquainted with General Kurt Student. The German parachute forces at this point were still small enough for all officers to be known to Student.

Shortly after Rudolf Witzig's promotion to lieutenant, German forces unleashed a massive surprise attack on Poland. In the early hours of 1 September 1939 Luftwaffe and Kriegsmarine units opened the offensive, heralding the beginning of the Second World War in Europe. The massive air attacks in the opening hours of the war destroyed the bulk of the Polish Air Force on the ground. Shortly afterwards, five armies of

The Parachute Battalion passes in review in Stendal, 1938.

the German land forces swept across the frontiers of East Prussia, Pomerania, Silesia, and Slovakia into Poland. In view of the superiority of the Wehrmacht, especially in modern tanks and aircraft, the speed of the German advance, and that fact that their own forces were exposed to German outflanking thrusts, the Poles could do little more than yield as little territory as possible, conserve their forces, and inflict the maximum casualties on the enemy pending the expected British and French offensives in the West. But the Allied attacks against Germany never materialised and the sudden Soviet invasion of eastern Poland shattered any hope the Poles had of holding out until they might. The last centre of Polish resistance, the Hel peninsula, fell on 1 October when 4,500 defenders surrendered unconditionally.[36]

At the beginning of the Polish campaign, Germany's parachute forces had been concentrated in camps on the highway between Berlin and Breslau (now Wrocław), ready to move to airfields near Breslau, from which they would emplane for a series of contingency operations planned by General Student. One of these was the capture of a key bridge spanning the Vistula River and the destruction of the Polish troops guarding it. The paratroopers assigned to this mission were already loaded and waiting to take off when the operation was cancelled. Later they learned that the Wehrmacht's fast-moving Panzers had seized the bridge first. It was the same for the other planned airborne operations. There was considerable disappointment among the

Fallschirmjäger, which soon turned to anger when various airborne units were sent off to perform what they considered to be relatively menial tasks, including guarding the headquarters of Luftwaffe Generalmajor Wolfram von Richthofen, a cousin of the legendary 'Red Baron', Manfred von Richthofen. Mid–September found the airborne troops protecting a series of forward airfields between the Vistula and Bug Rivers. The Fallschirmjäger thus saw little action in the Polish Campaign. In the course of the fighting one patrol of paratroopers clashed briefly with a Polish artillery regiment resulting in the first casualties for the German airborne corps. Sergeant Meusel was the first paratrooper to be killed in action.[37]

In Poland Witzig's platoon was was mostly occupied with building and repairing roads and bridges, and guarding prisoners. Unlike the majority of airborne troops, however, it did see some action:

> At first we were placed on standby in Upper Silesia. Even after marching into Poland, we still did not know whether there would be a [parachute] operation or not. Then, surprisingly came the order for Volarudowska. This was not an airborne operation, but a ground attack. From Upper Silesia, we drove in a convoy up to the [Vistula] river into the region of Dęblin. Outside Vola-rudowska [?] we made contact with Polish troops. They were the remainder of a unit that had pulled back, but they had to be fought and destroyed. It was with these that we had a battle. We took casualties on our side. It might have been fifteen casualties, one from my engineer platoon; the first one from the platoon. Then the Polish war was over.

In October the 7th Fliegerdivision returned to Germany and dispersed to its peacetime garrisons. Anxious to see action before the war ended, some of the paratroopers applied for transfers to the infantry. Witzig's battalion returned to Braunschweig and was soon after transferred to the Luftwaffe. 'They, the Wehrmacht, must have made the decision', reasoned Witzig afterwards. 'Göring was the strong man. He wanted to have them [the paratroopers] under his wings.' It was just as well. Soon afterwards the Army doctrine manual eliminated the independent engineer platoon in the infantry and Jäger [hunter] battalions altogether. 'That is why I had to leave my engineer platoon', lamented Witzig. 'The 7th Engineer Platoon; that is what they named it. It was then combined with the 1st Company, 1st Parachute Regiment, under Captain Koch and was moved to Hildesheim.'[38] Witzig's new company commander was Captain Walter Koch, one of the pioneers of Germany's airborne arm. A former policeman, Koch had joined the *General Göring* Regiment in 1935 and then completed the Parachute-Rifle Course in Stendal the following year. On 1 April 1938 he assumed command of the 1st Company, 1st Parachute Regiment and on 20 April he was promoted to captain.[39]

Unbeknownst to them, Adolf Hitler was already planning for the participation of his airborne troops in future campaigns. 'I told him of the paratroopers' disappointment and frustration during the campaign in Poland, and of the effect on their morale', wrote Student. 'Hitler listened attentively. "The paratroopers are too valuable," the Führer declared. "I shall employ them when I think the time is opportune. The Wehrmacht managed very well on its own in Poland, and I did not want to disclose what amounts to a secret new weapon." Hitler then went on to add: "They will certainly see some action in the West! And it will be a big show!"'[40]

Chapter 3

EBEN EMAEL

Planning for an attack against the Western Allies began even before the conquest of Poland was completed. On 27 September 1939 Hitler informed his commanders that he intended to unleash an offensive in the West as soon as possible. On 9 October Hitler issued Führer Directive No. 6 calling for an attack on the northern flank of the Western Front with the objective of smashing large elements of the French and Allied armies and capturing as much territory as possible in Holland, Belgium and northern France. His strategic goal was to create favourable conditions for follow-on air and sea warfare against Great Britain and to ensure the defence of German industries in the Ruhr valley. By January 1940 Hitler's strategic vision had broadened to encompass an attack on Norway and Denmark in order to forestall Allied intervention in Scandinavia and the Baltic Sea area, obtain air and naval bases to extend the reach of the Luftwaffe and Kriegsmarine, exploit the area's rich mineral resources, and provide security for the sources of Swedish iron ore. An incident in February, in which a British destroyer entered neutral Norwegian waters and recovered British prisoners from the German tanker *Altmark* convinced Hitler to speed up planning for the German occupation of Norway.[1]

Hitler's 1 March Directive for Case Weserübung (Operation Weser) outlined an air, sea and land invasion of Norway and Denmark and gave a significant role to the fledgling German airborne forces. Some seven groups of Ju-52 transports, consisting of 500 aircraft, would transport parachute and air-landing troops to Oslo and Stavanger in Norway and to Aalborg in Denmark. Those troops included the 1st Battalion of the 1st Parachute Infantry Regiment, which was tasked with seizing two airfields in North Jutland and the bridges connecting the island of Falster with Zealand, on which is located the Danish capital of Copenhagen, with the support of three battalions of the 305th Infantry Regiment. Two other companies would drop on the Norwegian Fornebu

An aerial view of Fort Eben Emael from the south-west.

airfield, seize and hold it, pending the arrival of two battalions of the 324th Infantry Regiment. The Germans began landing troops in Denmark and Norway on 9 April 1940. That same day the Danish Army halted its resistance and by 9 June the Norwegian Army had surrendered as well. In general, the airborne operations went as planned, although inclement weather forced the Germans to make some improvisations.

The German paratroopers were blooded in Norway and the campaign there served to demonstrate their immense potential. However, weaknesses had been uncovered and the German High Command had learned that heavy casualties would result from their improper employment. 'For Kurt Student, who had been promoted to the rank of Generalleutnant on 1 January,' writes German historian Volkmar Kuhn, 'this campaign had important lessons for the impending operations by airborne troops on the Western Front.' Rudolf Witzig and his colleagues took no part in the Norwegian campaign. Instead they were preparing for a very special mission. It would be in Belgium that the German Fallschirmjäger would display their greatest effectiveness and lethality in combat.

Located between Maastricht and Visé, Eben Emael was built between 1932 and 1935 to cover the Visé Gap to the north and the major crossings over the Albert Canal from the Netherlands into Belgium to the south. These crossings included the bridges at Veldwezelt, Vroenhoven, and Kanne. Situated atop St Peter's Hill, some sixty metres over the strategic Albert Canal near Caestert, the fort was in essence a reinforced artillery position and one of a series of four new strongholds constructed east of Liége after the First World War to defend Belgium. The most technologically advanced citadel of its day, it cost 24 million Belgian francs to build, the equivalent of about £2 billion today. Constructed in the shape of a rough equilateral triangle, with sides of 800 metres, Eben Emael had a surface area of 75,000 sq m, with the superstructure itself measuring 45,000 sq m.[2]

A small, self-contained, underground city, Eben Emael consisted of three levels. The lowest level, located almost sixty metres underground, was the living area. It was made up of large galleries, central stairs and

This model depicting Belgium's mightiest fort was used by Hitler's paratroopers to plan their assault on Eben Emael.

elevators, oil and water tanks, an electrical power plant powered by six diesel engines, barracks for the men and separate sleeping quarters for the officers, toilets, showers and washrooms, an armoury, and even a prison. The second or intermediate level, located forty metres underground, consisted of a system of tunnels and galleries four kilometres in length. With a few exceptions, all the fighting bunkers were accessible only via this level, which housed ammunition storage rooms under each bunker. These storage rooms were connected to the bunkers with lifts and stairs. The intermediate level also housed the air ventilation system. Finally, the upper level consisted of all the firing and observation cupolas and machine-

gun bunkers. Thick, hermetically
sealed armoured doors, resembling those found on a battleship,
separated the various levels and
parts of the fort.

Eben Emael's technical innova-
tions included air conditioning,
central heating, and a filtration
and overpressure system designed
to filter the air constantly and vent
dangerous gases. With its 1,200-
man garrison, including 1,000
artillery and 200 support
personnel, underground tunnels,
and robust defences, the fort was
thought by many at the time to be
impregnable. Indeed, in the event
of a war with Germany, the
French General Staff relied on the
fort to hold out for at least five
days.[3] And the Belgian Army's
eighteen divisions counted on its
border forts and their artillery as
their first line of defence. The

*Aerial photographs such as these were also
used for planning the assault on Eben Emael.*

forts, however, were never intended to stop the German Army alone,
but rather first to deter an attack by making the cost of offensive
operations too great and then to delay an advance and win time for the
Belgians and their allies to mobilise their forces.

On paper, Eben Emael appeared well designed and equipped to
accomplish this mission. Its defences included an intimidating array of
moats, anti-tank ditches, trenches, minefields, barbed wire,
blockhouses, real and false artillery cupolas, and observation cupolas.
Provision had been made for an emergency evacuation by the garrison
with the construction of three major exits and six emergency exits. In
addition to the seventeen bunkers in the fort, there were also two other
bunkers, at Kanne and Hallembaye, and six observation posts (at Loen,
Caestert, Opkanne, Vroenhoven, and Briegden) outside Eben Emael.
All were connected to the fort by telephone. Eben Emael was also
connected to the Belgium Army General Staff in Liége by both telephone

and radio. The fort literally bristled with guns, which provided a 360-degree defence. Eben Emael's main mission was to provide artillery support to the troops in the field. Its inventory thus included an impressive array of artillery pieces, including two 120-mm and sixteen rapid-firing 75-mm guns, a dozen 60-mm anti-tank guns, more than two dozen heavy machine guns and six light machine guns. The fort also boasted 19 searchlights for night combat. The 120-mm artillery pieces, mounted in a non-retractable cupola, had a range of more than 17 km, while the 75-mm guns, mounted in both retractable and non-retractable cupolas, could shoot 8 km, well within the range of the farthest bridge at Vroenhoven, only 7.5 km away. Finally, the 60-mm anti-tank guns could fire out to a range of 3 km.[4]

The fort's guns were manned by two groups of artillerymen numbering 500 men each. The men rotated on a weekly basis between duty in the fort and rest-and-recuperation at their barracks in the small village of Wonck, 4 km to the south. There were also 200 electricians, armourers, cooks, medical personnel and administrative staff. These men were billeted on civilians in the village of Eben-Emael or stayed in the wooden barracks located at the entrance of the fort. Commanded by a Belgian Army major, they worked eight hours a day.

The command relationship between the Belgian Army and the various batteries of the fort was excessively complicated and convoluted, diluting Eben Emael's tremendous firepower. The reason for this is unclear. While Eben Emael's commander and his fire-control office could give fire commands, the targets were determined by the Belgian field commanders themselves. Thus, Cupola 120, a non-retractable cupola with two 120-mm guns capable of revolving 360 degrees, was under the direct command of the Belgian I Corps, while Cupola North and Cupola South, retractable cupolas each containing two rapid-fire 75-mm guns capable of revolving 360 degrees, were allocated to the commander of the Belgian 7th Infantry Division. Maastricht 1 and 2, each containing three 75-mm guns, were under the commander of the 18th Infantry Regiment, while Visé 1 and Visé 2, each also containing three 75-mm guns, were controlled by the commanders of the 2nd Grenadier Regiment and the Lower Meuse Region respectively.[5]

Defending the Albert Canal in conjunction with the garrison of Fort Eben Emael were the men of the Belgian 2nd Grenadier Regiment. Although the unit was authorised 3,400 men (including 3,000 enlisted

Eben Emael. This retractable armoured cupola mounted two 120-mm guns.

personnel, 300 NCOs, and 100 officers), it was, like many Belgium formations at the time, understrength and numbered only 2,600 men. These grenadiers were responsible for defending a front 9 km long and 1·5 km deep. The regiment defended in depth along the Meuse River and Prince Albert Canal, with the 2nd and 3rd Battalions on the front line running from Kanne to Emael, Leon and Lixhe. The 1st Battalion was positioned on a line farther to the rear running from Fall to Weer and then Wonck. The 2nd Grenadier Regiment was supported by the 105th Artillery Battalion of the Belgian Army's 20th Motorised Artillery Regiment, located at Sichem.[6]

Thus, on paper, the defences of Eben Emael appeared imposing. Yet the fort and its garrison suffered from a number of critical deficiencies. There was, for example, insufficient barbed wire, minefields, or trenches near the bunkers or on the superstructure, where they were the most needed. Indeed, although Eben Emael's designers had never envisioned an airborne assault on the structure, the commander of the garrison, Major Jean Fritz Lucien Jottrand, had recognised the utility of the large flat meadow atop the fort's concrete roof and had considered using it for aerial resupply. It served, however, as a football

Another of Eben Emael's massive forts.

field for the garrison's soldiers, a morale booster in a unit and an army plagued with questionable esprit de corps, and it was probably for this reason more than any other that obstacles were not placed on the superstructure. Other critical defects were also evident. Some of the cupolas were missing their firing periscopes, rendering them useless. Furthermore, there were insufficient explosives in the fort to seal off its main gallery in the event of a breach by an enemy force, as called for by the Belgian Army regulations for its forts. And many telephone sets had been removed for use at a rifle range some 30 km distant. Moreover, the hilly terrain surrounding the fort blocked the garrison from firing effectively on Aachen or Maastricht, should the latter city fall to the enemy. In addition, the original ventilation system was defective, while a new one had not been fully installed. Finally, the fort lacked sufficient means to defend itself against an aerial attack. Its anti-air defences consisted of only four anti-aircraft machine guns situated atop the superstructure.[7]

The poor state of the Belgian garrison only aggravated Eben Emael's weaknesses. Training was at a very low level with many of the soldiers having never fired live ammunition. Furthermore, although they had been trained as artillerymen, the men of the garrison were also expected to fight as infantry and immediately launch local counter-attacks in the event of a penetration. As a result, morale among the men was low. Also, many of the soldiers were frequently absent from the their posts due either to throat infections, a common malady among those constantly exposed to the dusty and mouldy atmosphere of the forts, or special leave commonly granted to miners, farmers, and fathers of families with many children. All these shortcomings were well known to the Belgian senior leadership, which was attempting to rectify them when the war began.[8]

Planning for the assault on Eben Emael began on 27 October 1939, when Hitler summoned General Student to Berlin for consultations. Student remembered that Hitler presented his views on the use of airborne troops during the discussion that followed. Student's own philosophy on the use of his Fallschirmjäger would soon be put to the test.

> His opinions were explained with a clear sighted lucidity and with his own inimitable persuasiveness. I was astonished at his knowledge of what was virtually a new field – of the potential of gliders in particular. To begin with the Führer himself stressed that one had to realise that paratroopers and the airborne arm were a completely new, untried and – so far as Germany was concerned – still secret weapon. The first airborne operation had to employ every resource available, and be delivered boldly at a decisive time and place. It was for this reason, Hitler said, he had refrained from using airborne troops until there were appropriate objectives.[9]

Hitler had ordered planning for the war in the West to commence and wanted to know if Student's gliders and paratroopers could take Eben Emael by landing on the large grassy field on top of the complex and then storming the works. The rapid breakthrough of the German Sixth Army between Roermund and Liége depended on capturing the bridges over the Prince Albert Canal undamaged. In order to accomplish this, Eben Emael had first to be neutralised. Student replied that he was not sure and needed time to consider the proposal. Hitler, no doubt perturbed at having his competency questioned, responded: 'Go away and sleep on it and come back in the morning.' Returning the next day, Student told the Führer that he thought it possible, but only if the landings were made in daylight. Hitler agreed, then surprised Student again by telling him about the development of a fantastic new explosive, which weighed 50 kg and could blow through any known steel or ballistic concrete fortification. Called a *Hohlladung*, or hollow charge, this secret weapon would guarantee the success of the operation. Hitler then issued his order to Student outlining what he expected of the Fallschirmjäger in the coming offensive:

> 1. The 7th Fliegerdivision and the 22nd Airborne Division under Generalmajor Student will seize the Reduit National [the chain of forts along the Belgian border] and hold this important line of fortifications until the arrival of the mechanised columns of the Wehrmacht.
>
> 2. Parachutists and a glider-borne force are to launch surprise attacks on Eben Emael, and the bridges across the Albert Canal north of it, and the Meuse Bridges near Maastricht. The aim is to facilitate the speedy passage of the Sixth Army across the Maas and Albert Canal.[10]

After the war, Rudolf Witzig told two U.S. military officers interviewing him for the Army Center of Military History that there was another reason for the airborne assault on Eben Emael:

> It was essential to land on the fort and attack the artillery positions that protected the river and canal crossings in order to convince the French and the British that the Germans were making their main effort in the north. That is, attacking through Belgium as they did in the First World War. In fact, they did believe that, and to make it more believable, the Sixth Army had to strike into Belgium as quickly as possible, driving as far to the west as it could. Thus the enemy would say 'Ah, they are coming again just like in 1914. Move everything forward quickly!' Then the two armoured groups in the south could attack and set the 'Sichelschnitt [Sickle-Cut] Plan' into motion. In operational terms, that was the real mission of Koch and Witzig and the attacks on the bridges and Eben Emael.[11] * VON MANSTEIN,

Together with Colonel Bruno Bräuer, Commander of the 1st Parachute Regiment, Student selected Captain Walter Koch to seize the Albert Canal crossings and Lieutenant Rudolf Witzig to seize Eben Emael. 'The task came to my platoon simply because there were no other engineers in the airborne forces, which were still very small in 1940', Witzig explained. 'The [German] air force engineers simply didn't have the type of training we had undergone ... In our eyes they were not really engineers, but I suppose the correct expression would be "infantry engineers" – while we were real "black engineers".' Witzig was referring to the black piping worn on their uniform epaulettes by German Army engineers, though now his fully qualified Army combat-engineer platoon had been transferred to the Luftwaffe.[12] As a result of their long and comprehensive training and preparation, especially for assault missions, Witzig described his unit as 'a self confident' and 'proud group of men'.[13]

> My engineers, like Koch's infantrymen, were superior soldiers in every respect. There is no other way to describe them. There was not a single case of one wanting to withdraw. That was so because every one of my soldiers was a volunteer. They had first volunteered for parachute training, joined the parachute infantry battalion, and then came as volunteers into the parachute engineers. They were volunteers, high quality soldiers of good morale. I believe one could say in general that this was true not only of the airborne units, but also for the entire [German] army, air force and navy alike. The armed forces were at that time at their peak morale. Not that we necessarily reacted coolly to everything, but simply and plainly, the morale of the German army was, at that time, absolutely first rate.[14]

Witzig went on to observe that unlike his Army engineers, the Luftwaffe's parachute engineers, at least initially, had a far more restricted mission and thus restricted training. 'They were organised only for the so-called "demolition missions",' he noted after the war, pointing out that they had been originally trained and organised as 'human smart bombs':

> The parachute troops jumped in, marched to their objective, blew it up, and then tried to return to their own lines. How they got back was their own business. In the 1937 manoeuvres, parachute troops were supposed to have been picked up by aircraft after blowing up their targets. In fact, they wound up being given train tickets [for their return]! The army, on the other hand, organised its parachute units from the beginning for a full

range of tactical and strategic missions. Therefore, my engineers had expected more than just to supplement the standard air force missions, and had the training to do more than that. They were so well qualified that they were called upon in the winter of 1938–1939 to teach demolition techniques and certain engineer skills to other soldiers in the regiment.[15]

For the assault on Eben Emael, Witzig's platoon, which originally numbered 40–50, was reinforced to 70–80 strong. The additional personnel were all paratroopers from Captain Koch's parachute infantry company.[16]

Witzig received his orders directly from General Kurt Student in November. 'I was summoned to a discussion at the division staff at Berlin-Templehof, and was told about it then,' he recounted. 'At the same time Hauptmann Koch and Oberst Bräuer, the [1st Airborne Regiment] regimental commander, were informed. It was at that time we were given the mission.' Afterwards both Koch's 1st Parachute Infantry Company and Witzig's reinforced parachute-engineer platoon were detached from the 7th Fliegerdivision.[17] Later that month, Student ordered the creation at Hildesheim of a special battalion-strength airborne task force, Sturmabteilung *Koch*, consisting of hand-picked officers and men from the German airborne forces. Security was tight and Witzig and his men began practising assault techniques using the Polish fortifications at Gleiwitz. Commanded by Captain Koch, the detachment consisted of 11 officers and 427 men. This included 42 glider pilots and four reserve gilder pilots under the command of Lieutenant Walter Kiess.[18] The air component for the operation consisted of another 16 officers and 182 men and included a flying group of 44 Ju-52 tow pilots with four in reserve and a second reserve group of 6 Ju-52 tow pilots with one pilot in reserve. In all, some 84 tow aircraft and gliders were allocated to the operation. The air component was organised into four *Staffeln* (squadrons), one for each of the assault groups. Each squadron consisted, in turn, of two *Startegruppen* (sections), with three to six Ju-52s in each section. Thus the first squadron consisted of 11 aircraft, the second of 10 aircraft, the third of 9 aircraft, and the fourth of 10 aircraft for a total of 40 tow planes. A fifth squadron held all the reserve aircraft and pilots.[19]

For the assault on Eben Emael, Koch had divided his detachment into four *Sturmgruppen* (assault groups), each made up of roughly an understrength company of paratroopers. Each group was to seize and hold an objective pending the arrival of elements of the German 61st Infantry Division. Assault Group 1, code-named Granite, was commanded by Witzig and had the mission of eliminating the outer ring of forts at Eben Emael and neutralising the position until relieved by the 51st Engineer Battalion. Consisting of two officers and 83 parachute engineers, it would be transported into battle in eleven gliders. Assault Group Iron was commanded by Lieutenant Martine Schächter and had the mission of securing the bridge at Kanne and holding it until relieved by the German 151st Infantry Regiment. It consisted of two officers and 88 men and would be transported in ten gliders. Assault Group Concrete was commanded by Lieutenant Gerhard Schacht and had the mission of securing the bridge over the canal at Vroenhoven and holding it until relieved by the 162nd Infantry Regiment. The largest of the assault groups, it consisted of five officers and 129 men. The German High Command placed the highest importance on the capture of the bridges at Kanne, Vroenhoven, and Veldwezelt. For this reason the task force commander, Captain Koch, would accompany Assault Group Concrete into battle. Finally, Assault Group Steel was commanded by Lieutenant Gustav Altmann and had the mission of securing the bridge at Veldwezelt pending the arrival of the 176th Infantry Regiment.[20] It consisted of one officer and 91 men. With Assault Detachment Koch deployed in Belgium, the remainder of the 7th Fliegerdivision was assigned to attack Dutch airfields and bridges.

Each man in Witzig's platoon, which Koch had designated the 17th Reserve Squadron, was an experienced paratrooper, a veteran of the Polish campaign, and an expert in demolitions. 'We were the only parachute unit composed entirely of sappers, and all of us were volunteers,' Witzig wrote after the war. 'Among us were the best amateur glider pilots from prewar days when Germans already excelled in the sport of gliding; and during the two years of the unit's existence, it had grown into a sturdy, close-knit community in which each man had confidence in his fellow soldiers.'[21]

At Hildesheim, Witzig's company lived in a gymnasium at the airfield. It was there that he informed them of their mission without ever mentioning their objective – Eben Emael. Special restrictions were imposed on Koch's command and the area was surrounded with security troops. 'No one was permitted to leave the gymnasium without permission,' remembered Witzig. 'One could not send letters freely. Every letter, every postcard, everything that went out, I had to read. Everything that came in, I had to read. Total censorship, and for the soldiers, no permission at all to send mail or use the telephone.'[22] The paratroopers also had to divest themselves of their cherished airborne insignia and distinctive uniform items, a move which proved highly unpopular. 'My men wanted to wear their uniforms after duty hours' explained Witzig. 'They were proud of their first decorations and medals, their parachute badges. People recognised them for what they were and their uniforms drew women.'[23] In addition, special meals were arranged for Koch's command and the men were not allowed to associate with any other units on the base or even to take a stroll outside their quarters. And the punishment for any violations was severe. 'Just for example, three soldiers decided to leave the Kaserne for a cup of coffee,' recalled Witzig. 'They were apprehended, tried, and sentenced to death. Although the sentence was never carried out, it does indicate how seriously the authorities took our security measures.'[24] Witzig was also provided with a cell to incarcerate without food any soldier he placed under arrest. But because of the security arrangements, only his paratroopers could guard the cell. 'Naturally, my guards provided their friends with food as soon as I wasn't watching,' he recounted.[25]

> Security was vital, since our success – indeed our survival – depended on taking the enemy by surprise. No leave was granted, nor were we allowed out, or to mix with men from other units. The sapper detachment was constantly moved around under different code-names, and all parachute insignia and uniforms were left behind. Even glider practice in the Hildesheim area was carried out on the smallest scale possible; the gliders were then dismantled, moved to Köln in furniture vans, and reassembled in hangars surrounded by wire entanglements and guarded by our own men.[26]

As there was not enough transport available to move Witzig's platoon quickly in the event of an alert, it was transferred to Köln and Düsseldorf in order to shorten its travel time to the departure airfields at Köln-Ostheim and Köln-Butzweilerhof. 'In these places we were living a secret life under false names,' remembered Witzig. 'No one was allowed to know who we were and what we were doing.'[27]

Under Witzig's watchful eye, his assault group trained relentlessly, practising glider landings and developing and rehearsing tactics, techniques and procedures for neutralising their objectives. 'I was given only ten to fourteen days to prepare for the planned attack,' revealed Witzig. 'The anticipated date of the attack was 13 November [1939].'[28] Initially Witzig thought this was sufficient time to prepare for an assault on Eben Emael:

> In 1940 I was a 23-year old Oberleutnant. My knowledge of tactics and strategy was not really comprehensive. I was unaware of the large considerations. I was absolutely restricted in what I knew I had to have, and placed an uncommonly great trust in the command structure that assigned the mission. Expressed in another way, we had no misgivings that any part of our assignment was impossible or unreasonable. We were certain that we could succeed in such an attack . . . What we didn't know, we didn't consider unreasonable. This is something of a question of morale and trust as well as operations . . . What we had was sufficient.[29]

Witzig reported to Captain Koch periodically to inform him of his platoon's progress and how he planned to proceed with his training. 'Still, I was the specialist and not he,' Witzig noted. 'I had certain experience with attacking formal fortifications on the basis of my training, from my knowledge of theory, and from practice. He had none.'[30] Koch listened to Witzig's plans and facilitated logistical and administrative support to the parachute-engineer platoon, but left the matter of training and assaulting Eben Emael to his eager subordinate. 'When a mission is assigned an officer in the Germany Army, it is typical that the responsibility for training, planning, and execution are his alone,' recounted Witzig.[31] Witzig in turn sat down with his sergeants and discussed the entire operation thoroughly, working out how best to accomplish the mission using a sand-table model. 'They made suggestions and put forward ideas,' Witzig noted. 'And out of all of that our plan arose.'[32]

By February 1940 Witzig and his men had honed their demolition skills on the casemates of the Czechoslovakian Beneš Line, along the former Czech–German border, where they practiced assaulting strongpoints with flamethrowers and a large arsenal of explosives, including Bangalore torpedoes. This was a fortunate opportunity for the parachute-engineers. 'The Czech fortifications were considerably better secured and protected against infantry and engineer assaults than the Belgian ones turned out to be,' remembered Witzig. 'At the time I could only hope that the Belgian positions would be weaker. But I had no certainty about it, because the data available to us were not really sufficient.'[33]

Although this was an important part of their training, the preparation programme for the parachute-engineers also included other venues. 'Lectures at the sapper school at Karlshorst introduced us to the principles of fortress construction,' Witzig recorded. 'Finally deserters from Belgian fortifications were interrogated and we were able to check what we had been learning against the information they supplied. Thus, the picture became complete, and the sappers acquired confidence in their weapon: none of us would have changed places with anyone, not even with the men in the armoured forts.'[34] Witzig's papers reveal the full extent of German intelligence on Eben Emael. They include overhead photographs of the fort and detailed engineering diagrams of all aspects of the stronghold, inside and out.

> At first there were stereoscopic photographs [remembered Witzig]. Once you put on your stereoscopic glasses, you could see elevations and depths. Out of those photographs [the Luftwaffe Intelligence section] highlighted . . . particular factories or places . . . No single person in the engineer platoon even knew what this objective was called or where it was. The name of Eben Emael or Albert Canal was crossed or cut out of all documents or pictures. Nothing was left.[35]

For the assault, Witzig and each of his paratroopers would carry miniature maps of Eben Emael in a pocket-sized case.

Training was comprehensive and relentless. 'We exercised lifts, loading and unloading, and quick exiting of the plane,' remembered Witzig.

> As for all the preparation, the training was never executed in one complete step. The functions or tasks were broken into parts, so that a spectator would never even know what was going on. In the Pioneer School in Dessau, we trained in demolitions and attacking from the ground and air. In Sudetenland, we practiced on Czech fortifications, which were a lot more difficult than the ones at Eben Emael. We also trained with our glider pilots. They had to learn infantry/pioneer warfare; not just learn it but also master it.[36]

For the assault, Witzig organised his men into eleven squads, each consisting of two or three NCOs and four to six enlisted soldiers, a move necessitated by the number and carrying capacity of the Ju-52 and the load assigned to each squad to accomplish its mission. Each squad was tasked with capturing two emplacements or casemates and, in addition, to be equally ready to take over for any squad out of action. The first nine squads were given specific objectives to seize, while the tenth and eleventh squads were designated as the company reserve.

> Moreover, unlike other pilots, a glider pilot, who is in command up to the time of landing, cannot stand aside during the actual battle. So our pilots took their turn as sappers in the detachment and the section to which they were allocated so that they would be reliable in action.[37]

Witzig planned to position himself initially with the eleventh squad. His deputy company commander, Lieutenant Delica, would accompany the first squad into battle. 'X-Day was several times postponed, but our time was fully occupied in practising new techniques', Witzig went on to write, 'such as pin-point landing with explosives on an airstrip and in open country, or rapid disembarkation when fully armed.'[38] In addition to flamethrowers and collapsible assault ladders, which Witzig's men had constructed themselves, the special equipment for the operation consisted of some two-and-a-half tonnes of explosives, predominantly hollow charge devices, which were used for the first time at Eben Emael for penetrating the armoured cupolas.

Hitler's paratroopers would use two secret weapons in their attack on Eben Emael. The first were combat gliders. The Germans had developed the DFS 230 to insert squads of paratroopers armed and equipped to go immediately into action as a group, a task impossible to achieve with conventional airborne operations and the limitations imposed by parachutes. The DFS 230 was a fabric-covered glider with a tubular fuselage. Some 11·3 m long and with a wingspan of 29·1 m, it had a maximum towing speed of 160 km/hr and when released descended at 72 m per minute. The glider transported ten men, including the pilot, copilot, and eight fully loaded infantrymen sitting uncomfortably astride a wooden bench running down the centre of the interior. The last four infantrymen faced to the rear of the glider, where the door was located.[39] The one-tonne DFS 230 could also carry its own weight in supplies, a handy capability in light of the fact that Witzig's men would be

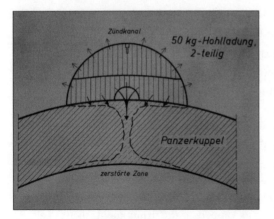

A German schematic depicting the explosion of a shaped charge on an armoured cupola.

transporting around 5 tonnes of explosives, including 28 x 50-kg shaped charges, 28 x 12·5-kg charges, 83 x 3-kg charges, and more than 100 other explosive charges. In addition, the assault group would be armed with six medium machine guns, 18 sub-machine guns, 54 rifles, 85 pistols, more than 30,000 rounds of ammunition, and almost 750 hand grenades. Each airborne engineer squad was literally a walking arsenal.[40]

Witzig's paratroopers were equipped with a second secret weapon, the shaped charge. 'We were the first soldiers to use them,' remembered Witzig. 'There was no experience for use of shaped charges in the attack, no doctrine for their use, and no programme of instruction. There were only the workers from the factories that made the explosives and the engineers and technicians from the Explosives Branch who had developed them.'[41] Although the theory of the shaped charge had been known since 1883, its first-ever military use would be by Witzig's airborne engineers in their attack on Eben Emael in May 1940. When a shaped charge detonates its energy is concentrated to the centre of the hollow space in front of and along the axis of the charge. A powerful jet of explosion gases results, which strikes the target at super-high speed (8,000 m/sec) and with tremendous penetrating pressure (in excess of 10 million kg/cm^2). To be most effective, the shaped charge has to be detonated at the right distance from the target. If detonated too close, the jet will not form properly before hitting the surface and the effect is lessened. If detonated too far from the surface, the jet is unfocused and weakened.

Witzig and his men were issued two types of shaped charge, one weighing 50 kg and the other weighing 12·5 kg.

> The 50-kg shaped charges, carried in two parts, were in the shape of hemispheres [Witzig wrote]. They could penetrate armoured domes 25 cm thick, and even where this armour was 28 cm thick, it was likely that weapons and troops below would

be put out of action by flying splinters. Where the armour was thicker still, several explosions in the same hole would be necessary. Even the smaller 12·5-kg charge penetrated armour of 12–15 cm and it was also suitable for precision blasting of loop-holes and heavy artillery. All charges were detonated by ten-second fuses.[42]

The men of Witzig's platoon were required to place the charges on Eben Emael's armoured cupolas, the large one in two halves which were joined. Upon detonation, pieces of the interior of the cupolas would be blown off to fly around with great speed, destroying and damaging equipment and wounding and killing the defenders. 'Remember that it wasn't necessary for us to force an entry into the cupola,' explained Witzig. 'It was only necessary for us to put the position out of action, and we could do that in some cases without breaking through the armour. That would be sufficient.'[43] Witzig's men conducted experiments to determine how close a man could be to a shaped charge so as to reduce the interval between ignition and detonation to as little as possible. They determined that ten seconds was the appropriate interval. Every soldier trained with the shaped charges, although not all had the chance to detonate one as available stocks were, according to Witzig, 'unbelievably small'.[44] Only a few of the soldiers carried the shaped charges. The rest of the assault detachments carried standard infantry weapons. 'A final stroke of ingenuity, characteristic of our thorough preparation, was the plan to drop by parachute several groups of uniformed dummies behind the Albert Canal to the west,' recalled Witzig. 'As we had guessed, this caused considerable confusion to the Belgian command.'

After six months of strict isolation and several postponements, the alert came in the afternoon of 9 May. That day Hitler issued a proclamation to the German soldiers on the Western Front, ending with: 'The battle which begins today will decide the fate of the German nation for the next thousand years. Now do your duty. The German people give you their blessing.'[45]

'We drove in trucks from Seldorf Flakkaserne – we were living in a new building, which wasn't occupied by anyone else – to Köln-Ostheim,' remembered Witzig. 'We had to load our machines in the hangars and had to wait and see what would happen.'[46] Platoon leaders checked their troops and ensured everything was ready. 'Having reported 'All

The effect of a 50-kg shaped charge on an armoured cupola.

ready' to Lieutenant Witzig at 2100, I paraded my troop and addressed them as follows,' remembered Lieutenant Ernst Arendt, commander of Witzig's 3rd Platoon: "'Comrades, we will be going into action tomorrow morning. We have to prove that we haven't wasted our time and that we have learned everything that we were supposed to learn." Then I dismissed them, telling them to get some rest.'[47]

Reveille the next morning was at 0245. The men of Assault Detachment Koch gathered at the airfields of Köln-Ostheim and Köln-Butzweilerhof. 'We paraded in full kit ready to emplane at 0330,' continued Arendt. 'Lieutenant Witzig then said a few words, concluding with the order *"An die Maschinen!"* ["Board the aircraft!"] We walked over to the gliders, climbed in, and at precisely at 0430, the eleven aircraft tugs took off towing us up towards the morning sky.'[48] The 0430 take-off had been planned to allow the four assault groups to land simultaneously, at 0525 hours, at Eben Emael and the bridges – five minutes before the German Army crossed the border. 'From that moment on we were in the hands of our pilots,' remembered Witzig, 'whom we expected to take us to the right altitude, at the right time and location ... Morale was good [but] tense. We were sure we had prepared ourselves as well as possible. The rest was up to us ... We were full of confidence.'[49]

The aircraft took off in complete darkness and started their journey through the night. They gained height by circling to the south then turned westwards, following a route which had earlier been marked with beacons and searchlights. By the time they reached Aachen the aircraft and gliders were at a height of 2,500 metres, giving the gliders a range of 30 km. The Belgian border was only 10 km away and Eben Emael only 25 km. Assault Group Granite travelled to its objectives in eleven DFS 230 gliders. The gliders were towed into battle by the tri-motor Ju-52. Beginning life as a Lufthansa airliner and evolving into an ad hoc Luftwaffe bomber during the Spanish Civil War, the Ju-52 found its greatest success during the Second World War as a troop transport. With a top speed of 276 km/hr and a range of 870 km, the Ju-52 could land and take off from very small airfields. Some 18·9 m long and with a 29·25-m wingspan, its most distinctive feature was its corrugated aluminium fuselage, which amplified the sounds of the three engines and forced the paratroopers inside to rely on hand-signals, klaxons, and lights. The stripped-down interior featured basic canvas seats on

The Germans experimented with various sizes of shaped charges on fortifications in Poland and Czechoslovakia before their assault in the West. Here a German worker sets a charge on an armoured cupola at Katowice in Poland in late 1939.

Eben Emael was impervious to German machine-gun and cannon fire, whose effects are visible on the outer walls of this fort. Shaped charges, however, brought the fort and its garrison to their knees.

which the German paratroopers flew into battle. At 0515 the tow planes released the DFS 230s, which still had some 30 km to go before reaching their objective. Two gliders were lost during the flight, including that of Lieutenant Witzig. Ten minutes later, at 0525, the nine remaining gliders began arriving over the fort, where they were greeted by belated fire from the four anti-aircraft machine guns located atop the superstructure.

Though surprised by the glider assault, the Belgian soldiers of the fort had not been caught napping. Indeed, the garrison had been alerted by their headquarters in Liége at 0030 – three hours before Witzig's force had taken off. 'Alert Fort Eben Emael!' had come the order. 'There are German troop movements along the border.' Two minutes later klaxons had begun sounding throughout the interior of the fort and Belgian artillerymen had begun moving to their positions. By 0315 the batteries were firing blank rounds at thirty-second intervals alerting members of the garrison in surrounding villages, the defenders of the bridges, and civilian personnel to the existence of a military emergency. The break of dawn heralded a clear sky with a wispy haze blanketing the fort.

At around 0500 hours a Belgian outpost north-west of Kanne reported 30–50 aircraft approaching from the direction of Maastricht at 1,200–1,500 metres. Soon afterwards an observation post called Eben Emael and reported: 'Aircraft overhead! Their engines have stopped! They are almost motionless in the air!' The DFS 230s descended to a height of almost 350 metres then flew over their objectives, executed a 180-degree turn, and completed their final approaches from the west, diving the last twenty metres and skidding to halt close to their objectives. The fort's machine gunners fired belatedly on the gliders as they came into sight, but the light aircraft were too low, too close, and approaching too fast to make effective targets, especially since the machine guns had been set for high-angle fire.

The skids of the gliders had been wrapped in barbed wire to help the aircraft stop more quickly. Even before they had stopped moving, however, the paratroopers in each aircraft hurtled out the rear doors with their weapons firing. Once the gliders had come to a complete halt the pilots and copilots quickly ejected the cockpit cover and joined the assault groups.

> We had been thoroughly drilled in our tasks [wrote Rudolf Witzig afterwards] and in the strict orders which our small number – eighty-five men, including the pilots and allowing for no losses during the flight – made it imperative to observe. Our earlier study of aerial photographs and a relief model, made to scale on a sand table, had convinced us that our initial assault had to be restricted to the central installations. First, we were to destroy all infantry weapons and anti-aircraft guns firing in the open and after that the artillery, particularly where directed north. Speed was essential, since anything not accomplished in the first 60 minutes would be made practically impossible by the increasing strength of enemy defence.[50]

As Assault Group Granite was landing, Ju–87 Stukas were pounding the towns of Kanne and Eben Emael and the soldiers of the Belgian 2nd Grenadier Regiment to prevent them from reinforcing the fort. Only five minutes later, at 0430, Hitler's armies began pouring across the Dutch and Belgian borders.

Witzig's was one of two sections that had not reached the fort with the main body:

> Soon after the start, the [tow] rope of my glider ripped and I was separated from the squadron. There wasn't a lot of space in the air. My tow pilot went into an abrupt dive to avoid a collision. That's when our tow rope, [which] was under too much stress, broke. The squadron was descending westwards and I was alone in the air with my glider. I told the pilot 'Turn back towards the Rhine! Try to get over the Rhine again!' because Köln–Ostheim and Köln–Butzweilerhof were on the eastern side. In order to start again, we had to get to the east side of the Rhine.[51]

Witzig's squads moved quickly into action and the specially trained airborne engineers began assaulting their assigned objectives using flamethrowers, special explosives, and shaped charges.

> Anti-aircraft Post 1 was captured immediately [he reported]. The occupants of Hut 2 offered some resistance, but were soon silenced, and in the first ten minutes the sections successfully attacked nine occupied and defended installations . . . although [one] installation . . . later started firing from its sunken dome. Charges were placed on seven armoured domes and five exploded with complete success; nine 7·5-cm guns in three casemates were destroyed, and in installation 8 – a flat armoured dome 6 metres in diameter, which was not penetrated by the 50-kg charge – the twin 120-mm guns were effectively attacked by two 1-kg charges thrown into the barrels, jamming breeches as they detonated.[52]

Within ten minutes of landing the paratroopers had both silenced and blinded Belgium's mightiest and most modern fortress, capturing or neutralising Maastricht 1 (equipped with three 75-mm guns), Maastricht 2 (three 75-mm guns), Mi North (machine guns), Mi South (machine guns), Cupola North (two 75-mm guns), Cupola South (two 75-mm guns), and Block IV. Only seven sections of fifty-five men took part in the action, while two other sections had been sent to destroy what turned out to be dummy positions in the northernmost complex of the superstructure. 'We came across no mines anywhere', remembered Witzig. 'The only installations protected by barbed wire were in the north, where the sappers had to free themselves with wire cutters and turn their flamethrowers on a machine-gun position firing from an embrasure, before they could place charges.'[53] Still, not all went as well as it could have. According to Witzig, the dummy positions diverted the efforts of two squads for ninety minutes. 'If they had been on the southern side of the fort where there were worthwhile objectives they would have been more effective,' observed Witzig. 'And perhaps we might have taken position 23 [Cupola South] earlier and forced an earlier surrender.'[54]

Meanwhile, having come this far, Lieutenant Witzig was not about to quit and let his men take Eben Emael without him. He instructed his pilot to look for a meadow large enough not only to land the glider but also to take off again and begin the mission anew. Once the aircraft was on the ground he instructed his soldiers and pilot to unload the aircraft, move it to the edge of the meadow, and load it once again, then to tear down any fences which might hinder a take-off. In the meantime, Witzig started to make his way back to Köln–Ostheim. He began by walking and then confiscated a bicycle from a railwayman. Next he confiscated a car from 'a very astonished medical officer' and was able to reach the

The Veldwezelt Bridge was the objective of Group Steel. Commanded by Lieutenant Gustav Altmann, it consisted of ninety-two men and nine gliders. The group accomplished its mission, again, against heavy Belgian resistance, suffering eight dead and thirty wounded.

Capture of the bridges spanning the Albert Canal was critical to the success of the German campaign in the West. The Vroenhoven Bridge was the objective of Group Concrete, commanded by Lieutenant Gerhard Schächt and consisting of ninety-six men in eleven gliders. The group accomplished its mission despite heavy Belgian resistance, suffering seven dead and twenty-four wounded.

Luftwaffe headquarters in Köln-Ostheim. 'There I was lucky enough to find a flight commander who knew what we needed to do,' he remembered, smiling. 'He managed to get a reserve Ju–52 ... from General Student, all on his own responsibility. Meanwhile I got a parachute in the event we would not be able to land. And so I started again!' Witzig explained the situation to the pilot while the two were still in the air and told him where to land. The pilot landed the Ju–52 and rolled to the edge of the field where the glider was waiting. 'My orders to the Ju pilot were to fly to Aachen along the same course to the western border [of Germany] at an altitude of 750 metres. What happened after that I didn't care!' And so Witzig and his men started the mission once again under a beautiful morning sun and released over the German border. 'During our flight we saw squadrons of the Luftwaffe fly westwards. The war had obviously already begun,' he remembered. 'We could see every now and then small black clouds [flak] in the air. None of them hit us. We then flew to Eben Emael; our pilot knew the way.'[55] Witzig arrived at the fort more than three hours late. The other 'lost' section was not so fortunate, landing near Düren, where they joined the first ground troops advancing to the west. They crossed the Maas River at Maastricht and eventually fought with the storm detachment on the western bank of the Albert Canal.[56]

By the time Witzig arrived, most of the fort was in German hands, as he recalled:

> There wasn't much shooting at the time. I went to Objective 19, where our command post was supposed to be. I went to Feldwebel Wenzel to receive all battle information. He had taken over the position, in the meantime, and was already receiving reports from some of our troops. We established our fighting position. The essentials – such as [overhead] photos, call signs, radios and whatever else needed to keep a platoon alive were with me.[57]

Later, Witzig described Wenzel, who would serve with him in North Africa and win the coveted German Cross in Gold, as 'a first-rate man ... [an] old engineer with vast experience' as well as 'a vigorous troop leader'.[58]

Assault Group Granite's two remaining tasks were to blow in the fortified entrances in order to press the attack into the depths of the fortress and to hold all captured positions until relief arrived. 'During some hours of moderate fighting, we managed to reconnoitre the entrances and we penetrated the installations already captured,' Witzig reported, 'but then the Belgian artillery started to shell our positions and their infantry attacked us repeatedly over the north-western slope, which was covered with dense undergrowth.'[59] A series of belated Belgian counter-attacks, beginning at 1000 hours, were indeed launched to regain control of the fort's surface. The first assault was smashed by Ju-87 Stuka dive bombers. A second counter-attack by reserve troops from near Wonck also failed. The situation, however, forced Witzig

Another view of the Vroenhoven Bridge.

and his men to defend themselves in the north-western sector of Eben Emael, which they occupied against the advancing Belgians.

In the meantime, his command continued with their mission of penetrating the fort. 'During the afternoon and night we detonated charges up to 100 kg each at the bottom of the ascent shafts, each about forty metres deep, below installations 3, 4, and 6, defended by barricades of rails and sandbags,' he recorded. 'In the narrow passages the explosions had a devastating effect.'[60] In fact, the explosions caused huge shock and sound waves, which reverberated throughout the tunnels and underground galleries, knocking out electricity and producing panic among the garrison. The situation inside the fort further deteriorated with the sympathetic bursting of barrels of calcium chloride, a disinfectant stocked throughout the fort, which filled the air and acted as a choking agent. According to the official Belgian report by Major Jottrand, commanding the garrison: 'The first contact with the enemy made a disastrous impression on those who lived through it. They had always thought themselves safe and secure under their steel and concrete. Now they felt like prisoners of their own fort.'[61] The Belgian commander felt that his troops could not offer an effective defence against the Germans armed with shaped charges.

Meanwhile, the paratroopers who had landed at Vroenhoven and Veldwezelt had successfully accomplished their mission. The bridges were captured undamaged and small bridgeheads were established and defended with the assistance of machine-gun detachments dropped later by parachute. During the afternoon of 10 May, these troops were relieved by German infantry. At Kanne, however, the Belgians succeeded in blowing up the bridge and the attacking paratroopers were engaged in a long day of hard fighting, which prevented the 51st Engineer Battalion, detailed to relieve Witzig's men at Eben Emael, from crossing the Albert Canal. The engineers' attempts to cross in rubber dinghies were prevented by Emplacement 15 (Canal North) on the western side of the canal. 'We ourselves could hear the gunfire far below us,' remembered Witzig. Eventually he and his men managed to neutralise the emplacement by lowering charges in front of the observation slits and detonating them. The resulting smoke and dust obscured visibility and the explosions no doubt encouraged the defenders to move elsewhere.

At 2000 hours, with the Germans firmly in control of the superstructure and his garrison trapped in the bowels of the fort, Major

A German soldier stands in front of one of Eben Emael's massive artillery fortifications.

Jottrand called for further counter–attacks and, shortly afterwards, issued orders for defence during the night. Belgian guns and mortars from Forts Pontisse, Barchon, and Evegnée fired almost 1,000 105–mm and 150–mm rounds at Eben Emael during the night, but Witzig's men were well protected inside captured casemates.[62] 'I expected a massive attack by well-trained [Belgian] infantry during the night,' Witzig remembered. 'If that had happened we would have been lost.'[63] Fortunately for the Germans a concerted attack failed to materialise.

> The night was uneventful [recorded Witzig]. After the hard fighting during the day, the detachment lay exhausted and parched, under scattered fire from Belgian artillery and infantry outside the fortification. Every burst of fire might have signalled the beginning of the counter-attack we expected, and our nerves were tense.[64]

Witzig was fortunate that an aerial resupply drop earlier that day had provided him with additional ammunition, although no food or water had been received. Witzig also discovered his single medic could not meet the unit's medical needs.[65]

At 0700 hours on 11 May, the advance elements of the 51st Engineer Battalion arrived at Eben Emael, having crossed the ditch in front of installation 4 in a rubber dingy. They silenced the position, which Witzig's men had twice tried to destroy, and thus opened the way for the entire battalion to enter the fort. Towards noon, other reinforcements arrived from the west and the last Belgian installations, Canal North

and Canal South, ceased firing. Major Jottrand surrendered the fort at
1227 hours. Five hundred Belgian soldiers walked out of the fort and
into five years of German captivity. The prisoners were kept in strict
isolation until 4 July 1940, as the Germans wished to keep their use of
both glider troops and shaped charges a secret. Twenty-three Belgian
soldiers died and another 62 members of the garrison were wounded in
the fighting.[66]

> As we retired, after burying our dead and handing over 30
> Belgian prisoners to the 51st Sapper Battalion, we saw scattered
> around the entrance installations the weapons of the garrison
> forces, who, with their commander, Major Jottrand, were taken
> away into captivity, According to a Belgian source, there had
> been about 750 men initially present out of a regular force of
> 1,200; it seems that some 15 per cent were absent on leave and
> that others were quartered in nearby villages — many arrived
> later.[67]

Of the 85 German paratroopers who had set out on 10 May to subdue
the fort, 6 were killed and, apart from injuries sustained in hard
landings, 20 were wounded.[68]

In the campaign as a whole, the Belgians finally capitulated to the
Germans on 28 May; the Dutch had already done so two weeks days
earlier, after the Luftwaffe had levelled Rotterdam. Perhaps the Dutch
received some small satisfaction in the fact that the man who had
planned the airborne invasion of their country that had proven so
effective, General Kurt Student, had been seriously wounded by a
German soldier in Rotterdam, only moments before it was surrendered.
A Dutch doctor saved his life after several hours of surgery.

Witzig wrote afterwards:

> Although an attack was clearly not expected, our use of tactical
> and technical surprise made the destruction of the vital surface
> installations, artillery, and observation posts possible, and this
> in turn made the enemy uncertain about the general situation.
> Damage to the ascent shafts and ventilating system only
> increased their confusion; all help from the outside, including
> the field artillery, failed. They felt captives in their own fortress
> and their fighting spirit was stifled. Although defeated only in
> their surface positions, they were not prepared to make a

counter-attack in the open field, even before the fortress was surrounded; while they may have been trained only to fight under cover, this nevertheless reveals shortcomings. Certainly an attack by night would have hurt us considerably . . . The disposition of the fortification itself seems to have been a disastrous mistake: defended trenches in front of the casemates would have made entry into the gun embrasures much more difficult for us – but there were no such close defences, even for the heaviest guns. Moreover, the defenders should have had sufficient imagination to cover the surface with mines and wire entanglements. On the other hand, the two dummy installations . . . were extremely effective in deceiving us, and the canal defences, which were immune to attack at close quarters, ensured for a long time the security of the canal.[69]

The shaped charges played an important role in the fall of Eben Emael. Witzig himself describes their effects as 'tremendous':

We hadn't expected such destructiveness. We later saw what had happened inside the Belgian positions, and that the effects of the

Adolf Hitler with (left) the commander of the 51st Engineer Battalion.

Lieutenant Gustav Altmann, shown here wearing the Knight's Cross presented to him by Adolf Hitler, led Group Steel's attack on the Veldwezelt Bridge.

explosions reached throughout the interior of the fort. I attribute the precipitate surrender of the fort to the effects of these shaped charges and the fact that the defenders did not know where and when the next explosion would come.[70]

After the war Witzig would tell his son: 'If more time had been devoted to indirect defensive measures atop Eben Emael – including more machine guns, wire, anti-personnel mines, and obstacles – we would have run into real problems taking the fort!'[71] However, once ensconced first atop and then inside the superstructure, the German paratroopers proved impossible to dislodge. With hindsight, Witzig also thought little of the Belgian defenders:

> An examination of Belgian sources suggests that, in spite of all preparations, the Belgian soldiers did not believe in the war, and, furthermore, that what happened at Eben Emael was typical of the whole 18-day campaign. Morale in Belgium had been weakened by neutralist politics, and an ill-prepared army fought badly because it was badly led. For the most part, it lacked the will to fight.[72]

Witzig went on to note that Major Jottrand had few options available to him in the defence of Eben Emael:

> With good units, long occupation of the position, good training, he might have abandoned the fort except for a couple of bunkers that would still fight – all the others being unimportant – and fought us in the open, on top of the fort. It could have been done, because we were not besieging the entrance to the fort. With well-trained soldiers and careful orders given inside the fort, he might have marched out and fought as infantry and, with artillery support, anything would have been possible. But it required a good troop unit and requisite training . . . I assume, however, that all of this was not the Belgian commander's fault . . . He could not, at the last moment, turn the Belgian fortress artillery into another sort of unit . . . He couldn't do that, and I can't reproach him for it. The planning of the Belgian General Staff for the defence of the Albert Canal and its bridges was faulty: a big, modern fort with an unclear mission, inadequate weapons and no support.[73]

A Belgian history of the Second World War supports many of Witzig's conclusions and provides further insights. It notes, for example, that at the tactical level the fort was poorly equipped to deal with the threat from the air. 'From the onset of operations, the Belgians were dominated from the air,' writes Professor Luc De Vos from Belgium's École Royale Militaire (Royal Military College). 'The consequence was the loss of all initiative.' Also, reliable liaison between the Belgian infantry and artillery was lacking, leading to the loss of a number of artillery pieces without a shot being fired. In addition, troop training in the Belgian Army was weak in many aspects in 1939 and 1940 and exercises almost non-existent. In comparison, the Germans trained twelve hours a day, six days a week and incorporated realistic and demanding live-fire exercises into their programme of instruction. Finally, the use of obstacles on the superstructure of the fort had been badly neglected, allowing the attacking paratroopers rapidly to establish an airhead directly atop Eben Emael.[74]

If the Belgian Army and garrison of the fort were caught unprepared, the same cannot be said of their opponents. The Belgian history points out that the German Army achieved its objectives in a 'magnificent' manner, using a small force to accomplish 'spectacular' results. Assault Detachment Koch is credited with achieving almost total tactical surprise and local fire superiority through the use of gliders, paratroopers, shaped charges, sub-machine guns and flame-throwers. Surprised was achieved despite the fact that the fort was on alert when the Germans landed. The crack-of-dawn timing of the attack, in conjunction with an early morning fog, added to the confusion of the defenders. German air superiority, and especially the use of Stuka dive-bombers as aerial artillery, robbed the Belgians of the initiative and more than compensated for the lack of heavy fire-power amongst the glider troops, with air power used to prevent reinforcements from reaching the fort in strength or launching effective counter-attacks. Detailed planning, preparation and training ensured the parachute-engineers were more than prepared for the challenges of seizing Eben Emael. Finally, the valour of the German paratroopers, many of them receiving their baptism of fire, was, according to the Belgian historian, 'conspicuous'.[75]

'The storming of Eben-Emael was the first sapper attack ever made from the air,' Witzig boasted afterwards, lauding the achievements of his command and the German airborne engineers. 'That it was

The heroes of Eben Emael returning to garrison on 12 May 1940 after having seized the greatest of Belgian forts. Eben Emael capitulated the previous day with some 1,200 Belgian soldiers surrendering.

successful is due to the efficiency and enthusiasm of the parachute sappers, using new weapons and new means of transport, aided by careful preparation, the participation of the Luftwaffe, and clear conditions of command.'[76] Student agreed wholeheartedly. 'So far as Germany was concerned the paratrooper and airborne assault on Fortress Holland, the bridges across the Albert Canal, and Eben Emael justified the airborne force concept,' he wrote after the war. 'Everybody sat up and took notice, including the Wehrmacht. During the Polish campaign nobody had much faith in the idea, and the prestige of the parachutists suffered a setback. But after the operations in the West morale soared and the paratroopers became an elite corps.'[77]

The fall of Eben Emael and its associated bridges dealt a tremendous psychological shock to the Allies. Indeed, one historian, James Mrazek, author of a book on the fall of Eben Emael, goes as far as arguing that it led directly to the Dunkirk evacuation and sealed the fate of France in May 1940 by allowing the Wehrmacht to slice its way across Belgium and France, stopping only when its panzers reached the English Channel.[78] This is overstating the case. The Allies, with their overwhelming quantitative superiority in infantry, modern tanks, artillery, and aircraft, could still have turned the tide against the Germans at

Sedan or Arras had they been better prepared or their forces more aggressively employed. However, according to Field Marshal Albert Kesselring, who served as the commander of the German Second Air Fleet during the Netherlands campaign and later as the German Commander–in–Chief, South–West:

> With the capture of Fort Eben Emael, the enemy flanking actions against the Maas crossing were eliminated. The capture of the most important bridge guaranteed that the Maas River would be crossed according to plan and thus established the necessary conditions for the coordination of ground and air operations in Holland. The dawn missions succeeded surprisingly well.[79]

According to one postwar report written by a group of German generals, which included General Student:

> This success was connected not so much with the achievement of the tactical objectives, such as the capture of a number of bridges, which were important to the attacking ground forces, as with the moral influence exerted upon the enemy by a wholly new method of fighting. The very fact that, in this way, large forces could penetrate deep behind Dutch defences at the outset of the fighting undoubtedly broke the resistance of the Dutch and saved the German Army the cost of a serious fight in capturing Holland. Success is attributed mainly to the surprise achieved by this method, which was used for the first time in the history of warfare.[80]

Hitler's decision to use airborne troops against Eben Emael was an inspired one. But a quick German victory was not as inevitable as many historians suggest, even in light of the many shortcomings of the Belgian Army, as shown by the concurrent events in Holland. In May 1940 the Germans employed some 5,000 paratroopers to seize three key Dutch airfields – Ockenburg, Ypenburg and Valkenburg – ringing the Hague in the north of the country, as well as to secure nearby bridges across the Maas River at Rotterdam, Dordrecht and Moerdijk. Student's airborne forces consisted of four parachute battalions and one air-transport regiment of three squadrons. In five days of fierce resistance the Dutch Army, whom few observers would have rated more effective than their Belgian counterparts, inflicted some 2,735 casualties on the German paratroopers and air–landing forces in the Hague sector alone, capturing no fewer than 1,745 enemy soldiers, of whom 1,350 were sent back to England as prisoners. According to reliable Dutch and German sources, as many as 525 aircraft, including many of the valuable Ju–52 transports, were damaged or destroyed during the battle for the Hague.[81] This figure appears to be extremely high. Nonetheless, one Dutch historian, Lieutenant–Colonel Eppo Brongers, asserts that the Luftwaffe's losses precluded the Germans from marshalling enough transport aircraft to conduct an airborne assault on England that year and that, even a year later, during their costly attack on Crete, Hitler was critically short of Ju–52s as a result of losses in Holland and was forced to commit his paratroopers piecemeal. There is evidence to support this statement. The Luftwaffe's Ju–52 transport fleet in 1939 consisted of approximately 1,000 aircraft, a number which the Germans tried to maintain throughout the war. Monthly production of new aircraft ran at 80–120 planes but this was only sufficient to offset 'normal' losses.[82] Approximately half of the available transport had been used for the attacks in Holland and Belgium.[83]

There also appears to be a great deal of truth to the rumour that the Dutch were forewarned by German officers and diplomats about the impending German invasion of their country. Indeed, Rudolf Witzig indicated to U.S. Army interviewers after the war that he believed that Admiral Canaris, the head of German military intelligence, had tipped off the Dutch military attaché as to the date of the German assault on the Low Countries. 'Happily,' Witzig concluded, 'they didn't believe the reports.'[84] In the end, however, the Wehrmacht's preponderance on the ground and in the air prevented a complete disaster. Senior German commanders blamed their difficulties on 'the inadequate strength of parachutists in the air attack group' as well as 'the command technique of General Student' who 'neglected liaison with the Second Air Fleet, especially during the most decisive hours', for the operation's failures and losses.[85] These same deficiencies would resurface with a vengeance at Crete a year later.

Thus, a successful attack on Eben Emael was not as predestined as many believe. Indeed, had the German Army used traditional infantry and artillery attacks against Eben Emael or had the Belgian defenders and the fort simply been as well forewarned as their Dutch brethren, a bit better prepared, or even more fortunate the outcome might have been very different. The smaller and weaker Belgian fort at Aubin-

Neufchâteau, east of Visé, for example, held out until 24 May against an entire German infantry division and surrendered only when the enemy were already at the beach near Abbeville in France.

Several days after their return to their home base, Walter Koch, Rudolf Witzig and all the officers of Assault Group Koch were ordered to report for a special ceremony. Adolf Hitler addressed the group and then awarded each officer the prestigious Knight's Cross, then the highest class of the Iron Cross, awarded for exceptional gallantry in the face of the enemy, for their successful accomplishment of their mission. The enlisted men were awarded the Iron Cross by General Albert Kesselring. In addition to the award, each participant was promoted one rank. There was only one exception, a member of Witzig's command, a paratrooper named Grechza, when it was discovered that he had carried a canteen full of rum with him into Eben Emael. Within nine months of the outbreak of the Second World War in Europe, Witzig and Koch had thus joined the ranks of a new

The commanders of Sturmabteilung Koch returning from receiving their Knight's Crosses. Rudolf Witzig is the first fully visible paratrooper on the left.

Captain Koch being pinned with the Knight's Cross.

and select few. They were also awarded both the Iron Cross First Class and the Iron Cross Second Class. And the government even printed postcards, suitable for autographing, with faces of its new Knight's Cross winners on them. The heroes of Eben Emael and the Albert Canal were lionised by the German public as celebrities. In May, shortly after receiving the Knight's Cross, Witzig was assigned as adjutant to Reichsmarschall Göring, Hitler's second-in-command and the Commander-in-Chief of the Luftwaffe.

Although the head of the German Air Force was always kind to him and Witzig found him to be 'a good family man' and even 'interesting', the hero of Eben Emael also believed the Reichsmarschall to be a 'salon soldier', in self-designed uniforms of white and powder blue. As a result, Witzig wanted very much to return to his paratroopers. Jürgen Witzig told the author how his father contrived to do so. One day, as Witzig was driving Göring to a hunt near Höxter, a large deer stepped onto the road nearby. The Reichsmarschall immediately grabbed his gun and attempted to shoot the animal without getting out of the car. However, Witzig, who hated hunting, leaned on the horn 'accidentally', scaring the deer away. A furious Göring, who could not have been unaware of his adjutant's desire to return to his unit, bellowed out: 'Witzig! It is better that you go back!' The young captain did not leave empty-

Adolf Hitler shakes hands with Captain Koch following the German seizure of the Belgian fort and surrounding bridges.

handed, however. Göring asked Witzig if he liked the car that they were riding in, a BMW two-seat sports convertible. When Witzig admitted to admiring the vehicle, Göring said: 'It's yours!'According to Jürgen Witzig, his father took the car to Braunschweig in 1940 and paid to have it garaged there for the duration of the war. When he returned after the war to claim his property, he found the city completely devastated from Allied air raids. Miraculously, the garage holding his car, and the vehicle itself inside, survived! However, Witzig soon lost the vehicle to a British officer, who claimed it as 'reparations'![86]

Witzig's tenure with the head of the Luftwaffe lasted only three months, but was nonetheless a fruitful one in othger ways also. On 16 August 1940 Witzig was promoted early to captain.

That summer of 1940 Witzig attended a ball in Höxter honouring Germany's airborne victory at Eben Emael. The large hall where the event took place was decorated with parachutes and the young and handsome Captain Witzig was the guest of honour. Gerda Remmers, to whom he had grown quite attached, was absent, however, as she was in Münster diligently studying for her medical exams. When the hero of Eben Emael asked her younger sister, Hanna, now sixteen, to dance, she and her friends were 'astonished'. After the dance, the young woman purchased a Rudolf Witzig postcard for 50 Pfennig and had him autograph it. Witzig only danced once with Hanna. 'He did not like dancing,' she remembered with a laugh, almost sixty-five years later. 'He acted like a young boy!'[87] She would not see him again for almost two years.

Chapter 4

CRETE

The success at Eben Emael had moved airborne operations to the forefront of Hitler's thoughts, and after the conclusion of the Western Campaign in 1940 the Wehrmacht began preparations for the invasion of England, Operation Sealion, which included an airborne operation. Two trains of thought governed the selection of objectives. The first idea was to establish airheads to assist the naval landings. Two divisions of airborne and air–landing troops were to capture from the rear the locations suitable for landings from the sea. The second idea was to capture airfields in order to paralyse the Royal Air Force, while at the same time obtaining landing fields for the Luftwaffe. A large number of objectives thus emerged, including simultaneous airborne landings at Dover, Beachy Head and Brighton, as well as the seizure of numerous airfields. However, these could not all be supported due to the limited number of paratroopers and transport aircraft available. In the end the objective selected was the establishment of an airhead at either Folkestone or Dungeness.[1] The airborne landings were initially part of a thirteen–division assault, but this was later scaled back to nine divisions with two airborne divisions.[2]

The airborne troops selected for the invasion of England were the 7th Flieger and the 22nd Air–Landing Division. By August the Luftwaffe had been able to make up some of the losses in personnel suffered in May 1940. According to German sources those losses included some 1,000–1,500 paratroopers. In reality they probably exceeded 2,000 men.[3] The paratroopers would have been supported by some 400–700 transport aircraft, depending on whether the operation would have taken place in July or August, along with some 100–150 gliders.[4] The number of transports and gliders available for Sealion was not enough to carry the entire airborne force in one lift and multiple sorties would have been required.[5]

Witzig at Göring's Karinhall some time between May and August 1940.

The prospects of success were variously assessed, with Field Marshal Kesselring favouring an invasion of England, believing that while an airborne assault, as in the Western Campaign, would not have decided the whole campaign; it would have helped, perhaps very effectively, to attain final success. While an essential condition for Operation Sealion was the achievement of German air supremacy over southern England, it is questionable whether the Luftwaffe could have effectively protected the airborne and air-landing forces against the extremely aggressive and lethal Royal Air Force. The Battle of Britain disclosed that the strength of the RAF had been dangerously underestimated by Hitler and Göring. Furthermore, the Kriegsmarine, which for the most part had been annihilated by the Royal Navy off Norway, would have been unable to launch or safeguard an amphibious landing across the Channel. In the end, an airborne operation against England was cancelled with the termination of Sealion. 'It is unlikely that the airborne landing would have been really successful,' concluded a panel of senior German officers after the war. 'Any minor local successes would have been balanced by heavy losses in personnel and material.'[6]

Soon after Sealion was shelved, Hitler asked General Student to study the possibility of capturing Britain's greatest overseas fortress,

General Milch decorating a Luftwaffe officer at Karinhall, summer 1940.

Gibraltar, by airborne assault much in the same way as the Germans had captured Eben Emael. That such an operation, code-named 'Felix', was under serious consideration was verified by Hermann Göring, after his capture by American forces. 'Lack of shipping had prevented us from invading England, but before the difficulties with Russia we could have carried out the "Gibraltar" plan ... The entire Italian Army, which was unfit for a major war, could have been used for occupation forces,' he explained to U.S. interrogators. 'The loss of Gibraltar might have induced England to sue for peace. Failure to carry out this plan was one of the major mistakes of the war,' he continued. Göring claimed the plan as originally his and noted that the Kriegsmarine was in favour of it as it would have provided the Germans with better naval bases. 'Instead of being cooped up in Biscay and Bordeaux, it could have had U-boat bases much farther out in Spain and on the Atlantic islands,' explained Göring. 'If the campaign succeeded, I personally wanted to attack the Azores to secure U-boat bases there, which would have crippled British sea lanes.' Göring stressed that the main task in seizing Gibraltar would have fallen to the Luftwaffe and his Fallschirmjäger. 'So I was chiefly concerned and I would have eagerly carried out the operation. The Luftwaffe had many officers who had participated in the war in Spain a year and a half [sic] before and knew the people and the country.'[7]

Once the invasion of the British Isles was deemed impractical, planning for the seizure of Gibraltar was moved to the forefront and on 14 August 1940 Hitler consented to a proposal by the Wehrmacht Operations Staff for the seizure of the fortress and ordered that an operational study be prepared. The study was completed on 20 August and approved by Hitler four days later. 'The High Command of the German Wehrmacht anticipated a successful outcome to the undertaking,' recorded Helmuth Greiner, the keeper of the War Diary in Hitler's headquarters from August 1939 to April 1943. Indeed, an estimate produced by the Armed Forces Operations Staff concluded: 'If Spain decides to enter the war, Gibraltar can easily be captured by specially trained German troops.' This, however, was not the conclusion of General Student, well aware that tentative plans called for the use of his airborne forces to capture and hold the Rock, pending the arrival of the ground forces, which included formations from the *Gross-deutschland* Regiment, the 98th Mountain Infantry Regiment and particularly strong artillery elements grouped together under General Keubler's XLIX Infantry Corps. Part of that study included an assessment ordered by Student, as commander of German airborne forces, and written by Rudolf Witzig. On 1 August Witzig had submitted a concise, three-page report, complete with a photograph of one of the potential landing zones, concluding that the capture of Gibraltar from the air was not feasible. 'The use of parachute and air-landing units to seize or assist in the seizure of Gibraltar,' he wrote, 'is precluded for the following reasons: The terrain, except for the windmill flat to the south of the peninsula, is not suitable for air landing [operations]. Even the exception allows only for the use of gliders in a small number ... The [aircraft] exit/drop point would be very difficult to determine due to unpredictable wind conditions and the fact that the approach is hindered by southern hills.' Witzig concluded that the lack of sufficient landing space for gliders and paratroopers, the steep terrain, the heavy British fortifications and defensive armament, the low speed of the Ju-52 transports, and the probable loss of surprise would result in the failure of the operation. According to Jürgen Witzig, prior to writing the report his father conducted a reconnaissance of the potential drop zones in person under the very noses of the British themselves, assisted by the Armed Forces Intelligence (Abwehr), which shuttled him through diplomatic channels into Spain. Witzig carried out his on-the-spot assessment in mufti prior to writing his report.[8] While difficult to believe, this story is very much in keeping with Rudolf Witzig's nature and that of most Fallschirmjäger officers, who valued boldness. The venture was also consistent with Hitler's Directive 18 of 12 November 1940, which mentioned the possible German seizure of Gibraltar. 'Reconnaissance parties (officers in plain clothes) will draw up necessary plans for action against Gibraltar and for the capture of airfields.'[9]

It is unclear how much Witzig's report, which stressed that surprise was the key to success and that such surprise would be impossible in any airborne attack on Gibraltar, contributed to Hitler's eventual cancellation of Operation Felix. When General Franco made it clear that Spain would not enter the war on the side of the Axis unless Britain was on the eve of collapse, Hitler postponed Felix. On 11 December 1940 Hitler ordered the Armed Forces High Command to discontinue preparations for the seizure of the island. On 28 January 1941 General Jodl informed Hitler that an attack on Gibraltar could not be launched before mid-April if preparations were not completed by 1 February and stated that the forces needed for Operation Felix would not be available for Operation Barbarossa, Hitler's planned invasion of the Soviet Union scheduled for mid-May. Hitler then decided to drop thoughts of taking Gibraltar.[10]

General Milch at Karinhall with two officers who are to be decorated by Göring.

After its return to Germany the 7th Fliegerdivision was expanded to three parachute regiments, each with three battalions. In addition, Assault Detachment Koch became the 1st Battalion of the newly formed Luftlande-Sturmregiment, or Air-Landing Assault Regiment, comprised of four battalions of paratroopers trained as a glider-borne infantry air-landing assault force. Command of the new regiment was bestowed on Colonel Eugen Meindl with the newly promoted Major Walter Koch assuming command of the 1st Battalion. The 7th Fliegerdivision and the 22nd Air-Landing Division were then incorporated into the XI Fliegerkorps, established that summer, along with the six transport groups of the 7th Fliegerdivision, each equipped with 52 Ju-52s.[11] Upon his return from Göring's personal staff in August 1940, Witzig was assigned to the Air-Landing Assault Regiment as commander of the 9th Company, 3rd Parachute Battalion. Witzig's company and a good part of the 3rd Battalion consisted of parachute engineers. Captain Witzig's company spent the winter of 1940–1 conducting winter-warfare training in the Harz Mountains. An artillery officer and veteran of the First World War, Meindl, by now a legendary figure in the German airborne forces for his exploits in Norway, had served in both the Imperial German Army and its successor, the Reichswehr. After ten years of working in the Reichswehr Ministry he went on to command a mountain artillery regiment.

Hermann Göring, Commander of the Luftwaffe, with his Chief of Staff, General Hans Jeschonnek, May 1940. Jeschonnek would commit suicide in August 1943.

During the invasion of Norway, he had led Group *Meindl* at Narvik, where he parachuted into combat without any previous airborne training. Appointed commander of Assault Regiment *Meindl* of the Army's parachute troops in August 1940, he and his command were transferred to the Luftwaffe shortly afterwards.[12]

During the second half of the 1930s the Balkans became the centre of conflicting interests of Germany, Italy, Russia, and Great Britain. From the beginning of the war Hitler had consistently stated that Germany had no territorial ambitions in the Balkans. Indeed, his primary interests in that area were economic and included vital oil and food supplies. As the war progressed, the Balkans constituted the southern flank for an invasion of the Soviet Union. Hitler was thus prepared to do his utmost to preserve peace in that part of Europe. For this reason he attempted to keep Italy's aggressive Balkan strategy in check, to satisfy Hungarian and Bulgarian claims to Romanian territory by peaceful means, and to avoid any incident which might lead to direct British intervention in Greece. However, Mussolini's invasion of Greece on 28 October 1940 and the almost immediate setbacks suffered by the Italians at the hands of the hard-fighting Greeks brought the Balkans to the forefront of Hitler's strategic thinking. On 4 November, seven days after Italy had attacked Greece through Albania and four days after the British had occupied Crete and Limnos, Hitler made the decision to intervene militarily. He ordered the Army General Staff to prepare plans for an invasion of northern Greece from Romania via Bulgaria to deprive the British of bases for possible ground and air operations across the Balkans against the Romanian oilfields. Moreover, such an invasion would assist the Italians by diverting Greek forces from Albania. The plans for this campaign, together with Hitler's intentions for Gibraltar and North Africa, were incorporated into a master plan to deprive the British of all their Mediterranean bases. On 12 November 1940 the Armed Forces High Command issued Directive 18, which outlined Hitler's plans for future operations to the three services.

On 25 March 1941 the Yugoslav government yielded to German pressure, joined the Axis Alliance, and agreed to let German troops cross its territory – despite growing opposition among the Yugoslav people to closer association with Germany. Two days later, a coup d'état toppled the government. The new leadership was determined to stay out of the coming German–Greek conflict and went to great lengths to assure Hitler that it was friendly. Hitler, who harboured a long-standing antipathy towards the Yugoslav nation and was furious over the government's change of face, added Yugoslavia as a target of invasion.

On 6 April 1941 the Wehrmacht therefore invaded Greece and Yugoslavia, quickly overrunning both countries, despite determined Greek and British resistance. Hitler attempted to justify his invasion of Greece by accusing the country's leaders of cooperating with the British. In the case of Yugoslavia, the Führer was determined to destroy it as a nation and ordered the Luftwaffe to demolish the capital city of Belgrade. On 17 April the Yugoslav government surrendered and six days later the Greek Army capitulated. Between 24 and 29 April the British evacuated some 50,000 British and Greek soldiers from mainland Greece. The Germans had suffered some 5,000 casualties against 12,000 British and 16,000 Greeks killed, wounded, missing or captured. Hitler had crushed Yugoslavia, conquered Greece, and shored up his Italian allies, while establishing a military presence in the Mediterranean area that Mussolini had tried to avoid.

Although the invasion of Crete was not part of Hitler's original attack plan, he sanctioned Operation Mercury while the invasion of Greece was still under way. Although Gibraltar was not deemed ripe for capture by airborne assault, Hitler felt that the island of Crete was. Its possession would allow him to control the Aegean, secure the sea route from the Danube through the Dardanelles and the Corinth Canal, so essential to Italy – especially for its oil, limit the influence of Allied air and sea power in the eastern Mediterranean, and use the island as a base on the flank of the North African theatre and of the sea route between Alexandria and Malta, for future conquests. Furthermore, it would prevent the British from using the island as a staging base for bombers to strike at the Ploesti oilfields in Romania.[13] Even Witzig agreed, long after the war, that the Germans had to capture the island. 'Taking Crete was essential and made sense from the strategic point of view of the war of the German Reich,' he emphasised in an interview. 'The British fleet ruled the Mediterranean Sea, the Italian fleet was weak from the beginning ... One had to keep the British out of the Balkans, the Black Sea and the Aegean. Crete could not stay in British hands. Crete had to be eliminated as a British attack base!'[14]

Crete is approximately 260 km long and 12–55 km wide. The interior is barren and covered by eroded mountains, which rise to an elevation of 2,470 metres in the west. There are few roads and water is scarce. The south coast descends abruptly towards the sea and the only usable port along this part of the coast is the small harbour of Sphakia. There are hardly any north–south communications and the only road to Sphakia which can be used for motor transport ends abruptly 400 metres above the town. The sole major traffic artery runs close to the north coast and connects Suda Bay with the towns of Maleme, Canea, Rethymnon and Heraklion. Possession of the north coast is vital for an invader approaching from Greece, if only because of terrain. The British, whose supply bases were situated in Egypt, were greatly handicapped by the fact that the only efficient port was in Suda Bay. The topography of the island therefore favoured the invader, particularly since the mountainous terrain left no other alternative to the British but to construct their airfields close to the exposed north coast.[15]

According to General of Mountain Troops Julius Ringel, commander of the 5th Mountain Division, who later became the ground forces

Göring with Koch and Witzig, May 1940.

commander on the island, the plan for the invasion of the island consisted of five phases. The first was an air supremacy campaign. The second part called for the employment of paratroopers via parachutes and gliders to capture the airfields on Crete with the main effort at Maleme. In the third phase, mountain troops would be landed to complete the conquest of the island and conduct mopping-up operations. Next, additional reinforcements would arrive by sea on small vessels, landing on the open beach at Maleme. Finally, once a harbour suitable for unloading had been seized, a naval force transporting artillery, tanks, pack animals, and wheeled vehicles would follow. According to Ringel, no definitive plan was developed for these follow-on ground operations, and the sites for the landings of mountain troops, either Heraklion or Maleme, would depend on the success of the paratroopers.[16]

Hitler placed Hermann Göring in overall command of the operation. Its implementation, however, was left to Generaloberst Alexander Löhr, commander of Fourth Air Fleet and the senior Luftwaffe officer in the Balkans. A Knight's Cross winner, Löhr had served as an infantry officer before the First World War and as a staff officer during much of that war, ending it in command of an infantry battalion. In 1934 he had been assigned to the Luftwaffe, where he had excelled in a series of command assignments.[17] Available forces for the airborne assault on Crete consisted of VIII and XI Fliegerkorps. The actual operation called for a two-wave attack by three groups over four sectors on the first day of the operation. In the first wave, scheduled for the early morning, Group *West* would attack in the Maleme sector, while Group *Centre* would attack in the Canea sector. In the second wave, scheduled for mid-afternoon, the remainder of Group *Centre* would attack Rethymnon, while Group *East* would attack Heraklion. This assault would be carried out by some 11,500 men of the 7th Fliegerdivision, augmented by 3,500 men from the Air-Landing Assault Regiment. The attack would be supported by 228 bombers, 205 dive-bombers, 114 twin-engined and 119 single-engined fighters, and 50 reconnaissance aircraft from VIII and XI Fliegerkorps, a total of 716 planes, of which 514 were reported serviceable on 17 May. In addition, XI Fliegerkorps possessed over 500 transport aircraft, mostly Ju-52s, and 72 gliders for the operation.[18] Once the key airfields and ports were seized, the airborne troops would be reinforced by some 14,000 mountain troops, including two rifle regiments from the 5th Mountain Division with a third from the 6th Mountain Division added later. These would be transported by relays of transport aircraft as soon as the captured airfields were prepared. Elements of the 5th Panzer Division, including a tank battalion, a motorcycle battalion and anti-aircraft detachments, would arrive by sea later.[19]

It was truly, as one German history notes, 'an ambitious, audacious, and risky plan'.[20] Ringel called it 'a historic, singularly hazardous enterprise without equal in the daring of its planning, but even more daring in its execution'.[21] However, as Ringel noted:

> The first few sentences of the Operations Order sent a cold chill down one's spine, for it was clear that the operation so laconically and soberly described would be a suicidal adventure. Anyone who had anything to do with Operation Mercury felt uneasy about it, to say the least, and those who actually had to go by boat regarded it with horror. Officers and men alike said they would rather fly to Crete than risk going by sea.[22]

The plan was indeed risky. The Germans had grossly underestimated the size of the island's garrison: 'So far as the Germans knew at that time, Crete had been occupied by British troops since the end of October 1940, and the approximate strength of the forces on the island was believed to be not more than 15,000 men, some of whom were believed to be exhausted from operations in Greece,' wrote Freiherr von der Heydte, who commanded the 1st Battalion of the 3rd Parachute Regiment. Von der Heydte was writing with the benefit of postwar hindsight.[23] In fact, at the time, the Germans believed there were no more than 5,000 combat-capable troops on the island. They were convinced, with good reason, that the island's defenders were disorganised and suffered from not only a lack of equipment, but also the will to fight. During Operation Demon, the evacuation of British and Commonwealth soldiers from the Greek mainland in April 1941, more than 50,000 military personnel had been rescued. 'Some 25,000 of these troops, the majority of whom had no equipment other than their rifles, were being re-organised in Crete,' reported Admiral Sir Andrew Cunningham, Commander-in-Chief of Britain's Mediterranean Fleet. 'A large number were useless for defence purposes and were awaiting removal.'[24] At the time of the airborne invasion the Germans faced almost three times the number of defenders they expected, including 15,000 British, 10,250 Greek, 7,700 New Zealand and 6,500 Australian soldiers, and a large number of Greek policemen. Not all, however, were equipped or prepared to contest an air- and sea-borne invasion. Three battalions of Greek Army recruits were, for example, poorly trained and badly armed, with rifles of many different calibres, and were short of everything from ammunition to clothing. Furthermore, malaria was endemic among those units. The 3,000 Greek policemen, on the other hand, were somewhat better armed and fed.[25]

Field Marshal Hermann Göring greets Luftwaffe recipients of the Knight's Cross following the Luftwaffe's successful assaults on Eben Emael and the Albert Canal bridges.

Allied ground troops were supported by 6 Matilda infantry tanks, 15 light tanks, and 85 serviceable anti-aircraft and artillery pieces, a not insignificant contribution to the defence of the island.[26] Against lightly armed parachute troops, reliant on large numbers of lumbering transports to deliver them to their objectives, the tanks and anti-aircraft artillery were particularly dangerous. At sea, four mixed naval task forces, three destroyer groups and a torpedo boat flotilla, under the command of Admiral Cunningham, stood ready to intercept and destroy any seaborne invasion. Furthermore, Ultra intelligence ensured that the Allies were forewarned about the impending German invasion. However, despite the availability of Ultra information General Sir Bernard Freyberg, commanding the Allied forces on the island, did not know precisely when the attack would take place. 'Although intelligence suggested that an attack on Crete was very likely, the exact date of the attack could not be forecast,' reported Admiral Cunningham. 'It was thought that the most probable date for the attack to begin was about the 17th of May.'[27] Furthermore, Freyberg had concluded that the real

Field Marshal Göring with a group of Luftwaffe officers. General Milch and Rudolf Witzig are to Göring's immediate right. General Jeschonnek is to Göring's left.

threat to his force was from the sea and not the air. This impression would later prove fatal to the defenders.

On 20 May 1941, a perfect summer day, Hitler unleashed Operation Mercury, the airborne invasion of Crete. During the previous ten days, the Luftwaffe had achieved total air superiority over the island. On the morning of the battle, Witzig and his paratroopers received a special ration, aimed at building morale and increasing physical stamina in preparation for their impending combat jump. The ration included items considered real luxuries by the German soldier, including white bread, milk, butter and fresh eggs. For most of the paratroopers, this was the last real meal they would eat for some time; for many it would be their last meal altogether. During the course of battle, those who survived would rely on their iron ration, intended to sustain them for three days. It contained cans of sausages and cheese, chocolate substitute, crackers, chewing gum, lemonade powder, coffee and sugar and fuel tablets.[28]

Prior to the jump, Witzig and every paratrooper of the airborne division and assault regiment received a copy of Student's 'The Parachutist's Ten Commandments';

1. You are the elite of the German Army. For you, combat shall be fulfillment. You shall seek it out and train yourself to stand any test.

2. Cultivate true comradeship, for together with your comrades you will triumph or die.

3. Be shy of speech and incorruptible. Men act, women chatter; chatter will lead you to the grave.

4. Calm and caution, vigour and determination, valour and a fanatical offensive spirit will make you superior in the attack.

5. In facing the foe, ammunition is the most precious thing. He who shoots uselessly, merely to reassure himself, is a man without guts. He is a weakling and does not deserve the title of parachutist.

6. Never surrender! Your honour lies in Victory or Death.

7. Only with good weapons can you have success. So look after them on this principle – first my weapon, then myself.

8. You must grasp the full meaning of an operation so that, should your leader fall by the way, you can carry it out with coolness and caution.

9. Fight chivalrously against an honest foe; armed irregulars deserve no quarter.

10. With your eyes open, keyed up to top pitch, agile as a greyhound, tough as leather, hard as Krupp steel, you will be the embodiment of a German warrior.[29]

Student's 'Ten Commandments' were no doubt meant to inspire his paratroopers on the eve of battle and to remind them that they were the elite of the Wehrmacht and that the eyes of Hitler would be upon them in history's first attempt to capture a fortified island by an assault from the air. The Commandments, however, had an unintended consequence that would forever influence the reputation of the Fallschirmjäger.

As part of Group *West*, Generalmajor Meindl's Air-Landing Assault Regiment was tasked with a number of missions. First, paratroopers arriving by glider in the Maleme area would destroy nearby British flak batteries and seize the bridge located south-west of the airfield. Shortly afterwards, the rest of his regiment would jump in the vicinity of Maleme to seize and hold that airfield as well as to establish contact with Kampfgruppe *Heidrich*, a regimental-size parachute combat group from the 7th Fliegerdivision scheduled to land later south-west of Canea. The union of these two forces would provide Generalleutnant Süssmann (commander of the 7th Fliegerdivision) with unified command of both groups.[30] Meindl's 3rd Parachute Battalion, commanded by Major Otto Scherber and to which Witzig's company belonged, was scheduled to drop north and east of Maleme, clear resistance in the town and secure the river bed to the east, and then, under the direction of the regimental commander, to advance east and link up with the Central Force.[31]

Witzig's 9th Company had a strength of about 144 men, including four officers and 26 NCOs, and had been allocated twelve Ju-52s for the flight to Crete. The company would fly in four flights of three aircraft each. Its mission was to parachute into the area east of the airfield at Maleme and support the 1st Battalion in its assault from the east.[32] The 3rd Battalion was also given the mission of seizing an attack position for the assauly on Canea. But as they boarded their aircraft, the officers and men of the 9th Company were unclear as to what exactly they would find once they hit the ground. 'There were no major preparations,' revealed Witzig in an interview long after the war,

Field Marshal Göring and Luftwaffe recipients of the Knight's Cross, May 1940.

... we knew very little of our enemy and the terrain. Our camp was in the south of Greece, which the British had just recently evacuated, but they had observation points and information [gathering] centres all over the country. The Greeks were not our friends, but friends of the British ... and they knew exactly what was going to happen.[33]

Scherber's 3rd Battalion experienced problems from the very beginning of the operation. It was the last in line at Megara airfield, one of six departure airfields in Greece, and its departure was delayed forty minutes due to heavy clouds of thick dust raised by the previous waves of aircraft taking off. 'These auxiliary airfields were not of an ideal type,' remembered General Ringel.

> The dust conditions presented quite a problem. Yellow-brown dust columns extended skyward with every start and landing and it was frequently so bad that, despite all measures, such as [the use of] fire hoses, salt water, etc, necessary intervals between aircraft taking off and landing had to be established to avoid collisions.[34]

The flight to Crete from the Greek mainland, depending upon the location of the departure airfield, took between seventy-five and ninety minutes. At first, Witzig and his men would have seen nothing but dust clouds from the windows of their Ju-52s. As they left the airfield behind, Athens and the Acropolis would soon have appeared. 'Suddenly, the blue shining sea, sky, and water,' wrote General Ringel: 'It was impossible to estimate if one was flying only a few metres over the blue surface or several hundred metres above the sea.' To the left and right, as far as the eye could see, and above them flew squadrons of Ju-52s and gliders, some 600–650 in all, protected by fighters and fighter-bombers. The island of Milos, in the blue Aegean, would have appeared next. 'And then finally, after endless minutes, greeted with great relief, land is sighted,' continued Ringel. 'Huge mountains emerged from the haze like a mighty fortress. It was the objective, Crete.'[35]

As a result of its delay, Witzig's 3rd Battalion did not arrive over Maleme until 1030 hours, well after the fighters and bombers of VIII Fliegerkorps finished their bombing and strafing runs. In order to avoid dropping paratroopers into the sea, a common occurrence during previous sorties due to unexpected winds, the 3rd Parachute Battalion was released over the hills to the south of the Maleme–Platanias road. A paratrooper assigned to one of the twelve gliders of the Assault Regiment's 3rd Battalion, which was tasked with seizing the airport, remembered: 'At 5 am we took off from Megara in Greece. My main concern was the landing. I hoped that we would not have too much trouble as we could carry out our mission. Unfortunately, we were not delivered onto the right spot, Maleme airport, but some distance away, in an olive groove midway down Ridge 107.'[36] The high losses among the 750 airborne troops who assaulted the island in gliders was a harbinger of things to come. In addition, many of the paratroopers dropped at Canea and Rethymnon were released from too high an altitude and had landed highly dispersed.

As the transports carrying Witzig's company approached the coast, the planes dropped to an altitude of 100–150 metres. The dangerously low altitude of the drop minimised the time each paratrooper spent in the air vulnerable to ground fire. On command each paratrooper stood up, attached the snap hook of his static line to the cable running down the length of the right-hand side of the aircraft, and awaited the final signal to jump. Unlike in the operation at Eben Emael, Witzig and a number of his men were now armed with MP40 submachine guns in addition to their P08 pistols. Ammunition for both would have been slipped into magazine pouches and attached to their brown leather uniform belts secured with an aluminium buckle. A spare magazine would have been carried in the right chest pocket and a hand grenade in the lower left-hand pocket of the paratrooper's jump smock. The pistol would have been carried in a back right pocket.[37]

The vast majority of Witzig's men, however, still carried only pistols and knives and counted on reaching the weapons containers to retrieve their rifles and sub-machine guns. As they approached their designated drop zone the jump master in each aircraft sounded a klaxon. The paratroopers immediately began taking turns assuming a good door position and hurling themselves, spreadeagled, out of the right-hand side of the aircraft. The parachutes deployed automatically five seconds later, by which time each man had dropped twenty-five metres. After they all exited, four equipment containers were thrown out the exit door of the Ju–52. Each contained weapons, ammunition and equipment for three or four men. At this early stage in the development of airborne troops it was still considered very difficult for a man to land safely if he carried any weapons other than an automatic pistol and a large knife, although the men in the first platoon to land were equipped with up to four hand grenades, and every fourth man carried a sub-machine gun. Other containers were used to drop disassembled light field guns and mortars in loads weighing up to 120 kg. Within ten seconds, each aircraft had been emptied of its twelve paratroopers and four containers. The sky was filled with silk parachutes of various colours, announcing the arrival of the 3rd Parachute Battalion and Witzig's 9th Company: green and brown for the Fallschirmjäger (to make them less conspicuous on the ground and to serve as camouflage for motor vehicles later); white for equipment containers; and pink for medical supplies. Witzig and his men would have reached the ground in 20–30 seconds, with very little control over their parachutes or the direction of travel. During this period, they were at the mercy of the wind and the enemy below.[38] Unbeknownst to them, the entire battalion was jumping directly atop two enemy battalions.

The 3rd Parachute Battalion's drop zone was defended by the 21st and 23rd New Zealand Battalions, which German reconnaissance photos had completely failed to detect. The Kiwi infantry were well entrenched and camouflaged along the terraced slopes and had been manning their positions for some time when the German transports arrived overhead. As the paratroopers leaped from their Ju-52s, they were met by a dense and lethal barrage of fire. Richard Kienzen, a member of the 3rd Battalion's 11th Company, recalled the ordeal experienced by hundreds of paratroopers like him: ' [Lieutenant] Jung, my company leader, was killed in action. I was wounded during the descent (hit in the arm by a bullet which struck between the elbow and shoulder). I landed in an olive tree and was hit again. The bullet struck with such force that I could no longer use my arm. Dangling from my harness, totally defenceless, I was then captured by the British.'[39] Kienzen was one of the more fortunate ones. Many of the paratroopers were dead before they even hit the ground, while a large number died within seconds of landing. The commander of the 23rd Battalion, Lieutenant-Colonel D. F. Leckie, for example, reported shooting five of the descending Fallschirmjäger from his headquarters, while his adjutant, Captain R. M. S. Orbell, killed another two 'without getting up from his packing-case deck'.[40]

The New Zealanders responded quickly and aggressively to the German airborne assault, which had been expected for some time. 'Suddenly they came amongst us,' remembered Captain C. N. Watson,

A lone Ju-52 over the Mediterranean en route to Crete. Almost 300 were destroyed or damaged during the battle for Crete, crippling the Luftwaffe's transport fleet prior to Hitler's invasion of the Soviet Union.

Commander of Company A, 21st Battalion. 'I was watching the 21 Bn. Area and a pair of feet appeared in a nearby olive tree. They were right on top of us. Around me rifles were cracking. I had a Tommy gun and it was just like duck shooting.'[41] Paratroopers who dropped farther east met the same fate at the hands of the New Zealand Engineers and the men of the Field Punishment Centre, commanded by Lieutenant W. J. Roach. The soldiers under sentence were given rifles along with the promise of a pardon if they fought well. They were then released to hunt down paratroopers scattered in their area. Sixty prisoners killed 110 Germans in less than an hour.[42]

'The [21st] battalion's own casualties were light because their positions were under cover of the olives and the men moved into aggressive action so quickly,' remembered D. M. Davin, a platoon leader with the battalion, who would later write New Zealand's official history of the battle. 'Even so the companies had plenty to do outside the perimeter, clearing up prowling bands of paratroopers.'[43] Two-thirds of Witzig's battalion had been killed and the unit ceased to exist as a coherent fighting force even before it reached the ground. 'What a welcome they gave us!' remembered Witzig. 'Our battalion took heavy losses at Hill 107. From my company only one-third survived. I was the only one who survived, severely injured, from my plane load of ten men.'[44]

Few Germans escaped the New Zealanders and, during the course of the day, the 3rd Parachute Battalion was almost completely annihilated. According to an XI Fliegerkorps report, many of the paratroopers were killed or wounded while still in the air or when caught in trees. 'Those parachutists who landed in the valleys unharmed had no opportunity of joining up or searching for their weapons containers. The greater part of the containers fell into the hands of the enemy who put the weapons into immediate use. All the officers were killed or wounded.'[45] With the loss of virtually all of their key leaders, the survivors of the battalion, though of considerable nuisance value, were unable either to launch their planned attack against the airfield or make their way farther east to join Group *Centre*. Although some 10,000 paratroopers had landed by parachute, glider or troop transport by the end of the first day, only 6,000 were still in action by last light and the survival of the entire German force on the island hung precariously in the balance.[46] Forty per cent of the first two assault waves had been killed, wounded, or captured. The casualties included General Süssmann, who was killed during the approach flight to the island, and General Meindl, who was in command of the Maleme group and was critically wounded shortly after landing. As a result, both the Maleme and Canea groups were left without their commanders.[47]

By the evening of 20 May not a single airfield was securely held by the Germans. The most favourable reports came from Maleme, where the defenders were falling back from Hill 107 and their defences around the airfield, which, however, was still under British artillery fire. Moreover, parts of the airfield were obstructed by crashed and destroyed transports and gliders. There was thus no field available for the landing of elements of the 5th Mountain Division, scheduled for the next day. The division was scheduled to be transported to Crete by both sea and air. Canea was still in enemy hands and the troops there had landed at four different points and remained isolated and unable to form airheads. But while the attackers had run into unexpectedly strong resistance and had failed to reach their first day's objectives, the defenders were surprised by the fury and strength of the onslaught.[48] 'It was apparent that due to heavy casualties, the fighting power of the

FS [Fallschirmjäger] would hardly suffice to capture an airfield,' wrote Ringel. 'Maleme offered the best chance as the airfield had been mopped up and somewhat secured in the west and the south. Only the east was troublesome [as] the British were still able to cover the field in that direction with MG. [machine-gun] and Arty [artillery] fire. One had to start where the easiest success could be expected.'[49]

Student thus decided to form a battalion of paratroopers from his last available and uncommitted reserves and to employ them, under the command of Colonel Bernard Hermann Ramcke at Maleme, where he would relieve the wounded General Meindl. A tough and experienced veteran of Germany's Imperial Navy in the First World War, Ramcke had been commissioned during that war and then distinguished himself as a member of the Marine Assault Battalion Flanders in its last year. On 10 May 1919 he had joined the Reichswehr and transferred to the Army as an infantry officer after serving as a member of the Freikorps. In 1940 he transferred services once again, joining the 7th Fliegerdivision after commanding an infantry battalion. Ramcke earned his Parachutist-Rifleman's Badge that year at the age of fifty-one.[50] There was little else that Student could do but commit his remaining reserves under this battle-hardened, skilled and reliable officer. Ringel and Student would have agreed with British newspaper assessments that day emphasising that there was more at stake on the island than strategic deliberations. 'A German defeat here on Crete would mean a severe and presently quite disastrous setback to German prestige.'[51]

'It was obvious that the British were tougher and much stronger than we thought,' reported Student later, in a gross understatement aimed at justifying the near-failure of the Crete operation, 'but at that moment there was nothing we could do but hold our breath and leave the conduct of the battle to the commanders on the ground.' There was little fighting left to be done by the 3rd Battalion, which had suffered catastrophic losses. Three of its four company commanders had been killed during the battle and the fourth, Rudolf Witzig, had been seriously wounded in the right leg shortly after landing, losing a sizeable portion of his inner right thigh. Despite the severity of the wound, he managed to drag himself out of sight into a shell hole hidden by brush, attend to his wound, and await assistance. With his battalion almost wiped out, Witzig decided his best hope for survival lay in hiding until the arrival of German reinforcements. 'I was lucky to be picked up by our soldiers after one-and-a-half days and to be brought to a field

German wounded during the battle of Crete. According to German after-action reports, their casualties on the island were estimated at between 4,000 and 6,500 men, with two-thirds of those killed.

hospital,' he recounted afterwards.[52] In the interim the wounded Witzig had to endure, along with his Fallschirmjäger comrades, all the miseries Crete had to offer.

> The sun beat down merciless from the clear blue sky during the day [remembered General Ringel]. The thermometer registered from 40 to 50 degrees [Celsius, 104–122 °F] in the shade. Even the night did not bring relief. Blistering hot, burnt-out rocks emitted during the night the heat they had stored up during the day. Vermin and gnats, the lack of drinking water, the heavy cloth uniforms of the paratroopers drenched with sweat, heavy equipment, heavy weapons, lack of roads and the difficult desert-like terrain made life unbearable.[53]

In the meantime, the beginning of the second day of the operation brought little relief to the attackers. By late afternoon, however, the German paratroopers were in control of Maleme airfield, despite several fierce counter-attacks by the two New Zealand infantry battalions. During the night a convoy carrying the men and equipment of the 5th

Mountain Division to Crete was engaged and destroyed by the Royal Navy, killing 330 men and forcing the surviving ships to turn back. Only the timely and energetic rescue of survivors by the Italian Navy averted greater loss of life among the German troops. By 22 May the Germans were in complete control of Maleme airfield and using it to pour reinforcements into the island by Ju-52, despite heavy losses to the air transport fleet. By the following day, twenty Luftwaffe transports, each laden with troops, light artillery and other heavy equipment, were landing every hour and returning to the Greek mainland loaded with wounded German soldiers, including Rudolf Witzig.

The temporary grave of Major Scherber, commander of Witzig's battalion, on Crete.

By 24 May Operation Mercury had gathered sufficient momentum that a German victory was no longer in doubt. That night Admiral Cunningham advised the British Chiefs of Staff that the scale of enemy air attacks was such that the Royal Navy could no longer operate off Crete in daylight. The following day considerable resistance, from Cretan civilians, unexpected by the invaders, resulted in the first executions, pillaging and burning of villages by German troops. A British air attack on the Maleme airstrip destroyed twenty-four Ju-52s, but such efforts were no longer enough to prevent the Germans from taking the island. On the morning of 27 May the Royal Navy managed to land 750 Special Forces commandos at Suda Bay and later that day the New Zealanders and Australians counter–attacked to stop the German advance west of Suda Bay. But the end was now in sight. On the 28th the Allies began evacuating the island, in an operation which cost the Royal Navy dearly. By 30 May Crete was in German hands. The final capitulation order for British forces on the island came at 0900 hours on 1 June. By that time the Royal Navy had evacuated 7,000 British,

4,500 New Zealanders, and 3,000 Australians from Crete to Egypt.[54] A large part of the defending force would thus live to fight another day.

'Mission completed. Crete is clear of the enemy as of today,' reported General Löhr the same day. After General Freyberg departed the island and the British War Office announced its fall: 'After 12 days of, doubtless, the hardest fighting of this war so far, it was decided to withdraw our troops from Crete.'

> The battle of Crete had been concluded [wrote General Ringel after the war]. A victory without equal was achieved through the sacrifices of the soldiers. With the capitulation of the British and the Greeks, the guerrilla groups also disbanded or retreated to the impassable hideouts of the White Mountains.[55]

Chapter 5

THE SPEARHEAD SHATTERED

At a victory parade in Germany following the epic battle Student praised his Fallschirmjäger.

> Our victory banners wave over Crete, You, my paratroopers and airborne troops, have, under your proven leaders, achieved unprecedented feats. Paratroopers! Filled with an unstoppable offensive spirit you, entirely on your own, defeated the numerically superior enemy in an heroic, bitter struggle. Wherever you landed on Crete you both stormed heroically and held stubbornly.

After the war, however, when he had had time to reflect, on the operation, he confessed:

> I find it very hard to write about Crete. For me, the commander of the German airborne forces, the name of Crete conjures up bitter memories. I miscalculated when I proposed the operation, and my mistakes caused not only the loss of very many paratroopers – whom I looked upon as my sons – but in the long run led to the demise of the German airborne arm which I created.[1]

As Student said during his post-war interrogation: 'Crete was the grave of the German parachutists.'[2]

The Battle of Crete had indeed been a disaster for the German airborne forces. For weeks after the battle newspapers all over Germany published black-bordered statements announcing the names of the dead. One military family lost three sons during the battle. At twenty-four years old, Lieutenant Wolfgang Leberecht Graf von Blücher was a veteran of Holland, where he had been awarded the Iron Cross First Class for storming and conquering a nest of bunkers. Assigned as the commander of the 2nd Company, 1st Parachute Regiment, he was

Lieutenant Rudolf Witzig reporting to Colonel-General Milch following a parachute jump of the Engineer Parachute Platoon in Lippstadt in May 1939.

killed in action on the second day of the battle after capturing a key hill at the eastern end of the Heraklion airport. Three days later he was awarded the Knight's Cross. His two brothers, Private Leberecht Graf von Blücher, nineteen years old, and Rifleman Hans Joachim Graf von Blücher, only seventeen, were also killed on Crete. The body of the youngest brother was never found.[3] 'Beyond all human conception, great and overwhelming is the watch of the dead,' wrote Ringel, 'who sacrificed their lives for their fatherland and the conquest of Crete.'[4]

According to German after-action reports, their casualties on Crete were estimated at between 4,000 and some 6,500 men. Generalmajor Burkhart E. Müller-Hillerbrand, adjutant to the Chief of the Army General Staff, wrote that these included 4,000 men killed and missing and another 2,000 wounded.[5] Ringel cites a figure of some 6,000 men for both the Army and the Luftwaffe.[6] Student's own figures for the battle were 3,250 killed and missing and another 3,400 wounded.[7] Those casualties included Generalleutnant Süssmann, commander of the 7th Airborne Division and highest-ranking German officer killed at Crete. He died, along with almost his entire staff, when one of the wings of the glider they were riding in snapped off, sending it plummeting to the rocky ground below.[8] Another high-ranking casualty was

German Airborne School, Stendal, 1938. A German paratrooper descends to the ground under his fully inflated canopy.

Generalmajor Meindl. Refusing to accompany his own staff into battle on their glider, he jumped instead with his 4th Battalion. So fierce was the fighting on the ground that, within an hour of landing, he had been wounded twice, including once in the chest. And out of the 500 men of Witzig's 3rd Battalion, some 400 had been killed, including its commander, Major Scherber, and its adjutant, Captain Heinz. Witzig himself was fortunate to have survived and to have been transported back to a German military hospital in Greece aboard a Ju-52.

German Airborne School, Stendal, 1938. Paratroopers of a Fallschirmjäger company descending to the ground. The vulnerability of German paratroopers in the air would become all too evident during the Battle of Crete, where thousands would be killed or wounded.

Losses to the Luftwaffe's transport fleet were equally heavy. Of the 600–650 Ju-52 transports used in the operation, some 270 were destroyed, seriously damaged or missing.[9] This represented more than a quarter of the entire Ju-52 transport fleet available to the Luftwaffe. The Ju-52 fleet would never again be used on such a large scale in support of airborne operations but instead would spend the remainder of the war hauling reinforcements and supplies. Generalleutnant Walter Warlimont, the Deputy Chief for Operations of the Armed Forces High Command, admitted that the loss of so many transports meant a considerable depletion in the strength of the Luftwaffe at the beginning of the Russian campaign.[10] Furthermore, their absence precluded any airborne invasion of Cyprus as a follow-on operation to Crete, a venture favoured by Göring and Mussolini. 'We could have taken Cyprus, too,' boasted Hitler's Reichsmarschall after the war. 'I would have taken it right after we took Crete. We could have also taken Malta easily. Then the Atlantic islands would have been a further protection for the coast of Africa. But fear of Russia stopped us.'[11]

In light of the debilitating losses suffered by the Fallschirmjäger and the Luftwaffe's transport arm in the Crete operations, Göring's claim was an empty one. Still, statements like these would give rise to a myth that only the lack of an order from Hitler prevented his paratroopers from continuing their airborne blitz across the Mediterranean to take Cyprus and Malta as well.

Nor was Göring alone with regard to myth-making; in view of the high losses suffered on Crete it is astounding that, in his order of the day for 12 June 1941, Löhr announced: 'True to our oath to the Führer and supreme commander of the Wehrmacht: "We stand ready for new tasks."'[12] This was clearly impossible as the loss in officers and NCOs alone precluded the commitment of the German airborne troops on any meaningful scale for some time to come. 'Our proud paratroop unit never recovered from the enormous losses sustained on Crete,' admitted Martin Pöppel frankly.[13]

Churchill was closer to the truth when he told the British people after Crete: 'The very spearhead of the German lance has been shattered.' However, he too engaged in myth-making, when he wrote after the war that the Germans had suffered well over 15,000 casualties.[14] According to the British official history of the battle, out of the 8,060 paratroopers from 7th Fliegerdivision and the Air-Landing Assault Regiment deployed on Crete, more than 4,500 became casualties. Yet Churchill was in effect correct when he wrote: 'But in fact the 7th Airborne Division was the only one which Göring had. This division was destroyed in the Battle of Crete. Upward of five thousand of his bravest men were killed, and the whole structure of this organisation was irretrievably broken.'[15] Indeed, the 7th Fliegerdivision never appeared again in any effective form. In comparison, British and Commonwealth forces suffered almost 16,000 casualties in the battle. Some 14,800 men were evacuated from the island by the Royal Navy, a task it was becoming quite proficient at accomplishing, to fight another day.[16] Of the more than 10,200 members of the Greek Army and Gendarmerie who fought with the British, some 1,500 were killed and another 5,000 taken prisoner.[17] The German victory was thus as lopsided as it was close.

Although Witzig believed the German attack on Crete was 'essential,' he called the execution 'weak'. 'Everyone thought the Fallschirmjäger could do everything; they would be able to master this as well,' he remembered. 'Our preparations were weak' he added, ever the meticulous planner. 'We were dropped at the wrong places … the wind had not been calculated correctly and many paratroopers fell with their parachutes into the water and drowned.' Furthermore, the 3rd Battalion jumped on top of 'many British defensive positions' and 'there was nothing known about their strengths and locations. Everything had to be figured out on the ground.'[18]

German after-action reports of the battle substantiate Witzig's observations and conclude that the operations 'many deficiencies' gave it the characteristic of an improvisation. 'German air reconnaissance during the period preceding the invasion was inadequate and the intelligence picture presented by the Luftwaffe did not correspond to the actual situation on the island,' noted a group of senior German officers, including Student and von der Heydte, who compiled the report. The British had succeeded in concealing fortifications and camouflaging their gun positions. Dummy flak positions were extensively bombed, while the real ones were not discovered. Some British positions were erroneously marked as artesian wells and the prison on the road to Canea was thought to be a British ration dump. The German Twelfth Army had a more accurate intelligence picture from local agents, but the Luftwaffe, believing that the British garrison consisted of only 5,000 combat troops and that they intended to evacuate the island immediately after the first airborne landings, refused to consider other estimates of enemy preparations. The same report went on to note that troops had indeed jumped at the wrong places 'in most instances', with some landing as far as 15 km to the east; others were dropped from too high an altitude and were exposed to enemy fire for much longer than necessary. 'Their conduct', noted the report, referring to the German transport pilots, 'jeopardised the success of the operation.' The report also concluded that a strong and well-integrated defence system could not be overcome by landing on top of it 'unless it has previously been smashed by continuous bombing attacks' and recommended that better results could be achieved by jumping 'at a distance from the objective' which had to be reduced by customary infantry actions, thus necessitating that the paratroopers 'receive infantry training'.[19]

These deficiencies indicate a potential problem among the Fallschirmjäger with the tactics, techniques and procedures they used, resulting in higher casualties than might have been the case had they been trained differently. The need for readily available 'strong reserves,

Rudolf Witzig eating a meal in the field during training prior to deploying to Greece for the Battle of Crete.

including flying formations' is also highlighted, indicating a command deficiency in this area as well. It was also noted that the arms and equipment containers often fell onto enemy positions and were used by British troops against the paratroopers 'inflicting heavy casualties on them with their own weapons'. Other containers fell into gullies and deep streams and could therefore not be recovered. The report recommended that individual soldiers jump with light machine guns, recoilless rifles and rocket launchers since they might be forced to fight before recovering their weapons containers. Finally, the German paratrooper uniform proved unsuitable for the hot climate of Crete. During combat many men suffered from heat prostration. 'Every movement on the battlefield involved terrific physical efforts, and the efficiency of the troops was thus considerably impaired.'[20]

While quick to point out deficiencies in the operation, Witzig was equally fast to praise those deserving it:

> The battle was won due to the initiative of the few: commanders, NCOs, even corporals and privates who took the initiative and did their best in the situation until the first landings in Maleme, under enemy artillery fire and with great losses of aircraft, could take place; until the landing of the mountain troops . . . These started the push from Maleme to the east, south-east and south that kicked the British off the island. This was not the task of the paratroopers any more but of the mountain troops.

Witzig was also not afraid to praise his opponent: 'Large parts of the British [Army] were captured in Greece,' he observed, and then asked in hindsight: 'What more could be left? Consequently, how difficult could this task be? But it was. The British defended their island vigorously. They did everything possible to hold Crete. They had the same exact reasoning we did for wanting Crete.'[21] General Ringel agreed to an extent with Witzig, but qualified his praise of the British: 'The enemy's stubborn defence could have led to our defeat if he had grasped the situation from the very outset and had made use of all his available forces and resources.'[22]

Commanders at all levels had their own explanations for the heavy German losses. 'Our losses had been caused by multiple reasons,' Freiherr von der Heydte later informed General Student, when the commander of Germany's airborne forces visited Crete after the battle:

Generalmajor Meindl was seriously wounded within an hour of accompanying his regiment into battle on Crete.

The troops had been inexperienced in parachute warfare. For many of them the Battle of Crete had been their first taste of action, and for most of them it had been their first drop against an enemy. The training of the officers had been none too thorough, and their personal bravery had not proved sufficient compensation for their lack of knowledge. But most important of all was the fact that in Crete we had encountered for the first time an enemy who was prepared to fight to the bitter end . . . It seemed almost a miracle that our great and hazardous enterprise had succeeded.[23]

Student partially agreed, later writing:

The capture of the island of Crete was the most interesting and eventful German airborne operation. The initial attack contained all the germs of failure. Only the fact that the defenders of the island limited themselves to purely defensive measures and did not immediately and energetically attack the landing troops saved the latter from destruction.[24]

Von der Heydte did not entirely agree:

On the other hand the German paratroopers demonstrated that it was possible to carry out an airborne operation on a large scale in which parachute units were not employed solely in support of ground forces, but on their own in order to solve unique and isolated strategic problems. They demonstrated that it was possible to attack an island – equal in area to one-fifth the size of Switzerland – and to take it by airborne operation despite the enemy's absolute supremacy at sea.[25]

Excessive casualties and the loss of large numbers of valuable transport planes, coming so close on the heels of the heavy losses suffered in Holland the previous year, convinced Hitler that airborne troops had lost much of their strategic surprise value and, thus, utility. 'The day of the paratrooper is over!' he declared to Student after learning the true extent of the casualties. 'The parachute arm is a surprise weapon and without the element of surprise there can be no future for the airborne forces.' Freiherr von der Heydte objected: 'Hitler and his military advisers did not draw the right conclusions from the experience in Crete,' he argued, though almost certainly not to Hitler. 'They saw only the losses, but not the reasons for the losses or the possibilities for the future.'[26] Interestingly enough, Witzig agreed with Hitler's reasoning, even more than sixty years after the battle:

We couldn't expect that a surprise like that [at Eben Emael and the Albert Canal] would be possible again anywhere during the war. One had to be prepared [for the fact] that our enemy had woken up and henceforth would be informed of how we were preparing to use our [parachute and air-landing] forces. And this is what happened. The attack on Crete with our air-landing forces was not a surprise at all for the English. They knew exactly what was planned, just not where the air-landing and parachute troops would land. They knew they had to face both. The surprise was gone![27]

Not surprisingly, it was the Führer who had the last word and, despite objections from his Fallschirmjäger officers, Operation Mercury was the death-knell of the German airborne forces in the role for which they had been created. 'After the Crete operation no German parachute division was committed in airborne operations as a whole unit,' protested Student. Indeed, according to him, only parts of the remaining divisions, of which there were six in 1944 and ten or eleven at the end of the war in 1945, were trained for airborne operations.[28] The decision was not as wrongheaded as Student would have his American and British counterparts believe after the war. Hitler realised, perhaps better than anyone else, that the training of an elite paratrooper was a long, arduous and resource-intensive process and one increasingly difficult for him to support as the scope of the war spiralled out of his control. The German leader realised too well that his Fallschirmjäger could no longer establish the strategic pre-conditions for success as had been the case in Norway, the Low Countries and Crete. From then on, the Fallschirmjäger would be used as fire brigades of elite infantry to attack and defend where the fighting was the toughest, such as the Eastern Front. There, in Russia, according to von der Heydte 'the greater part of those who survived the Battle of Crete bled to death'.[29]

Many historians consider it ironic that the German experience at Crete led Hitler to turn his back on the further development and use of parachute and glider forces, while at the same time prompting Roosevelt and Churchill to develop parachute and glider forces that would total almost eight divisions and include an airborne army and two airborne corps headquarters by the end of the war. But while Germany could no longer afford the expense and time involved in producing elite paratroopers, the Allies, and especially the United States, could. The expansion of the American armed forces, which would eventually total some fourteen million young men and women and be equipped on a lavish scale unprecedented for any army in history, was only just beginning. The Americans and British felt that they could provide the manpower and technology to ensure the success of future large-scale airborne operations. The dubious results of U.S. and British airborne operations in Sicily, Normandy, Holland and

Germany, however, would later cause many Allied commanders to question whether those elite soldiers might not have better served their armies in the ranks of the infantry. Indeed, after the near disaster of the Sicily drop, Eisenhower and other senior U.S. Army generals concluded that division-size airborne operations were impractical. Only the personal and vigorous intervention of the commander of the 82nd Airborne Division, Major General Matthew B. Ridgway, prevented the dissolution of his division.[30]

Hitler arrived at the same conclusion Eisenhower and his lieutenants had contemplated, and he implemented changes affecting the future employment of his Fallschirmjäger. The performance of his elite paratroopers, used as the backbone for regular infantry and even second- and third-rate formations in defensive operations in Russia, North Africa, Italy (especially at Monte Cassino), Normandy and finally inside the Reich itself, validated, to a large extent, Hitler's decision. The Allies learned that wherever they encountered Fallschirmjäger units, they could expect the fight of their lives against an unyielding, extremely skilful, and almost fanatical foe. It was a lesson the Allies themselves applied with equal success at Ste-Mère-Église, Carentan and Bastogne.

The heroism of the German Fallschirmjäger at Crete would forever be marred by the actions of some German soldiers against the island's population after its capture. According to German accounts, such actions were prompted by rumours of large-scale mutilation by Cretan partisans of the bodies of a number of German paratroopers. General Ringel was quick to exonerate his soldiers for the reprisals that followed: 'As long as the Fallschirmjäger occupied the island, which was until the end of the year 1941, there was not a single case of sabotage nor attack by the Cretans,' he told American interrogators. 'On the contrary, the attitude improved, relations with the population became more and more friendly and there were touching scenes when the Parachute Division left.'[31] It is clear, however, that Ringel was attempting to convince the allies that the Fallschirmjäger had not been involved in large scale atrocities on the island. This is simply not supported by historical evidence. As a result of the alleged mutilations, Student ordered harsh retaliatory measures against Greek civilians who participated in the fighting. 'The German units concerned were to return to the respective villages, exterminate the male population, and demolish or burn down all the houses,' notes the official postwar German history of the battle. Student expressly ordered the officers concerned not to wait for a special military court but to set a 'warning' example. 'He believed that in this way he could create the best conditions for his work as the future German commander on the island.'[32]

In the end possession of Crete was not as crucial to Germany's war strategy as Hitler, Student and even junior officers such as Rudolf Witzig had believed. The island proved of little value to the Axis powers because subsequent developments in the overall strategic situation prevented them from exploiting their victory. But all that was irrelevant to Witzig. Evacuated to hospitals first in Athens, then Berlin and finally Braunschweig, near his home, he spent almost a year recovering from his wounds. During this period he wrote articles on Eben Emael for the local schools and various papers. It is illustrative that so little is said about Crete in his informal memoirs. His only comment to his family long after the war was short, concise, and typical of Witzig: 'Right strategy, wrong tactics!'[33] It is perhaps natural that it is to Eben Emael, the site of his greatest conquest, that he returns, again and again, during and even after the war. Crete, the graveyard of not only the German airborne and so many of his own friends and colleagues, but also of Witzig's innocence with regard to the infallibility of Adolf Hitler and the Third Reich, appears best forgotten.

One wonders if contemplating the loss of so many of his men, as he lay hospitalised for months on end, caused Witzig to waver in his loyalty to Hitler or his faith in a victorious ending to the war. True, Germany was at the zenith of its power in Europe, the Balkans and the Mediterranean and, shortly after Witzig was hospitalised, the Wehrmacht began over-running most of Russia as well. To accommodate the Führer's latest act of aggression, the size of the Wehrmacht had ballooned to 8,254,000 men, a significant increase from the 6,600,000 men of the previous year.[34] At sea German U-boats were savaging Allied shipping. And at the beginning of December 1941, Japan gutted the American fleet at Pearl Harbor and then surged through Asia and the Pacific riding the crest of a tidal wave of victory, defeating one British and American force after another. In response, Hitler had declared war against the United States. But already, unbeknownst to the Axis and Allies alike, the tide was beginning to turn.

It is now clear that Operation Barbarossa, Hitler's invasion of the Soviet Union launched on 22 June 1941, soon after the end of the Crete invasion, was the beginning of the end of the Wehrmacht and the Third Reich. The start of the campaign in Russia was characterised by a series of unparalleled German victories that many believed spelled the imminent collapse of the Soviet Union. Within weeks the Wehrmacht had travelled half the distance to Moscow, killed half a million Russian soldiers and taken one million prisoners. The German successes prompted General Franz Halder, Chief of the General Staff, to exult: 'It is thus probably no overstatement to say that the Russian campaign has been won in the space of two weeks.'[35] Within a month the German Army conquered an area twice the size of Germany and by August the Russians had lost three million men. But Hitler and his generals had dangerously underestimated the fighting abilities and tenacity of the Russian soldier and by 13 August, Germany had suffered almost 400,000 casualties on the Eastern Front, including more than 83,000 killed. This represented 11·4 per cent of the total German strength in the east.[36] The Wehrmacht lost more soldiers killed between June and August 1941 in Russia than had died between September 1939 and May 1941, prompting Halder to lament: 'The whole situation makes it increasingly plain that we have underestimated the Russian colossus.' While Rudolf Witzig was well into his recuperation period, German forces had bogged down at the very gates of Moscow after advancing more than 2,000 km. The true situation was recognised by many, but especially by those serving in the armed forces, such as Rudolf Witzig, for what it was: Germany's first major setback in the war. It was soon followed by a massive Soviet counter-attack which succeeded in throwing the Germans back 100–250 km from Stalin's capital and proving that the Wehrmacht was far from invincible and the Red Army far from beaten. By the end of December 1941, less than six months after the beginning of Barbarossa, more than a quarter of the men of the German Army who began the campaign on the Eastern Front were dead, wounded, prisoner or missing.

The situation in North Africa, the Reich's other active front, was little better. Earlier in the year, on 18 November 1941, a British offensive, Operation Crusader, hit Rommel hard, throwing him back and relieving Tobruk. As a result the German High Command was forced to come to Rommel's aid, transferring the Luftwaffe's Second Air Fleet Headquarters, under Field Marshal Kesselring, from the Eastern Front to the Mediterranean in the critical days of early December.[37] Thus did the British contribute to reverses suffered by the Wehrmacht on the Eastern Front, at a critical time when every combat and transport aircraft counted.

As a result of severe manpower shortages, the German High Command was increasingly forced to use airborne formations in the

Rudolf Witzig recovering at the Berlin Hansa Clinic. Witzig spent four months at the clinic before being transferred to a hospital near his home. The sole surviving officer of his battalion, Witzig spent almost a year recovering from his wounds.

ground role in Russia. Towards the end of September 1941, the 7th Fliegerdivision received a warning order to have some of its units ready for deployment to Russia, where they would used as infantry. The unit selected was the 1st Parachute Regiment, based at Stendal and now commanded by Generalmajor Bruno Bräuer. The regiment deployed shortly afterwards to the Leningrad area, where it was involved in hard fighting before returning to Germany in January 1942. While still in Russia, it was joined by other elements of the division, now commanded by Generalmajor Erich Petersen. An Army infantry officer, Petersen had taken command of the 7th Fliegerdivision on 1 October 1941, the day he entered the Luftwaffe.[38] His selection to command the elite formation is indicative of the ground role Hitler had in store for his paratroopers. The units he took to Russia included the 3rd Parachute Regiment, the Parachute Engineer Battalion, the Parachute Artillery Detachment, the 7th Medical Detachment, and most of the division's attached panzer units. These formations were deployed to the Neva, where they saw bitter fighting, suffering some 3,000 casualties.[39]

The critical shortage of German infantry on the Eastern Front even necessitated the deployment of the understrength Air-Landing Assault Regiment, which had been brutalised in Crete. It was sent to Russia in December 1941, minus two battalions, which previously went with the 1st and 2nd Parachute Regiments, to defend an airfield. Like their paratrooper brethren, the glider troops also suffered extremely heavy casualties. And as soon as these depleted formations returned from Russia, they were replaced by other elements of the fully reconstituted 7th Fliegerdivision, which was at full strength with some 21,000 men, all trained as paratroopers. The division was stationed in Normandy and came under the command of Generalmajor Richard Heidrich, a parachute artillery specialist and the former commander of the 3rd Parachute Regiment.[40] Thus began a constant rotation of Fallschirm-jäger units through the Russian meat grinder that would last most of the war.

While in hospital, Witzig lost not only a portion of his leg, but a piece of his heart as well. He had fallen in love with and become engaged to Gerda Remmers, now a doctor of medicine in Münster, whom he had first met in Höxter, where she had been a medical student. Gerda died, however, from an infection in January 1942. Witzig was devastated. It was to her younger sister Hanna, now seventeen years old, that he turned increasingly. The two met again at Gerda's funeral, a sympathetic chord was struck, and they started to exchange letters on a regular basis. Hanna had attended the boy's high school in Höxter and received her diploma the previous year. She was one of only two girls in a class of twenty-seven students and only one of five students to remain in school long enough to complete the course. 'All the others were already soldiers, somewhere at the front,' she wrote in a short autobiography.[41] Hanna would have preferred to study medicine and everything had been arranged at Berlin University. However, as a result of 'the worsening military situation' and the targeting of Berlin by British bombers, her parents did not allow her to go. 'Therefore I attended the Housekeeping School in Höxter for one year until March 1942. In January 1942 my sister Gerda died. This was quite shocking for my parents and me.'[42]

In April 1942 Hanna, like all German men and women her age, reported for her Reichsarbeitsdienst (RAD, or Reich Labour Service) duty, to Herringhausen in Westphalia. Unemployed workers were 'voluntarily' drafted into service on public-works projects after the Nazis

Witzig enjoying an evening with friends in Berlin prior to the battle of Crete.

came to power and a compulsory six-month period of labour service was introduced for all young men in June 1935. Labour service remained voluntary for young women until 15 February 1938, when all single women under the age of twenty-five were required to undertake a 'duty year' of labour service.[43] Hanna worked alongside other young women in a warehouse and enjoyed her service 'despite the strenuous work and the many privations'.[44] After her RAD obligation was over, she supported her father, a doctor, during office hours and drove him as he made his house calls. 'Then I studied two semesters of medicine in Göttingen, but I had to stop because of the total war and I worked for the Red Cross as an assistant at the Protestant Hospital in Höxter.'[45]

In the meantime, her relationship with Rudolf Witzig soon blossomed into romance, a not unwelcome development for her parents, who liked him a great deal. She appreciated his strong personality and good sense of humour. He liked her beauty and musical talent. He liked to sit with her while she played the piano, and the two would sing the songs his mother used to sing to him when he was a child. True, there were important and major differences between them. Hanna and her entire family were staunch Lutherans, and she loved singing in the choir at the Protestant Church in Höxter. Witzig, on the other hand, professed to be non-religious and was put off by the clergy, whom he perceived as 'zealots' and 'fanatics' because they opposed the war and called on young German men to avoid service in the military.[46] His attitudes towards religion and the clergy were in lock-step with those of the Nazi Party, which believed priests and pastors were nothing more than 'viruses and agitators' and 'closet reactionaries misusing religious beliefs in order to fish in dark waters'.[47] Yet Witzig had never been a member of the Nazi Party and he was in love nonetheless. With his full recovery imminent, the war and his paratroopers started calling once again and any doubts about the future he might have contemplated were cast aside as he marched to answer, his upper right leg wrapped tightly to prevent thrombosis.

Although his wound would plague him for the remainder of his life, it failed to slow him down. On 10 May 1942 he was posted as commander of the newly formed Corps 11th Parachute Engineer Battalion. The battalion had been formed earlier that year in Dessau. Some officers, especially engineers and intelligence and communications specialists, were transferred to the new battalion from the Army and the Luftwaffe, while a number of others volunteered. An entire company from the Independent Engineer Battalion in Tangermünde was assigned to the battalion. A number of its officers and NCOs had taken part in the attacks on Eben Emael and the Albert Bridges in Belgium as well as the German air assault on Holland and the invasion of Crete.[48]

Chapter 6

NORTH AFRICA: FIRST BATTLES

By the beginning of 1942 there were some 21,000 trained paratroopers in the ranks of the German airborne forces. Activation of a second parachute division raised this number to somewhere between 30,000 and 40,000 men.[1] A robust structure of schools and experimental institutions under the command of XI Fliegerkorps provided support for these forces. These included three parachute schools (at Wittstock, Salzwedel, and Stendal), an airborne combat observers' school, three transport-glider schools, a parachute proving centre, a transport-glider proving centre, an Me-321/Me-323 experimental detachment, an Me-321/Me-323 loading detachment, a supply dump, and a parachute depot. With a permanent strength of approximately 200 men, each of the parachute schools was capable of training 300–400 men a month, representing a tremendous potential for further and rapid expansion of Germany's airborne forces. To provide support for large-scale operations, the parachute depot stored and maintained 120,000 parachutes, enough for two parachute divisions.[2]

The Me-321 Gigant was designed and constructed in 1940 to carry heavy loads, including artillery pieces, small assault guns, light tanks, and other motor vehicles or an entire company of soldiers. The world's largest glider and first oversize transport aircraft, it had a wing-span of almost 55 m and a length of more than 28 m. Weighing some 12·5 tonnes unloaded, it could carry approximately 22 tonnes of cargo. The six-engine Me-323 was a motorised version of the Gigant.

Certainly one of the reasons for the expansion of the parachute arm was that, at the beginning of June 1942, the German High Command had ordered the commander of XI Fliegerkorps to initiate preliminary measures for the capture of Malta. The island had been under constant air attack since the summer of 1940 because it constituted a steady and serious menace to the supply lines of the German–Italian forces fighting in Africa, by now under General (soon to be Field Marshal) Erwin Rommel. Indeed, Kesselring believed the Italians should have captured Malta before setting out to conquer North Africa. Planning to capture Malta had begun early in the war but took on new urgency in the spring of 1942.[3] The idea was to capture the island before Rommel would be allowed to advance on the Suez Canal. Malta's garrison consisted of some 30,000 men, supported with artillery and anti-aircraft guns as well as combat aircraft. Operation Hercules, as it was named, was to be carried out by five parachute regiments and one parachute-engineer battalion, supported by parachute artillery, mortar, flak, and machine-gun units, along with an 'armoured para-chute' detachment. The assault would commence with a German-Italian air offensive against the island. Luftwaffe aircraft support consisted of 2–3 transport groups, equipped with He–111s, and 7–8 airborne groups (later raised to 8–12) equipped with Ju–52s, as well as DFS 232, Go–241 and Me–321 gliders.[4] In all, some 500 transport aircraft would support the assault.[5] It was also planned that an Italian parachute brigade would participate using its own Savoia transport planes.[6]

A detailed May 1942 memorandum by Kesselring to General Count Cavallero, Chief of the Italian High Command, indicated that the Germans had learned some lessons from Crete and were determined not to repeat their previous mistakes. The plan called for intensified reconnaissance 'so that no defensive works escape notice', aerial suppression of enemy defences 'day and night', achievement of surprise as to the time and place of the initial airborne landings, a mass parachute assault by both German and Italian paratroopers, and the timely delivery and protection of seaborne troops. By the second half of June all reconnaissance for the operation had been completed and it appeared likely that Witzig and his parachute engineers would soon be part of another big show.[7] But the Italians claimed that they had not finished their preparations and successfully requested a postponement until after 20 July 1942. Rommel had, by this time, been allowed to attack once more, but had been brought to a halt in front of the El Alamein line. The most favourable moment was thus missed and soon afterwards the planned airborne invasion of Malta was cancelled as the forces needed for the operation, especially the airborne forces and transport squadrons, were required for other purposes.[8]

It is unlikely a German–Italian victory in Malta would have come cheaply, if at all. Plans for the airborne invasion of the island were nothing more than Crete on a larger scale. True, the ad hoc nature of the Crete operation would have not been present during the invasion of Malta, but if the Germans and Italians were better prepared offensively, the British were equally better prepared defensively. By the end of April 1942 British aerial reconnaissance had detected marshalling areas for airborne and glider troops in Sicily. Ultra ensured that the British would have been forewarned with regard to the exact timing of an invasion.[9] And in May the island was reinforced with Spitfire and Hurricane fighters flown from the carriers USS *Wasp* and HMS *Eagle*. These aircraft managed to bring down sixty-five Axis aircraft in a single day and allowed the RAF to establish air superiority over the island.[10] It was this fact, more than any other, in combination with Hitler's fears of another Crete-like massacre of his airborne elite, and his lack of confidence in his Italian allies, that caused him to blink, calling off the invasion of the island.

The cancellation of the German airborne invasion of Malta was a tremendous blow to General Student, who was trying to regain a major role for his devalued Fallschirmjäger in Hitler's war plans. 'Since the operation in Crete I have been concentrating on the future development of the Paratroopers and on improving the methods of their operational employment,' he wrote in 'The Future of German Paratroopers and Airborne Operations' addressed to Hermann Göring on 10 November 1942. Student's report was comprehensive and addressed a number of subjects. The first was a quick-release parachute harness, which took only 10 seconds to jettison and could be released in a prone position, as opposed to 80 seconds for the older-model harness. 'With the parachute then in use, a paratrooper could only release himself from the harness by standing upright, and thus presented an easy target for enemy fire,' wrote Student. Furthermore, new jump techniques had been pioneered, which allowed German paratroopers not only to land with all their weapons, including rifles and sub-machine guns, but also allowed them to employ their weapons as they descended. 'The throwing of hand grenades with percussion fuses was also experimented with,' wrote Student: 'Firing from the air now forms an integral part of all paratrooper training.' Great strides had also been made in replacing the Ju-52, which the commander of airborne troops described as 'a slow, unwieldy aircraft with unprotected fuel tanks', thus making it an easy target for enemy fighters and anti-aircraft fire. According to Student, several thousand jumps had been made with the He–111, which could carry twelve paratroopers, and the Go–242 glider, which carried sixteen. 'The use of gliders represents a further step forward towards the solution of the urgent problem of air transports,' wrote Student, 'and indicates the great possibilities of giant aircraft such as the Me–321 and Me–323 in the future conduct of war.'[11]

Improvements had also been made to the weapons used by the Fallschirmjäger and included the development of a new assault rifle, light artillery, and air–transportable heavy mortars. Furthermore, greater emphasis had been given to airborne operations at night. Special clothing had also been further refined to reduce personal injuries on landing and now included protection for the face, shoulders, elbows, knees, ankles and pelvis. A new family of light, medium and heavy gliders was produced, which featured two machine guns in some models to provide them with defensive firepower during descents and landings. 'The German Paratrooper Corps has demonstrated its value in all theatres of war,' argued Student. 'Trained for special tasks and accustomed to fighting engagements in which there can be no surrender, its offensive spirit is probably greater than that of the Army – which can usually afford to be more cautious.'[12]

Student's arguments fell on deaf ears. Göring had no desire to support a force or concept abandoned, to all intents and purposes, by Hitler. Furthermore, strategic events were unfolding which led the German High Command to send the rapidly deployable and still dependable Fallschirmjäger into action. Once committed as regular infantry in conventional ground operations they would never again perform their original role on a large scale.

In the meantime, in July 1942, the Corps 11th Parachute Engineer Battalion shifted its headquarters from Dessau to the Flak Kaserne at Wittenberg. That same month, Witzig's 2nd Company, commanded by Lieutenant Tietjen, was deployed to Libya to strengthen Colonel Ramcke's paratrooper brigade, which had been sent to reinforce Rommel's Afrika Korps.

On 1 September Rudolf Witzig was promoted to major and that same month the battalion gathered in Wittenberg to participate in a training sports festival under the watchful eyes of Colonel Walter Barenthin, who was no doubt evaluating its combat readiness. A German Army engineer officer for most of his military career, Barenthin had been transferred to the Luftwaffe and was serving as the Chief Combat Engineer officer for XI Fliegerkorps. By October Witzig's unit had reached a high level of training and was deemed proficient in engineer, combat engineer and infantry tasks. However, it was still lacking its full establishment of engineer equipment, wheeled vehicles and bridging equipment. Furthermore it had never trained with its parent parachute corps or with other units.[13] But there was little more that could be done, as time had now run out.

In late October the unit was alerted for movement to Italy. Like the 2nd Company, the remainder of the battalion was bound for Libya as reinforcement to the *Ramcke* Brigade. An advance party consisting of the battalion's staff, communications platoon, and 1st Company traveled to Athens and then to Lecce and Brindisi in southern Italy, bound for a transport ship heading to North Africa. However, it was held in place, while a second element consisting of the 3rd and 4th Companies, was delayed in Naples. 'The situation of the Afrika Korps, and of the *Ramcke* Paratrooper Brigade, had worsened,' wrote Witzig, in his history of the battalion, 'and [safe] transport to Libya became questionable.'[14] Witzig was referring to the British attack against Rommel's Afrika Korps at El Alamein, which opened on 23 October, shattering the German–Italian defences. Besides being critically short of fuel, Rommel was also out–gunned and out–manned by British General Bernard Law Montgomery's Eighth Army and by 4 November his defeated army was in headlong retreat across Libya. Some 30,000 Axis soldiers fell prisoner to the British. The climax of the Western Desert campaigns, El Alamein was one of the major turning points of the war. The victory did a great deal towards influencing the Vichy French ultimately to cooperate with the Allies in the North African campaign.[15]

Although hampered by his wounds, Witzig had completed the Battalion Commanders' Training Course at the Engineer School in Dessau. Command of the 11th Parachute Engineer Battalion was his first experience as a battalion commander and the physical requirements of his new job caused him to suffer a relapse, forcing him to return to the hospital at Wittenberg in October with inflammation of his leg. This was about the same time the advance party from his battalion was departing for Italy. Ten days later, he left hospital and followed the battalion, reporting in person to Field Marshal Kesselring, Commander-in-Chief South, in Rome. 'The Allied troops had landed in

Morocco,' remembered Witzig, 'and Kesselring was desperately looking for troops to throw against them.'[16] Reporting that his scattered unit was now all in Italy, Witzig was given his orders: Tunisia.

On 8 November 1942 American and British soldiers began landing on the beaches of North-West Africa as part of Operation Torch. They were part of an Allied expeditionary force, which brought together ground, sea and air forces from the United States and Great Britain under the overall command of Lieutenant General Dwight D. Eisenhower. The occupation of France's North African colonies was part of a series of operations aimed at Allied domination of the Mediterranean Sea and control of the coastal region. By landing behind, or to the west of Rommel's Panzer Army Africa, which was at the same time being hammered by General Montgomery's British Eighth Army from the east, the Allies hoped to finish off the troublesome Desert Fox once and for all. After liberating French North Africa and clearing Axis forces from the Italian colonies, the Allies sought to bring the French back into the war against the Axis and reopen the Mediterranean route to the Middle East. From there they would move to Sicily, Sardinia and Corsica, drawing more and more German forces away from Continental Europe and into the defence of Italy and Hitler's vulnerable ally, Benito Mussolini. Eventually, the Allies sought to deliver a solid blow from southern France against the German forces arrayed to oppose an Allied landing in northern France. All of this was intended to assist the Soviet Union by establishing a second front against the Germans, while at the same time creating the conditions for the success of the Allied landings in northern France.[17]

The Allied army which landed in North Africa consisted of 107,500 men supported by approximately 10,000 vehicles, and was organised into three task forces. Commanded by Major General George S. Patton and with almost 34,000 men and 250 tanks, the Western Task Force had the mission of securing the port of Casablanca and adjacent airfields and, in conjunction with the Centre Task Force at Oran, of establishing and maintaining communications between Casablanca and Oran. It was also to build up land and air striking forces capable of securing Spanish Morocco, if necessary. Commanded by Major General Lloyd R. Fredendall, the Centre Task Force, the largest of the three, had almost 41,000 men, including 37,000 Americans and almost 4,000 British, and 180 tanks. Its mission was to seize the port and city of Oran. Finally, the Eastern Task Force, commanded by British Lieutenant-General Kenneth Anderson, had a strength of almost 33,000 men. The smallest of the three task forces, it had the mission of seizing Algiers. The three task forces together were transported and supported by over 300 warships and some 370 merchantmen.

Instead of Germans and Italians, the Americans and British faced a French Army of 120,000 men. Of these 55,000 were believed to be in Morocco, 50,000 in Algeria, and 15,000 in Tunisia. These forces were supported by twelve batteries of motorised field artillery. Some 120–160 obsolete tanks and 80 armoured cars of the French mechanised cavalry were available in Morocco, 110 tanks and 60 armoured cars in Algeria, and only 20 armoured cars in Tunisia. In addition, there was a regiment of anti-aircraft artillery in each colony. Some 155–170 French combat aircraft, most concentrated on Moroccan airfields, could be expected on first contact, with an additional 170–200 aircraft available from locations further inland within two hours.[18]

The Germans had long debated what to do about the French territories in North Africa in the event of an Allied invasion, but had not yet arrived at any firm course of action. Instead, they 'sceptically' tolerated the state of affairs created by the 1940 Franco-German armistice, 'feeling confident that the British and the Americans would never dare to strike while the Reich was strong'.[19] The Italians, on the other hand, assumed correctly that a successful Allied invasion meant the loss of their North African coast and Italy as the next objective. The Allied landing thus caught the Axis by surprise. 'We had discussed the possibility of your attacking the west coast of Africa but did not think that you would enter the Mediterranean,' Göring told his U.S. interrogators after the war. 'When the big convoy was reported near Gibraltar, we knew some operation was imminent, but the objective might have been any part of Africa, Sicily, Sardinia, Corsica or Malta.'[20]

Hitler's initial reaction to Operation Torch and the presence of Allied troops in Rommel's rear was surprisingly feeble. Once the magnitude of the Allied landing in Morocco and Algiers became known, however, the Führer belatedly recognised that Allied possession of North Africa would provide them with a base from which to invade southern Europe. Italy in particular, the Reich's closest ally, was gravely threatened. Were the Allies to gain possession of the Tunisian peninsula, the Axis would sooner or later be defeated in the central Mediterranean.

With the success of Operation Torch, the British breakthrough at El Alamein, and the start of the Soviet autumn offensives, the war had taken an unmistakably unfavourable direction for Germany. According to Generalmajor Christian Eckhard, it was the Reich's military situation between October and November 1942, as well as the crisis in the Wehrmacht High Command during the same period that diverted their attention and caused Hitler and his generals to lose sight of a possible Allied invasion of North Africa. As a result of El Alamein, Germany's fortunes in North Africa were irrevocably shattered and the High Command was forced to divert troops and material to 'the sorely-pressed Army in Africa'. In order to accomplish this, the men and equipment, ships and aircraft, had to be taken from over-stretched German sources as Hitler distrusted both Mussolini's Supreme Command and the fighting ability of his much-criticised Italian troops.[21] To make matters worse, the German strategic situation in the East had continued to deteriorate with both Stalingrad and Leningrad continuing to resist fiercely. As a result the Germans were becoming painfully aware that they had failed in their primary objective of destroying the Red Army.

At the same time, Hitler feared a large-scale Allied landing in Norway and used, according to Eckhard, 'vast quantities of material and equipment urgently needed on other fronts to improve the defences there', while in the Atlantic the effectiveness of Hitler's wolf packs was being diminished by the increasingly effective Allied air forces and navies.[22] Finally, it was in the air that the greatest shift in the correlation of forces between the two sides was becoming noticeable. In action almost without a pause, the Luftwaffe was unable to build any significant operational reserves or maintain a flow of trained replacements and equipment that met or exceeded its losses, while the Allied air forces, 'fast growing' and 'well trained', according to Eckhard, were beginning to make their power felt.[23] On top of this, Hitler had lost confidence in his most senior officers and had taken command of the Army in the East himself.

Despite all these developments, the Führer refused to accept that the initiative had changed hands, even though, by November 1942, 230 of Germany's 260 divisions, or more than 88 per cent, were on the defensive. Instead, he clung to his illusions and, until the beginning of December, continued to dream of launching fresh offensives westwards from Tunisia, to drive the Allies back into the sea, and eastwards to the Suez Canal.[24] The Allied landings in North Africa could thus have not been better timed. According to Generalleutnant Warlimont, there had been no prior planning on the German side for military operations in

Tunisia and no guiding principles had been laid down on which to base immediate action. This was mainly because of uncertainty about the attitude of the French. Responding quickly to the Allied incursion, however, the Germans decided to use the Luftwaffe to slow down the Allied advance, while building up Axis forces in preparation for offensive operations.[25] On 9 November, having decided, by arrangement with Mussolini, to establish a bridgehead in Tunisia, Hitler gave Field Marshal Kesselring a free hand. Kesselring, one of Germany's most brilliant strategists, had anticipated such a move and had already made the appropriate preparations. He had brought a parachute battalion group and his own headquarters defence battalion to high readiness and concentrated a group of mixed transports, which included six-engined BV–222 seaplanes, Ju–52s and Ju–290s, in preparation for transporting the two battalions to North Africa. Later these would be joined by the Me–323, the six-engined variant of the Me–321 glider and the largest transport aircraft then in existence. Kesselring also directed the military members of the Armistice Commission in Tunis to conduct negotiations with the French Resident-General to accept German ground and air units from Sicily and southern Italy at once. That same day elements of the Luftwaffe began moving to Tunis.[26]

Meanwhile, German bombers had started attacking Allied targets in Algiers, while reconnaissance aircraft tried to ascertain the extent of the American and British advance towards Tunis. At the same time, Ju-52 transport groups, totalling some 200 aircraft, began ferrying troops to Tunis.[27] The first aircraft began landing with the lead elements of the 5th Parachute Regiment at 1000 hours on 10 November. These units occupied first the airfield and then, during the night of 11–12 November, the city of Tunis itself.[28] Leading German parachute reinforcements into North Africa was Colonel Walter Koch, commander of the 5th Parachute Regiment and one of the heroes of Eben Emael and Crete. His 1st Battalion, 1st Parachute Assault Regiment, had participated in the ill-fated German assault on Crete and, on the morning of the invasion, Koch suffered a serious head wound near Hill 107 close to Maleme. Evacuated to Italy and then Germany, he was named commander of the 5th Parachute Regiment on 11 March 1942 and selected to lead the unit to Tunisia.[29] Koch's regiment consisted of two battalions, the 1st and 3rd. The formation's 2nd Battalion had previously deployed to North Africa in July 1942 with the *Ramcke* Brigade to reinforce Rommel's Afrika Korps.[30]

Now concentrated in southern Italy, Rudolf Witzig's 11th Parachute Engineer Battalion was alerted to move to Tunisia:

> The American landings in Morocco began during the transfer to the south. One feared that they would gain the upper hand there and move east into Tunisia. Therefore the High Command had to find ways and means to conquer Tunisia and hold it clear of the British and Americans. From there Italy was only a stone's throw away. Consequently, my orders were changed and my battalion landed with many other different units, from South Italy and Athens, by plane at Bizerta.[31]

The battalion's organisation included a headquarters company with a signal platoon, four parachute engineer companies, and a light parachute engineer column. Each of the parachute engineer companies consisted of a headquarters element, three platoons, and a medium machine-gun section with two medium machine guns. In addition, each platoon consisted of a platoon headquarters, with a small flamethrower and an anti-tank rifle team, and three sections, each with one light machine gun. The battalion had an authorised strength of 716 all ranks and was equipped with 36 light machine guns, 8 medium machine guns, 12 anti-tank rifles, and 12 flamethrowers. All the men had been intensively trained in the use of mines and demolitions of all types.[32]

Witzig's command was 572 strong, including 14 officers, 115 NCOs, and 443 enlisted men.[33] The 1st Company was led by Lieutenant Hünichen and contained two veterans of Eben Emael: Sergeant Niedermeier, who had led the 1st Squad, and Sergeant Helmut Wenzel. Lieutenant Ernst commanded Witzig's 3rd Company and Lieutenant Hardt his 4th Company. The commander of the Light Parachute Engineer Column was Lieutenant Conrad. Other key officers included Lieutenant Braun, the Adjutant, Medical Captain Dr. Illing and Medical Lieutenant Dr. Bartels, and Lieutenant Heise, the Signals Officer.[34]

'We received our marching orders,' remembered Rifleman Bohn, who had volunteered for the parachute forces at eighteen years old and was assigned to Witzig's 2nd Company. However, as the 2nd Company had deployed to North Africa in July, Bohn found himself serving with the 3rd Company in Tunisia after training at the Wittstock jump school:

> We swapped our uniforms for tropical clothes while our helmets were repainted sand brown. We guessed that we were bound for

Africa. For security reasons, we were then transformed into the soldiers of a Flak unit. We were issued with red-piped shoulder tabs, and with our helmets concealed deep inside our rucksacks, entrained for Italy. After a two-day journey, we arrived at Reggio in Calabria and on the next day, were flown by Ju-52s to Trapani in Sicily. We took off for Bizerta on the next morning.[35]

Corporal Feigl, commander of one of 4th Company's heavy machine-gun teams, was recalled back to his unit from a four-day leave granted after he received his parachute qualification badge. Feigl was not an altogether typical Fallschirmjäger. After serving in the Luftwaffe and qualifying as a mechanic he had volunteered for the parachute forces. Arriving too late to depart with his unit to Africa, he entrained with members of the *Barenthin* Glider Regiment for Caserta near Naples. 'At Naples, take-off was delayed because the machine-gun position [in the aircraft] was unmanned,' he remembered.

> Fortunately I had been trained to operate this kind of weapon and stood in for the gunner in the MG position. From this vantage point I had a splendid view of the Bay of Naples and Mount Vesuvius. We spent the night in Trapani but in the morning, take-off was delayed again, this time on account of mechanical problems.

Feigl offered his services to the pilot as a qualified aircraft mechanic and fixed the problem:

> We took off on hour behind schedule but did not regret it, as the aircraft which had left before us were attacked by British aircraft as they were about to land at Bizerta. One of our aircraft was shot down.[36]

'Monday – on the way to Africa,' wrote Sergeant Helmut Wenzel on 16 November 1942, as the battalion began its North African adventure:

> I write from a (six-motored) flying boat en route to Africa. We started at 0550 hours from the port of Piraeus; now we fly over the Adriatic in complete radio silence just above the water. The aircraft is carrying 41 men, 20 weapons containers, 4 bicycles, one ton of medical supplies and 10,200 litres of fuel on board. The fuel is for the flight over [to Africa] because we will not make any intermediate stops. The sun comes up, the sky is partly

> cloudy, and the boat flies without any problems. Besides me
> sleeps Lieutenant Heise [the battalion signals officer], fast asleep
> from yesterday's alcohol.[37]

Behind Wenzel's BV–222 flew a long line of Ju–52s ferrying more German troops to Tunisia.

Command of ground forces in Tunisia was placed in the hands of Lieutenant–General Walther Nehring, former commander of the Afrika Korps. Nehring arrived in Tunis on 16 November and took command the following day of the newly formed, though non–existent, XC Army Corps Headquarters, a headquarters in name only. 'German and Italian troops have landed in Tunisia in full agreement with the French and military authorities,'[38] announced the German High Command the same day. Nehring's command authority extended to all German and Italian army formations as well as the Italian marines. The German and Italian air forces and navies, however, remained independent and were only requested to cooperate. However, the 2nd Parachute Regiment and the 11th Parachute Engineer Battalion, both Luftwaffe formations, were also placed under Nehring's direct command. Air support included a German fighter group reinforced by dive bombers, several air force security companies and an Italian fighter squadron, all of which had participated in the first occupation of Tunis. Navy support consisted of several German E–boats anchored in Bizerta. The closest friendly Axis command was Field Marshal Rommel's German–Italian Panzer Army fighting near Derna some 2,000 km away. There was, however, only intermittent signal communications with it and distance and terrain precluded coordination of operations.[39]

Nehring's orders were to advance immediately to approximately the Tunisian–Algerian border, seize the western slopes of the Tunisian highland and establish defensive positions with sufficient depth and with sufficient space for troop movements to prevent an enemy break-through.[40] Kesselring hoped to establish a strong German bridgehead in Tunisia that, at best, would serve as a bridgehead for future offensive operations or, at worst, would allow Rommel's army to be withdrawn from Tripolitania to Sicily. To accomplish this Nehring established two separate bridgeheads; one at Tunis under Colonel Harlinghausen and the second at Bizerta under Lieutenant–Colonel Stoltz. However, soon afterwards, Stoltz was relieved by Colonel Friedrich (Fritz) Freiherr von Broich and Stoltz took command of the troops at Mateur. At about the

Battalion commander Rudolf Witzig receiving orders from Colonel Friedrich Freiherr von Broich in North Africa. In Tunisia Kampfgruppe Witzig's battalion was initially subordinated to Division Broich (later redesignated Division Manteuffel) and then to the Barenthin Glider Regiment.

same time Colonel Harlinghausen was relieved by Colonel Koch, freeing Harlinghausen to serve in his primary capacity as commander of all Luftwaffe units in Tunisia. Harlinghausen also retained command of the anti-aircraft troops and other units in Sousse, Sfax, and Gabès.[41]

In Tunis, Witzig's battalion was detached from Koch's command and subordinated to the newly formed Division *von Broich*, consisting of a hotch-potch of formations. No sooner had they arrived than Witzig and his men came under attack. 'We had hardly set foot in Tunisia when we were bombed by British aircraft, remembered Rifleman Bohn. 'Two comrades were killed. These were the first fatalities of our company. The war had started for good! We commandeered a large number of private vehicles and drove off in the direction of Sedjenane and Djebel Abiod.'[42] Within a short period of time Bohn, Feigl and Wenzel would find themselves in good company as German reinforcements continued to pour into Tunis and Bizerta. By the end of November the Axis order of battle in North Africa included the two battalions of the 5th Parachute Regiment, three companies of Witzig's 11th Parachute Engineer Battalion, and two-and-a-half battalions of the *Barenthin* Luftwaffe Rifle Regiment, commanded by Colonel Walter Barenthin. Manned by air force personnel, the regiment was chiefly composed of the staff and students of the Parachute School at Wittstock and the Glider School at Posen. As a result it was frequently referred to as the *Barenthin* Glider Regiment. Other reinforcements included Marsch Battaillonen (Personnel Replacement Transfer Battalions) 17, 18, 20, and 21, and miscellaneous artillery and anti-aircraft units.[43] Although 'march battalions' were organised strictly speaking for the transfer of personnel from the replacement area to the theatre of operations, the German situation in North Africa was so desperate that many of these units would be thrown into combat without sending the men to the field units for which they were intended.[44] Nehring reported that some of his march battalions were armed only with their personal weapons and lacked any anti-armour capability.[45]

Mobile and armoured units included two reconnaissance companies, detached from the 190th and 501st Panzer Battalions, and two companies of the 7th Panzer Regiment of the 10th Panzer Division. The only complete German formation still due to arrive was the 10th Panzer Division. German forces consisted of ten battalions, averaging 400 men each, supported by 130 tanks and 28 field artillery pieces.[46] In addition, on 12 November the Italians had started to send over the *Superga* Division, including four infantry battalions, commanded by General Lorenzelli. This move was still going on during December. They also sent the 10th Bersaglieri and two battalions of the *San Marco* Regiment of Marines, which were subordinated to Nehring on 2 December.[47] This gave the Italians a total of five battalions of unknown strength.[48] German and Italian combat troops were supported by reconnaissance, engineers and signal troops of undetermined strength. Some of these German units had originally been intended for Rommel's army. The march battalions, for example, had been destined to be reinforcement drafts, but were instead sent directly to Tunisia and put into the line, where they fought as infantry battalions. By 17 November the British estimated the enemy strength at around 500–1,000 combat personnel in the Tunis area and another 4,000 at Bizerta, with an unidentified number of tanks at each location. In addition, a large number of combat and support aircraft had been flown in. By the end of the month, the

Witzig outside his headquarters in Jefna with one of his airborne engineers.
Note the soldier is wearing the distinctive German airborne helmet, while
Witzig is wearing a soft garrison cap. Several of Witzig's soldiers told the
author that Witzig never wore a helmet in North Africa – only his cap.

Axis forces in Tunisia, exclusive of support elements, would total approximately 15,000 fighting troops backed by 130 tanks, 60 artillery pieces and 30 anti-tank guns.[49]

Despite the flow of German troops into North Africa, they remained heavily outnumbered by the Allies. A newly arrived British battalion, for example, had an authorized strength of 1,000 men, and many in fact fielded over 800, while a German battalion typically had only 400. Similarly, a British brigade had three battalions of approximately 2,400 men, while a German infantry division with nine battalions had only 3,600. A British infantry division normally had three brigades, while a British armoured division had three armoured regiments of battalion size and a motorised infantry brigade. In comparison, a German armoured division had only one armoured regiment and six infantry battalions, totalling some 2,400 men. 'If the strength of a British battalion dipped below 350 men, it was disengaged from the front and filled up,' wrote General von Arnim, while that same figure was the average strength of a

German battalion and this number decreased for as long as the Germans fought in Tunisia.[50] Yet despite their superiority on land, sea and in the air, the Allies had failed to exploit it in a timely manner due to their inexperience and caution, a mistake which would cost them dearly and seriously delay their inevitable victory.

If, like many, Rudolf Witzig had imagined North Africa as a dry country, he was in for a rude awakening. Winter was the wet season and the extent of the rains and their effects on the roads, on cross-country movement and on the airfields was as much of an unpleasant surprise to the Germans as it was to the British. In the northern zone, in which Witzig's troops and their colleagues faced the British First Army, the rains began early in December and would continue until April, with March the wettest month. Rain, mist and 'a particularly glutinous mud' formed the background to Allied and Axis operations during the North African campaign. Furthermore, both sides had to contend with a large, austere and extremely difficult theatre of operations. Northern Tunisia is a country of high mountains, narrow plains between the ranges, and few roads, with a limited scope for armoured action. In the south it becomes much more open and desert-like, but rocky hills occur everywhere. The distance between Algiers and Tunis is about 900 km and at first only two main roads and an inefficient railway were all that were available to the Allies and Axis alike in the extremely mountainous country. Both armies were completely dependent on what they brought with them in terms of transport, ammunition, fuel and supplies. 'Nothing whatsoever was available locally,' reported General Anderson, the British commander. 'Indeed, we had to supply the railway with coal, and our [French] Allies, out of our none-too-plentiful stocks, with rations, petrol and other supplies.' The Germans were forced to do the same with the Italians in order to keep them in the fight. The term 'front' was deceptive and, when defending, each side could only cover the main passes through the mountains with small forces of up to a brigade group. Gaps between these defended areas varied from 15 to 30 km as the crow flies, and these spaces were inadequately patrolled by both sides. General Anderson could have been speaking for the Axis as well, when he said of the Allies; 'Always the need was for more infantry.'[51]

The fighting in Northern Tunisia can be divided into three main phases. The first phase was a race for Tunis and Bizerta between the Allied and Axis forces. 'We just failed to win this race, after some bitter fighting in bad weather, which gave us our first experience of Tunisian mud,' reported Anderson. 'This phase ended after Christmas 1942.' The second phase lasted from 28 December 1942 to 27 March 1943. During this time both sides attempted to build up their forces and to hold or seize ground important for future operations, while struggling to improve their lines of communications. 'We were mainly on the defensive, suffered from an acute shortage of infantry, and were often very hard pressed in the mountainous country.' Finally, the third phase lasted from the Allied counter-attack at Djebel Abiod on 28 March through the final destruction of the Axis forces in Africa on 13 May 1943.[52]

Nehring initially expected the British to advance against Bizerta and Tunis along the two principal roads and believed they would try to capture Bizerta early. He decided to counter this move by attacking first. For this purpose, Witzig's battalion, reinforced with tanks, armoured cars and artillery and redesignated Kampfgruppe *Witzig*, was sent from Mateur towards Tabarka on 16 November with orders to drive the enemy back to Bône. The battalion was replaced in Mateur and Bizerta by Kampfgruppe *Stolz*. During the next few days the Axis occupied Sousse, Sfax, and Gabès, and raided Gafsa. In the meantime, the Tunis bridgehead continued to take shape. Gradually, all units in the Bizerta bridgehead coalesced to form the *Von Broich* Division, to which Witzig's 11th Parachute Engineer Battalion had been attached.

The Germans advanced along four separate axes towards Djebel Abiod, Béja, and Medjez el Bab as part of Operation Wild Sow. Witzig commanded the north-westernmost column. 'Hardly had we arrived [in North Africa] than the battalion received orders to march immediately after it was motorised,' he recorded.[53] Kampfgruppe *Witzig* had been motorised on short notice with requisitioned vehicles; its own motor park, having been left behind in Germany, was scheduled to arrive by sea. It had also been reinforced and now consisted of the 11th Parachute Engineer Battalion's 1st and 4th Companies (the 3rd Company having remained behind on the approach to Mateur), a battery of 105-mm guns, 16 light tanks, six 20-mm anti-aircraft guns, and 6 Italian armoured cars with 47-mm guns, totalling almost 600 personnel.[54] There was heavier armour too. While not mentioned in Witzig's official report, Matthias Scheurer, who served under Witzig in North Africa, remembers that Witzig was also reinforced with four Panzer IVs[55] and in his postwar history of the battalion, Witzig mentions

A street scene in Tunis. Both armies were dependent on what they brought with them; few supplies could be be obtained locally.

that he was reinforced with a company of Panzer IVs.[56] 'On 16 November the small combat team marched in the early afternoon, first, past the far superior French garrison at Ferryville, which reacted passively, and then past Mateur, approximately 35 km south-west of Bizerta,' recorded Witzig. 'We were enthusiastically received by the Arab and Italian settlers.'[57] As the Germans began their advance an Italian settler brought Witzig his beautiful white sports car and handed him the keys, remarking: 'I will not need it now. If all goes well, you can give it back. If not, it's lost anyway!' 'We used it until April 1943,' remembered Witzig.

The British had earlier attempted to beat the Germans to Mateur, but had been thrown back and were now dug in at Djebel Abiod. At 1500 hours on 16 November they spotted a column of German tanks and armoured cars approaching. 'They were by no means fully deployed, believing that Djebel Abiod was unoccupied,' recorded General Anthony Farrar-Hockley, historian of the British campaign in North Africa. 'Behind the tanks in transports was a detachment of parachute infantry.' The British opened fire at 200 metres, knocking out the two leading vehicles. Then a dog fight ensued around the village 'the powerful 75-mm gun of the Mark IV being particularly deadly in a long-range sniping at the British 2- and 6-pounder anti-tank guns'.[58] Heavy British artillery fire pounded Witzig's column, which deployed swiftly and then responded for the next three hours with accurate mortar and machine-gun fire, accompanied by effective shelling from the tank guns. Witzig and his men had been taken by surprise. 'Almost no reconnaissance!' recorded Helmut Wenzel angrily in his diary afterwards:

Our tanks engaged the target while we lay in a ditch. Our 88–
mm Flak was outstanding! It fired from the open road until it
received a direct hit and the crew were killed or wounded . . .
The British were well camouflaged in a village, while we were in
the open. Finally we occupied a small hill beside the road and
a few Arab huts.[59]

Their superior position and unyielding small–arms and artillery fire
decided the matter in favour of the British, despite the presence of the
Luftwaffe overhead, which contributed little to support Witzig. 'Due to
the lack of infantry, a further advance was not possible,' Witzig later
reported.[60] At dusk, the Germans and Italians retired, having suffered
some twenty casualties and eight tanks knocked out. 'Losses were
heavy,' reported General Anderson.[61] The British suffered the loss of
five field guns, most of their anti–tank guns, and a large number of
carriers and other vehicles destroyed or damaged.[62] The following day
Wenzel recorded the loss of two men from the 1st Company, including
Pionier Schumacher, who was 'so heavily wounded by artillery
fragments that he died'.[63] Within a short period of time the Germans
would learn to respect the British artillery. Fast, accurate, unrelenting,
and plentiful, it would make their lives in Tunisia miserable. Witzig's
positions at Djebel Abiod mark the westernmost points which German
forces would reach in the entire Tunisian campaign.

The battle continued at intervals during the next two days, with both
sides receiving reinforcements but neither being able to gain the upper
hand. 'The Kampfgruppe was forced to switch to the defence, between
high ground occupied by the enemy, which succeeded without the loss
of heavy weapons or motor vehicles due to the quality of leadership,'
Witzig reported. 'Despite unbelievably unfavourable positions (with no
covered approaches, no covered artillery positions, no favourable terrain
of attack or attack zone for our tanks), the Kampfgruppe held its ground
until 25 November 1942, some 50 kilometres forward of friendly lines
and with no other German or Italian units on its flanks.'[64] On 21 and
22 November Lieutenant Hünichen's 1st Company launched successful
night combat patrols. A reinforcement of 300 Italian paratroopers on
22 November did not improve Witzig's situation substantially. These
were probably the surviving elements of the Italian Air Force's 1st
Folgore Parachute Division, formed in September 1941 and deployed to
North Africa in July 1942. There the division served alongside Rommel's

Afrika Korps until November 1942, when it was largely destroyed during the battle of El Alamein and reduced to the strength of one small battalion.[65] It was probably these survivors that were sent to reinforce Witzig's battalion and it is no surprise that his Fallschirmjäger formed such a poor opinion of their Italian counterparts. According to Matthias Scheurer, the Germans found them poorly-armed, ill-equipped, and weakly trained and called them, derisively, '*Die Spaghetti Kameraden*'.[66] By the time the initial series of battles was over, Witzig's command had suffered 83 casualties, including 1 officer and 17 NCOs. The high percentage of killed, wounded, and missing among the leadership cadre was the result of the German belief in leading from the front.[67]

On 25 November the Allies attacked to drive back the Germans and Italians, capture Tunis, and reduce Bizerta. Witzig's reinforced 3rd Company in Mateur, acting as the division reserve, successfully repulsed an American tank attack 17 km south of the city and this was the closest Witzig would ever come to U.S. soldiers. That same day the British 36th Infantry Brigade attacked in Witzig's sector, only to find their bird had flown the coop. Witzig's orders to hold a position as far forward as possible had been changed, as the concentration of German forces around Bizerta had been completed. As a result, the 11th Parachute Engineer Battalion and its attachments had withdrawn in two stages to Djefna, some 20 km. west of Mateur, during the two previous nights, unnoticed by the British, who had been reinforced. To assist in covering their withdrawal, a night attack was launched by one of the platoons of Witzig's 1st Company, under the command of the company commander, Lieutenant Hünichen. Its mission was to determine the strength of the British and whether or not Abiod could be taken without heavy losses. The attack proceeded well, supported by artillery, and was executed with minimal losses. It determined, however, that Abiod could be taken, but not held without additional infantry reinforcements. As a result Abiod remained in British hands. Instead Witzig ordered an attack on the railway station at Nefza, which was located 2 km. forward of the German front lines in order to delay the Allied advance as long as possible. Well supported by artillery, the attack was conducted by the 4th Company, led by Sergeant Schürmann. According to Witzig's report, the station remained in German hands for the complete period needed to withdraw.

The British, estimated by Witzig at two to three battalions, two batteries of artillery, and a number of tracked vehicles, advanced cautiously for the next two days, slowed by numerous mines and booby traps, all expertly laid by the parachute engineers, before stumbling upon their opponent just west of Djefna. The Fallschirm-jäger, supported by a battery of Italian anti-tank guns and reinforced by the 8th Company of the *Barenthin* Glider Regiment,[68] were ready for a fight.

'Posted on top of the hills, we waited for the clash,' remembered Rifleman Bohn of the 4th Company.[69] Witzig had prepared the position with meticulous care, directing the construction of sheltered gun pits and ensuring interlocking fields of fire and excellent camouflage. A German account later called the fortified area 'a Tunisian Verdun on a minor scale'. Minefields were laid on both sides of the road, while the high ground was protected by wire obstacles and S-mines. Weighing about 4 kg, the anti-personnel 'S-' or Schu-mine contained 250–360 steel balls, short lengths of steel rod, or small pieces of scrap steel. Pressure- or remote-activated, the mine was propelled some 1–1.5 metres into the air by a secondary charge before detonating and scattering its load. It was capable of killing those within a 25-metre radius and wounding and maiming up to 100 metres.[70] Allied soldiers on all fronts soon learned to fear the S-mine.

Lead elements of the 36th Brigade attacked at dawn on 28 November. By 1200 hours they had advanced some 24 km, reaching their objectives, designated as Green and Bald Hills, on which Witzig's men were positioned. Witzig, who had been expecting the attack, waited until the two deployed companies of the 8th Battalion, Argyll and Sutherland Highlanders, were well within the kill zone before giving the order to open fire. Anti-tank guns ripped through the first and last carriers, trapping the column on the narrow road, and then dense 20-mm and mortar fire raked the column back and forth along its entire length. Within ten minutes the two British companies had lost almost a dozen tracked carriers and suffered 30 men killed, 50 wounded and another 86 taken prisoner. 'Eleven light tanks were destroyed, approximately two companies were dispersed,' Witzig reported without any elaboration. But the British fought back resolutely. 'It was terrible,' remembered Rifleman Bohn. 'The khaki uniforms worn by the soldiers of both sides were mixed in the battlefield. Our small group numbered only 28 men and so was grossly outnumbered by the foe. Fighting petered out about 4 p.m. Both sides had suffered heavy casualties.'[71]

Bohn was among the German casualties:

> I was captured by the British along with two wounded comrades.
> For us the war was over. In spite of their heavy losses the British
> treated us with fair play. Two of them tended my wound,
> expressing surprise on discovering that a "Green Devil" [German
> paratrooper] could be so young. It seemed to me that the British
> regarded us as gallant and loyal soldiers, certainly among the
> bravest they had to contend with.

In February 1943, Bohn was shipped to Britain on a hospital ship
and from there, in May, to a prisoner of war camp in the United States.
A photo of the young German soldier in captivity shows a handsome
and proud young man, glaring defiantly into the camera, wearing a
tropical tunic borrowed from a comrade lest the sight of his own,
tattered when he was wounded in Tunisia, might distress his parents,
for whom the photograph was intended.[72]

During 29 and 30 November the British continued their assaults,
invariably preceded by heavy artillery barrages. Three company–size
attacks were repulsed and a two–battalion assault fared little better.
'The enemy was repulsed after a heavy fight,' reported Witzig, noting in
his history of the battalion that these were the heaviest attacks his unit
endured during the entire North African campaign. Three of his officers
and a fourth from the 8th Company of the *Barenthin* Glider Regiment
were wounded in the fighting.[73] The British then withdrew some 2 km.
and proceeded to pound the German positions to pieces with generous
doses of artillery. 'Our greatest asset was our preponderance in
artillery,' reported Anderson accurately, 'and the front seemed at times
largely held by artillery fire.'[74] Within a short period, Witzig's command
had sustained 100 per cent officer casualties and the number of killed
and wounded among his men was so high that he had to merge the 1st
Company into the 4th, giving the combination a total strength of one
officer and 200 other ranks. The withdrawal of what remained of the
300 Italian paratroopers was more than balanced by the addition of a
separate company of 250 German soldiers.[75] On 30 November the
British 36th Brigade finally withdrew, unable to budge the Germans
from Djefna. Witzig and his paratroopers had stopped a British brigade
of more than 4,000 men dead in its tracks. 'For six months, the Djefna
position would remain as impregnable in fact as Eben Emael had been
in reputation,' writes Rick Atkinson, a historian of the campaign.[76]

Chapter 7

NORTH AFRICA: TO THE LAST MAN

In December Witzig's battalion was provided with some eighty Jews for use in building defensive positions. These had come from Tunis, where Jews had made up 60,000 of the city's population of 220,000 before the beginning of the war. Shortly after assuming control of Tunis, the Germans had arrested a number of Jews; the city's grand rabbi was ordered to provide a list of 3,000 young Jews for a labour corps and eventually some 3,600 were finally drafted as manual labourers. Hundreds toiled under Allied bombardment in Bizerta and at the Tunis airfield, while hundreds of others dug defensive positions for German soldiers. In addition, the Jewish community in Tunis was ordered to pay twenty million francs to cover Allied bomb damage to the city and the Germans began plundering Jewish gold, jewellery, and bank deposits.[1] 'They were neither suitable for this work nor had they been supplied, even with blankets,' remembered Witzig, writing of the Jewish labourers who had been sent to dig defensive positions. 'As the food supply for the battalion was already difficult, this presented a problem. After a few days I sent them back. They did not suffer any casualties.'[2]

The incident not only put Witzig at odds with the vast majority of German officers, who had no qualms about exploiting Jews in any way they could. It also serves as a stark reminder of the merciless racial war Hitler was waging against Jews, Poles, Slavs and others, a war vastly at odds with the *Krieg ohne Hass* ('war without hate') myth created by Rommel to characterise the war in North Africa. Indeed, a Wehrmacht conquest of the Middle East would have enabled the Germans to eliminate all Jews there before turning the area over to Italy.[3]

That same month Generalmajor Hasso von Manteuffel assumed command of the division from Broich and the unit was renamed Division *von Manteuffel*. Manteuffel was a highly respected panzer leader of great ability. Witzig reported that cooperation with Division *von Broich* had been 'good'. Furthermore, the *Barenthin* Glider

Regiment, which had been assigned to the German forces in the south, was transferred to the north and the Djefna defensive line. The 11th Parachute Engineer Battalion was subordinated to the regiment.[4]

Witzig presenting medals to his men in Tunisia in January 1943.
He awarded some thirty Iron Crosses and asked the High Command to
send him thirty more for his elite parachute-engineers.

On 8 December, Colonel-General Jürgen von Arnim replaced Nehring. Considered by many to be an excellent commander, Nehring had constantly infuriated his superiors with his outspoken criticism. Arnim arrived in Tunis unannounced on that day. He had been engaged in heavy defensive fighting with his corps of one panzer and three infantry divisions on the Volga in Russia at the end of November when he had received a telephone call directing him to report to Hitler's headquarters in East Prussia. There Hitler personally gave him his marching orders: 'General, you will leave immediately for North Africa,' Arnim remembers the Führer telling him. 'As you know the Allies have landed there . . . Our initial forces are too weak. I have decided to form a new Fifth Panzer Army from three panzer and three motorised divisions and you will take command.' Hitler further informed Arnim that he would be under the Italian High Command, but would work directly for Field Marshal Kesselring. The leader of the Third Reich then concluded with a description of the geographical and political conditions in North Africa and the effects he expected a new German army, located in the area between Tunis and Tangiers, would have. 'The change from North Russia to North Africa was totally unexpected,' Arnim wrote after the war.

Arnim's new command consisted of the composite infantry division in the Bizerta area, the 10th Panzer Division in the centre before Tunis, and Italian forces on the southern flank. The Allies had made strong efforts to prevent the Axis build-up, committing substantial air and sea forces to the task. However, Tunis and Bizerta were only 190 km from the ports and airfields of western Sicily, 290 km from Palermo and 480 km from Naples, making it very difficult to intercept Axis transports which had the benefit of substantial air cover. From mid-November through January, 243,000 men and 856,000 tons of supplies and equipment arrived in Tunisia by sea and air.

On 16 December, Kampfgruppe *Witzig* was pulled out of the line to act as a divisional infantry reserve and also serve as the division combat engineer battalion in Mateur. 'Our losses were heavy when we finally pulled out,' remembered Sergeant Feigl, commanding a heavy machine-gun team in Witzig's 4th Company. 'The withdrawal took place under artillery shelling. Once relieved by the infantry, we headed for Michaud, were we set up our camp.'[5] During this period of British attacks, Witzig's casualties included 3 officers, 18 NCQs and 57 other ranks. Since its début in North Africa, the battalion had sustained almost 200 casualties. The arrival of some 130 reinforcements by the end of the year alleviated somewhat the gradual haemorrhaging of the unit's strength. The reinforcements were in the form of the 1st Engineer Company, not to be confused with Witzig's own 1st Parachute Engineer Company, which joined the battalion in Bizerta on 26 December. 'They cannot carry out their regular tasks due to a lack of vehicles and engineer equipment,' Witzig reported. 'To reinforce the combat power of the battalion, these soldiers reconstituted the 1st [Parachute Engineer] Company under the command of Lieutenant Konrad. As a result, the battalion is comprised of three companies of 130 soldiers each.'[6] The average company strength at the beginning of the campaign had been 157 personnel.

On 30 December a small detachment of parachute engineers from Witzig's 3rd Company were dropped by parachute and gliders behind the Allied lines in eastern Algeria, to destroy two bridges. They were part of a little-known 120-man operation aimed at disrupting Allied lines of communications running from Morocco to Algeria and then Tébessa. The operation, however, was a complete failure. According to General Paul Deichmann, Kesselring's Chief of Staff, it forced the Allies to use some 100,000 men to guard key bridges along their main supply routes, but this is an exaggeration.[7] Indeed, this operation has received scant attention in Allied histories. Only two men, one of them Lieutenant Friedrich, the company commander, managed to make their way back to German lines. 'As they were being driven away by their captors Lieutenant Friedrich and a Tunisian scout jumped out of the back of the truck and made good their escape,' recorded Rifleman Pollman, who, although assigned to the 2nd Company, had missed deploying with his unit the previous summer and was posted to the 3rd Company upon his arrival in North Africa. Pollman kept a diary during his time in North Africa. 'Several days later, they were back in our camp in the Michaud farm, near Mateur.' Pollman goes on to note that Friedrich did not trifle with regulations and then continues: 'Instead of sharing my joy at being reunited, [he] was quick to point out that my boot laces were not properly secured but tied around the top of my boots!' After the failed night jumps, the 3rd Company suffered more casualties in the Djebel Azag region at the hands of British paratroopers. Later, the paratroopers of Pollman's company carried out a number of sabotage missions.[8]

For the rest of December and the early part of January 1943, Witzig's battalion worked on improving the division's battle positions, laying more than 2,500 T-mines. The Teller mine was a powerful pressure- or fuse-detonated weapon, weighing some 8 kg and containing 5·5 kg of TNT. It was normally laid on or near roads, buried about 5 cm below the surface, and was capable of destroying wheeled vehicles and disabling tanks and personnel carriers.[9] The 11th Parachute Engineer Battalion also conducted mine-laying operations behind enemy lines aimed at inflicting losses on the British, sowing the seeds of uncertainty, and causing them to tie down additional forces searching for and clearing these minefields. Both Teller mines and the anti-personnel S-mines were used in these operations, as well as dummy mines. Although the laying and removal of mines was a standard engineer mission, it was nonetheless still fraught with extreme danger. Witzig's command accomplished its missions losing two sergeants and two enlisted men.[10]

At the same time, Sergeant Feigl's heavy machine-gun team was detached and sent on air-defence duties to keep British aircraft from harassing reinforcements bound for the German front lines. The team was credited with shooting down one British Spitfire.[11] The incident is illustrative in that it shows the tendency of Witzig's superiors to detach elements of his battalion at random for use in other sectors, highlighting once again the ad hoc nature of the German defence in North Africa.

In the meantime, on 1 January 1943, the 3rd Company, which had remained behind in Bizerta, rejoined the battalion. The company had been subordinated directly to the army commander for almost two months for special parachute operations, but was only used in this role once due to the unfavourable weather conditions. Witzig reported that a group of his parachute engineers dropped behind enemy lines was missing and presumed captured, leading to the loss of a further eight men.[12] He was no doubt referring to the 30 December operation.

Witzig giving orders to his subordinate commanders in North Africa.
Witzig's battalion suffered heavily in the fighting and he was unable to get
enough replacements to make good his losses.

On 5 January 1943, the British penetrated the right wing of the Djefna position under cover of the heaviest artillery concentration the Germans had seen to date. 'The enemy was sitting behind our right flank with infantry and artillery,' Witzig reported. 'As a result, the battalion moved into position and took over command of the Kampf-gruppe.' The 1st Company, under Lieutenant Konrad, successfully seized the barren mountain on the endangered position. 'Even though it was bombed out, it was still key terrain,' noted Witzig. 'The company also successfully defeated two night attacks by British airborne troops.' The 4th Company, in the meantime, attacked and seized the right flank of the Djebel Azag position, defended by two British companies, losing Lieutenant Leute, the company commander. The already under-strength 11th Parachute Engineer Battalion suffered 61 casualties during this action, including 1 officer and 10 NCOs.[13] According to Witzig, this battle marked the first encounter between British paratroopers and his own Fallschirmjäger.

With the British attack blunted, the battalion returned to the rear as the division reserve once again. On 10 January Witzig's command numbered 10 officers, 2 civilian officials (*Beamter*), 87 NCOs, and 377 enlisted men. The strength of the 1st Company stood at 121, that of the 3rd Company at 142 and the 4th Company at 113. The battalion was short 2 officers, 28 NCOs, and 66 enlisted men. Witzig reported that, at this strength, the battalion was 'barely able to conduct routine operations'. None of the platoon leader positions in the 1st and 4th Companies were filled by officers, which he noted, was needed 'for special tasks'. 'Parachute assaults, which may always be necessary,' Witzig reported, 'can now only be conducted by the 3rd Company.' For this reason, it was held in reserve.[14] The manning situation was so critical that the Germans resorted to accepting Arab volunteers and on 22 January some twenty were assigned from a training camp in Tunis to Witzig's battalion. 'They wanted to serve voluntarily in the German armed forces,' wrote Witzig after the war. 'It is said that some were former [French] Foreign Legionnaires.' These Arab soldiers were equipped and assigned to the various companies in a support role. Witzig deemed the use of Arab volunteers with the German Army in North Africa a success: 'In no case did they surrender their ground in combat.'[15]

On 27 January Lieutenant Konrad and two other parachute engineers drove over one of their own mines, killing all three men and highlighting the prevalence and dangers of mines in the North African campaign. Former Sergeant Helmut Wenzel, now a second lieutenant, assumed command of the 1st Company. Less than a month later the commander of Witzig's 105-mm artillery battery, Captain Elson, was killed by an S-mine. A friend of Witzig's, Elson had attended the same War College course in Dresden.[16]

In addition to commanding the battalion, Witzig was also the division engineer. As such, he was responsible for expanding the division's defensive positions and constructing barriers and obstacles and building bridges throughout the sector. His elite paratroopers also served as a 'half motorised' mobile reserve for the division, being committed to those sectors where the situation was the most critical. Half the battalion's casualties had been suffered while fighting as an infantry reserve, the other half to artillery. 'The battalion was used as infantry,' he reported, adding: 'The men were fully capable of performing as infantry' and concluding proudly: 'The engineer companies have always been the best part of the *Witzig* Kampfgruppe.'[17]

With a lull in combat operations, Witzig departed to Höxter in January 1943 for a short leave which he spent with Hanna and her family. The two had continued exchanging letters during his brief absence in North Africa and their short time together was filled with a great deal of music and laughter.[18] Witzig was fortunate that throughout the war the Wehrmacht adhered to an extremely generous leave policy for its troops, given the circumstances, theoretically without distinction as to rank or seniority. Every member of the armed forces was entitled to fourteen days of annual leave. In addition, troops might quality for additional discretionary special leave of up to twenty-one days for convalescence or a death in the family. Unlike their British, American and Russian counterparts, who were in for the duration of the war and could not expect to return home from overseas unless they were killed or seriously wounded, the German soldier could expect to get home once a year. 'Thus at any one time approximately ten per cent of the German army was on furlough back home,' write historians Stephen and Russell Hart and their colleague Matthew Hughes. 'It was a rare German soldier indeed who had not been furloughed in two years and such troops received priority on the leave quotas. Commanders also gave priority status to frontline combat troops and to married men with families.'[19] The generous leave policy was designed to maintain troop morale and combat effectiveness by reducing personal distractions brought about by extended absences from loved ones and family. It was, no doubt, one reason why so many German soldiers like Rudolf Witzig and his paratroopers continued to fight so well long after any chance of a Germany victory in the war had slipped away.

Upon his return to North Africa, Witzig found himself engaged in a war of a very different kind, a battle with his own bureaucracy for replacements and the preservation of his much-loved parachute engineer battalion. In order to reconstitute the battalion's combat power, Witzig had asked XI Fliegerkorps, on 21 December 1942, for 10 officers, 2 officials, 25 sergeants, and 245 enlisted replacements. But by mid-January 1943 he had still not received any response to his request for replacements. He noted, somewhat testily in his official report, that the 1st Engineer Company, which had been attached earlier to the battalion, had not rejoined him since the fighting in early January. Furthermore, he had been informed by Lieutenant Reimann, his liaison to the Corps Engineer of XI Fliegerkorps that his battalion could not count on receiving any reinforcements in Tunisia. Witzig responded strongly to this information, noting:

1. The battalion will not get reinforcements from the home front until its fighting strength is at zero.

2. The establishment of a new battalion, if the original is wiped out, would be very difficult due to a severe lack of trainers; consequently, the quality of that battalion would be low.

3. With the increase of [German combat] power on the Tunis front, an offensive is again being considered. Once again, we would not have the troops required because we would not have been reinforced.

4. Cooperation with the Army is good. Only speaking to them in person will allow them to understand the value and tasks of the paratroopers, especially a parachute engineer battalion. This is why the battalion is asking for reinforcements in Tunisia.[20]

Witzig also demanded the return of his 2nd Company, which had been in Libya since the previous July: 'I believe that not reattaching this group, the remains of an engineer company, will mean the certain attrition of these soldiers, as they will be used as infantry reinforcement ... The best use of these soldiers would be to attach them to this battalion to use them as engineers.' He added that the 2nd Company would have to be retrained as engineers and that its strength, as of 29 November 1942, had been 86 men, including two officers, ten NCOs, and 74 enlisted. Demands for the return of the company were not included in Witzig's request for reinforcements as: 'the 2nd Company is a part of the battalion and can only be saved from disbanding by staying with the battalion'.[21] To his surprise the 2nd Company returned to the battalion in February 1943 but all that remained were fifty men. Having escaped the advancing British Eighth Army, the men of the company decided to make their own way back to the battalion rather than accompany Ramcke and his unit back to Germany.[22]

As if all of this were not enough, Witzig found himself demanding the return of officers seconded to other units. Lieutenant Tillman, who had joined the *Ramcke* Brigade on 10 November, was one such. Though ordered to return to the battalion when it arrived in Tunisia, Tillman had remained with the brigade, where he was serving as an ordnance officer, while the battalion needed 'every available engineer officer'. 'The battalion,' complained Witzig in his official report, 'does not appreciate this procedure of Brigade *Ramcke*. Tillman is now being requested by official channels through Fifth Panzer Army Headquarters.'[23]

Another officer Witzig wished returned to the battalion was his surgeon, Lieutenant Dr. Schostack, who had been ordered by XI Flieger–korps to join Kampfgruppe *Frankfurt* on special assignment and had not been returned. 'The battalion is of the opinion that a paratrooper doctor with schooling for medical treatment of ground troops in combat should belong to an airborne unit,' complained Witzig. 'Besides, the combat strength [of Kampfgruppe *Witzig*] rose to over 1,000 due to the reinforcement of the group. The battalion doctor alone could not keep up with the combat casualties. Consequently, the battalion requests that the urgently needed Lieutenant Schostack be given orders to return.' Nor did the matter of doctors end there. The battalion's second assistant doctor, Lieutenant Bartels, was also missing 'without a trace' since being ordered to join Witzig's 2nd Company with Brigade *Ramcke*. 'The battalion likewise asks that Doctor Bartels be reattached to the battalion, because he belongs to the battalion and is urgently needed.' Witzig also noted in his report that a civilian engineer attached to the 1st Parachute Engineer Battalion had been heavily wounded before Abiod and requested a replacement, noting the position 'is vital for the procurement of needed pioneer machinery and equipment'.[24]

Witzig's battle for replacements did not end there. According to information received from XI Fliegerkorps Headquarters, the Army had decided to open a War School in North Africa. This was to be a permanent institution requiring twenty good instructors to be retained by the school. 'Those officers will be training replacements for other units, while our replacement situation is still not solved,' noted Witzig.

German paratroopers inspecting knocked-out British tanks during Operation Ox Head
in February 1943. Intended initially as a corps-size attack, the operation mushroomed
into an all-out German offensive to widen the Axis bridgehead around Tunis.

'The battalion is requesting orders regarding this disproportionate
issue.' Witzig's command was slated to lose three officers, all
lieutenants, to the War School. In addition, he also reported one officer
with Brigade *Ramcke* and another assigned to the division rear area.
Thus five of the battalion's remaining twelve officers, not including the
two doctors, were assigned elsewhere with only seven serving in the
unit by the end of January. Of these, two each were serving with the
1st, 2nd, and 3rd Companies and one with the 4th Company.[25]

Relief did not appear to be in the offing, at least for Witzig's battalion.
The three officers detailed to the War School would be gone for three
months and replacement parachute engineer officers were being held
back by other parachute engineer formations. Additionally, out of the
four *Fahnenjunker* (officer candidates) assigned to the battalion before
the deployment to North Africa, three had been killed and one wounded.
Despite repeated requests, no additional officer candidates were
assigned to the battalion. 'The battalion is weakening,' Witzig reported
gloomily. 'If losses continue in the same proportion, we are doomed.'
He also asked for the transfer of Lieutenant Weber from the replacement

depot in Wittenberg to the battalion in North Africa. 'His current illness, which precludes him from serving in a tropical climate cannot be reason enough not to come out,' wrote Witzig, 'since it is now winter.'[26]

While Witzig was fighting for replacements, additional Axis units were flowing into Tunisia. During the first half of December, the remainder of both the 10th Panzer Division and the *Superga* Division had arrived, although each had lost a substantial portion of its heavy equipment at sea. 'The 10th had suffered considerable losses during transport,' recorded Arnim. 'So many ships were sunk that the soldiers now had to be transported by Italian destroyers or Italian aircraft.'[27] As a result, the 10th Panzer Division would never muster its full establishment and both divisions remained short of artillery throughout the campaign. Additionally, further march battalions arrived at regular intervals. Some were broken up as reinforcements, while others operated as independent infantry battalions. These independent battalions were either used to bring the original ad hoc force to the strength of a division or were used to reinforce the Italians. A number of Italian battalions were also brought over. The most significant arrival, however, was the German 510st Heavy Tank Battalion with 43 tanks, including 20 of the new Tigers. And, in the second half of December, the German 334th Infantry Division, a new formation of 'rather low quality', also began to make its appearance. Thus, by the beginning of January 1943, the estimated total of Axis ground troops in Tunisia, excluding aircrew and ground staffs, was almost 56,000 men. These were backed by some 160 German tanks, an unknown number of Italian light and medium tanks, and fourteen 12-gun battalions of artillery.[28]

Nonetheless, the entire German army in North Africa was facing the same predicament as Witzig's 11th Parachute Engineer Battalion. The flow of replacements into theatre was plagued by problems. Axis losses at sea were extremely heavy and it is reported that Hitler himself gave orders that personnel should travel only by destroyer or air. Most of those who arrived by air were transported by the approximately 500 Ju–52s that had been used since the beginning of the campaign in Tunisia to carry German troops and equipment to North Africa.[29] The daily intake of reinforcements thus varied greatly, as the Luftwaffe was responsible for carrying supplies as well as troops. By January the daily average of troops reaching North Africa was between 700 and 1,000 men, some of whom were destined for Rommel's Afrika Korps.[30] This influx of new formations and personnel, however, was simply not enough to staunch the chronic haemorrhaging of the Axis battle strength in North Africa. Furthermore, it reflected a policy of using replacements to create new formations rather than reinforcing existing units that had proven themselves, but had been decimated in combat. Indeed, a persistent shortage of replacements, especially infantrymen, bedevilled the Wehrmacht in North Africa for the duration of the campaign (although the Allies suffered to a lesser degree from the same problem). The policy of constantly creating new formations shaped the illusion that the Germans had a much larger force in North Africa than was the case. Perhaps this was intentional, aimed at instilling caution in the Allies, slowing their advance and delaying their inevitable victory. Perhaps it was an internal ploy, intended to convince Hitler that the North Africa front was more important in terms of manpower and equipment than it really was. Or perhaps it simply reflected the German policy of allowing units to fight until losses were so heavy that individual formations had either to be disbanded altogether or totally reconstituted. Nonetheless, after almost two months of battling the Allies, Hitler's defensive policy in Tunisia still reflected its extremely improvised nature.

If replacement difficulties made waging war in Tunisia problematic for the Germans, supply shortages crippled their war effort. 'Supply was the worse problem,' remembers Arnim:

> Every fourteen days the Allies had an entire supply convoy arrive. We were limited to individual ships. Instead of using the first element of surprise and not only transporting troops but also loading all available ships with ammunition and fuel – to transport them before the Allied Air Force arrived – we sent single ships. Most never carried more than 3,000 tons. Later, when there were more at sea, they were sunk by enemy submarines or by the Allied Air Force.[31]

He went on to complain that neither the German nor the Italian High Commands had a clear picture of the logistic conditions in North Africa, 'especially how little actually made it to the front'. As a result, reports on the sacrifices of German soldiers were considered 'exaggerated' or 'pessimistic'.[32] 'Hitler believed he could replace the missing material through the bravery of the German soldier – as if there weren't brave men on the other side as well,' concluded Arnim. 'Even the bravest soldier could not fight with his bare fists but needed enough weapons, ammunition, fuel, etc.'[33]

Field Marshal Kesselring confirmed the Wehrmacht's inferiority in logistics in North Africa. He accurately called Germany's efforts in the Mediterranean 'the war of the poor against the rich', with the Allies far superior in numbers, equipment and supplies. According to Kesselring:

> This was expressed by the number of army units, their strength and supply as regards personnel and material; the air superiority and – later on – the air supremacy of the Allies; our own lack of tonnage and naval security forces; and the limited aptitude of the Italian soldiers and units at the front. The insufficient technical equipment was not the least reason for this.

These weaknesses necessitated that German units remain employed on the front lines continuously. 'As a result,' noted Kesselring, 'their fighting qualities decreased and their reorganisation was rendered more difficult.'[34] Due to their weakness in numbers, German forces in North Africa were forced to occupy extensive defensive positions for long periods, making it almost impossible to organise any system for their relief, as reserves were insufficient, despite the exhaustion of the troops. Commanders were further plagued by a lack of armour, artillery and engineers. Consequently, the Germans were forced to conduct delaying operations, characterised by numerous counter–attacks.

This in turn led to the development of what Kesselring termed 'centre of gravity' tactics, in which less threatened sectors were almost entirely stripped of forces in order to strength those sectors under the greatest threat.[35] Still, Witzig and his men, like most German units in North Africa, gave as good as they got. 'If any success was to be achieved in the prevailing conditions, the leaders of all ranks had to act on their own initiative within the framework of the general combat task,' Kesselring told his interrogators after the war, discussing the North African campaign. 'In other words, they had to take advantage of any opportunity. In the training of German commanders and subordinate commanders lay the German strength, which, of course, was partly lost as the war progressed further.'[36]

Kesselring also provides insight into the decision by the German commanders to use highly trained engineer units, such as Witzig's 11th Engineer Battalion, as infantry:

> The all–around training of the Engineers and the lack of combat forces induced the German intermediate commands – although

sometimes erroneously – to use the engineers for infantry tasks in order to cope with a dangerous situation. In this case, they did not consider that the training of new engineers takes a very long time, thus causing generally a great lack of engineers and that, on the other hand, the employment of engineers for highly technical tasks exclusively – such as laying of mines, etc. – would outweigh by far the advantages of their commitment as infantry.[37]

Born of necessity in North Africa, the German practice of using combat engineers as infantry would become standard for the remainder of the war.

In addition to fighting a battle for replacements, Witzig also fought to receive his battalion's vehicles and equipment, which had still not reached him by January 1943:

The step-by-step transfer of vehicles of the battalion from Italy has been arranged, but the Italian Air Force and service posts take vehicles out of our convoy and detach them to different units. The battalion will need the motor park again and asks to be treated as a ground division, not like an air division, which is still tactical without vehicles. Consequently, the battalion asks for the relevant orders to prevent further reduction of our motor park.

Witzig went on to note that the vehicles of the 11th Parachute Engineer Battalion's 2nd Company, subordinated to Brigade *Ramcke*, had disappeared in the same way, 'and not through the sinking [of the transport ships] during the movement by sea'. He concluded this portion of his report with the following request: 'It must be acknowledged that procuring engineer vehicles is a lot more difficult than for normal vehicles. We request that the remaining vehicles of 2nd Company, 11th Parachute Engineer Battalion, are sent to the rear echelon of the battalion in Naples, to Inspector Müller, and that replacement vehicles are ordered by the *Ramcke* Brigade.'[38]

Witzig concluded his North Africa report by noting that, from the battalion's arrival in November 1942 through mid-January 1943, he had awarded the Iron Cross Second Class to 30 soldiers and the Iron Cross First Class to 3. In addition, he had requested another 30 Iron Crosses, wishing to make 26 Second Class and 4 First Class awards to his men. 'We are confident the awards will be approved,' he wrote. 'The engineers deserve this.'[39]

Few reports show as well the many challenges faced by German commanders in North Africa as Witzig's on his battalion's first three months in theatre. Committed to fighting an enemy growing ever stronger on land, sea and in the air, leaders like Rudolf Witzig also had to battle the German High Command for every individual replacement and every vehicle and were forced to watch their beloved units and elite soldiers ground further and further down until, it was clear to all, there would be nothing left. For the German army in North Africa, there was only one inevitable outcome to the fighting, as it became evident that Hitler had no intention of sending the massive reinforcements to Tunisia needed first to stop and then drive back and decisively defeat the Allies. And yet, despite all of this, the majority of German commanders and their soldiers, and especially Witzig's paratroopers, continued to fight with skill and almost fanatical determination, true to their oath to Hitler and Germany.

There was, in fact, little else they could do, for the tide of the war had irrevocably turned against Hitler and the Third Reich. On 19 November 1942, not long after Witzig and his colleagues had landed in North Africa, the Soviets launched Operation Uranus, which succeeded in encircling the German Sixth Army at Stalingrad. Attempts to break through to the Sixth Army were no more successful than the Luftwaffe's efforts to resupply it by air and on 31 January, with his army confined to two small pockets in the city, Field Marshal Friedrich Paulus surrendered. According to German Red Cross estimates, the Germans lost 200,000 troops at Stalingrad.[40] Soviet accounts, however, state that 147,000 German dead were counted on the battlefield and another 91,000 Germans were taken prisoner, including 24 generals and another 2,500 officers of lesser rank.[41] In addition, Field Marshal Erhard Milch, Director of Air Armaments, estimated that the Luftwaffe had lost almost 500 irreplaceable transports and 1,000 aircrew during the airlift.[42] Germany's allies were equally hard-hit during the offensives that followed, with Romania losing two entire armies, while Hungary and Italy each lost one. On 3 February 1943, Joseph Goebbels, Hitler's Minister for Propaganda, ordered three days of national remembrance for the German soldiers lost at Stalingrad. All places of entertainment were closed and traffic stopped completely for one minute. However, neither mourning nor sentimentality were allowed, 'only a dignified and new resolute devotion to further efforts'.[43]

One wonders what Rudolf Witzig and his soldiers, who were fighting what was clearly another hopeless battle in North Africa, made of all of this. For many, the German debacle at Stalingrad marked the moment in the war when the strategic initiative passed out of Germany's hands. General Warlimont, however, believed that Stalingrad was only one of three key events which presaged the decline of Hitler's already waning star. The other two were Rommel's defeat at El Alamein, where some 30,000 Germans were taken prisoner and the Allied landings in North Africa. 'It was November 1942, the month of doom in modern German history, when the enemy struck in both the East and the West,' wrote Warlimont. 'At the nerve centre of German strategy, people had shrugged off the effects of the September shocks [Hitler's sacking of various senior officers] and there was not the smallest recognition, least of all on the part of Hitler himself, that the war had now definitely turned against Germany, although this was clear to all the world.'[44] According to Percy Ernst Schramm, the keeper of the OKW War Diary, Generaloberst Alfred Jodl, Chief of the German High Command Operations Branch, acknowledged the decline of Germany's fortunes in November 1942, remarking: 'It was clear not only to the responsible soldiers but to Hitler himself that the god of war had now turned from Germany and gone over to the other camp.'[45]

Still, Witzig and his men were probably unaware of these strategic developments and were more concerned with ensuring the combat capability of their battalion. Some relief was forthcoming for the battalion at the beginning of February when the 2nd Company, commanded by Lieutenant Tiemens, rejoined the unit with fifty men. Tiemens and his men had escaped capture by the Allies along with some 600 men of the *Ramcke* Brigade by using Allied vehicles to reach the German forces to the east. Kesselring tried to decorate Ramcke with the Knight's Cross in recognition of the magnificent desert march but Rommel refused to allow him to do so.[46] On 15 February Witzig's battalion lost another officer when Lieutenant Hardt was killed by a land mine. 'A heavy loss for the battalion,' recorded Witzig. 'He was removing a mine for a war correspondent, who was filming the scene, when the device exploded,' remembered Sergeant Feigl. The mine was fitted with a tripwire which Hardt had not noticed.[47] That month the North African campaign began heating up once again. 'Beginning on 4 February we were used increasingly in the area north of the Djefna position,' remembered Witzig. 'A Bersaglieri regiment was positioned at that location but we did not believe it capable of much if the British attacked there.' Witzig ordered his 1st Company to conduct a reconnaissance forward of the Italian positions and discovered that his Italian allies were facing Algerians of the French Corps d'Afrique.[48]

In mid–February 1943 Arnim and Rommel launched a series of joint attacks at Faid, Sidi Bou Zid and Kasserine Pass, aimed at splitting the Allies in North Africa, driving a wedge through American defences, and destroying the U.S. II Corps, which guarded the southern flank in Tunisia. Kasserine Pass was a 3-km.-wide gap in the Western Dorsale chain of mountains in west central Tunisia. The battle was the first large–scale meeting between German and American forces in the Second World War. The untested and poorly led American troops suffered heavy casualties and were pushed back over 80 km from their positions west of Faid Pass. In the aftermath came sweeping changes from unit–level organisation to the replacing of commanders. When Germans and Americans next met, in some cases only weeks later, the U.S. forces would be considerably more effective.

Meanwhile, as the Americans were experiencing their first defeat at Kasserine Pass, the Germans launched a new attack, Operation Ox Head. This was originally intended to be a corps-size limited offensive aimed at improving German dispositions in Tunisia in preparation for the coming battles with the British Eighth Army in the east and the British First Army and American forces in the west. The German order of battle included elements of the 10th Panzer Division, the 501st Heavy Tank Brigade, the *Hermann Göring* Division, and the 5th Parachute Regiment. The operation, originally designed as a modest attack on Medjez–el–Bab, blossomed, under pressure from Kesselring, into an all-out German offensive to seize Béja and widen the Axis bridgehead around Tunis.

On 26 February the German army in Tunisia and the remainder of the Afrika Korps surged westwards. Reinforced with a number of smaller units, Witzig's battalion advanced parallel to the main attack in the north into the Sedjenane valley in an operation involving eight battalions and personally supervised by Arnim. The Germans swarmed out of their Djefna revetments and past the bones of British dead left on Green and Bald hills the previous November. Led by Rudolf Witzig, Italian soldiers and German parachute engineers flanked the British and the French at the mining hamlet of Sedjenane. The attack came to a halt in front of Sedjenane, where the British unleashed their own counter-attack, leading to fierce fighting. General von Manteuffel ordered Witzig to conduct a daylight attack from the north, but he responded that both the open terrain and the lack of heavy weapons precluded a successful daylight attack. 'We attacked under the cover of darkness and took the place without losses' remembered Witzig.[49] Manteuffel admonished Witzig, who led from the front and had been personally decorated by Hitler, for his recklessness in battle: 'This is the division with two Knight's Cross winners and you are one of the two!'[50] Afterwards, Witzig surveyed the battlefield with Lieutenants Timmermann and Müller and then awarded Iron Crosses to his men. After driving the British 46th Division back 16 km, Arnim pushed them another 15 km and closed within a few thousand metres of Djebel Abiod, the northern gateway to Béja. The British, however, refused to give ground further.

As Witzig's battalion continued attacking westward, it suffered heavy losses, including former Sergeants Wenzel and Niedermeier, veterans of Eben Emael, who were both captured in battle. By the beginning of March the battalion was so sapped for manpower that it went into reserve and was used to conduct local counter-attacks and mining operations in the division sector. In the end, Arnim and his forces were too weak and scattered to exploit their gains. The British fell back 30 km in the north, 15 km in the centre, and very little in the south. British casualties were heavy and included 2,500 men taken prisoner and sixteen tanks lost. German losses were heavier still and included 2,200 prisoners of war. Most of the German tanks used in Operation Ox Head had been destroyed or disabled. Arnim had managed to extend the German bridgehead and delay the inevitable Allied advance only slightly.

Witzig recognised that the North African campaign could not continue in this manner for long. 'The end was in sight,' he wrote. Shortly after the battalion went into division reserve he began to contact those soldiers due to rejoin the unit and ordered them instead to join the replacement battalion in Wittenberg. 'It may surprise some that I could take such measures, which were not within the powers of a battalion commander,' he wrote after the war.

> An explanation is necessary. My reporting directly to the Commander-in-Chief South [Kesselring] in September 1942 was already unusual. But the Corps Parachute Engineer Battalion

was, as a corps unit, very independent. The corps commander was located very far away. When the battalion was subordinated to a unit for operations, such as the *Von Manteuffel* Division in Tunisia, [it fell to the division to] conduct . . . operations and supply of goods, such as food, ammunition, and fuel. For personnel replacement, training, and equipment, such as weapons, engineering equipment and motor transport, the parachute corps remained responsible. Despite being assigned to an Army unit in Tunisia we were part of the Luftwaffe, so the division could only command units and personnel of the Corps Parachute Engineer Battalion for certain tasks and it could not transfer the soldiers of the battalion. II Parachute Corps showed no interest in the fate of the battalion after it moved to Africa. Thus, I was often forced to act on my own initiative if it were necessary for the well-being of the battalion and its soldiers. Finally, a special bond of trust existed between General Student, founder of the paratroopers, and his commanders and he insisted on 'leadership from the front' which obligated commanders, even if they were assigned some distance away and to other formations, to act loyally and conscientiously. In this special case the conclusion was to strengthen the replacement battalion in Wittenberg at the expense of the battalion in Tunisia.[51]

Witzig thus chose his loyalty to his paratroopers and the preservation of what little remained of his battalion over his loyalty to the *Von Manteuffel* Division and the German war effort in Tunisia. A difficult dilemma, his decision reflected the worsening strategic situation for Hitler and the Third Reich in North Africa and throughout Europe in early 1943. At the beginning of March, for example, RAF bombers succeeded in pounding the German capital, killing some 700 Germans and driving another 35,000 out of their shattered homes. And later that same month Witzig's war against the British in North Africa took on a more personal nature. On 25 March 1943 his younger brother, Kriegsmarine Lieutenant Ernst-Georg Witzig, perished in the North Atlantic south of Ireland along with the entire crew of *U-469* when a British aircraft sank their submarine with depth charges. Commissioned on 7 October 1942, *U-469* had only one patrol to its credit and had not sunk or damaged any Allied ships. Ernst-Georg was nineteen years old and was one of forty-seven crewmen who died when the boat was lost with all hands.[52]

Still, the Allied pressure in North Africa was relentless. By the beginning of March 1943 Eighth Army, advancing westwards along the North African coast, had reached the Tunisian border. Rommel and Arnim found themselves outflanked, out-manned and out-gunned and caught between two powerful Allied armies. Montgomery's Eighth Army shattered the Axis defences on the Mareth Line in late March, while Anderson's First Army in central Tunisia launched its main offensive in mid-April to squeeze and eliminate the Axis forces. By then the Allies had over 300,000 men in Tunisia and possessed a huge advantage in men, tanks and aircraft over the Germans and Italians. The Allied blockade of the Mediterranean continued to strangle the Germans and Italians in North Africa, depriving them of fuel, ammunition and food. On 23 April the 300,000-man Allied force, supported by 1,200 tanks and 3,000 aircraft, advanced along a 65-km front with the British driving on Tunis, while the U.S. II Corps, having recovered from its thrashing at Kasserine, advanced on Bizerta. 'The Americans have finally broken through in the east towards Bizerta,' Witzig recorded on 1 May. 'The division withdrew towards the south-east and gave up Mateur.'[53]

Less than a week later the 11th Parachute Engineer Battalion was instructed to extract itself from North Africa. All that remained of the proud paratroopers were 2 officers, including Major Witzig and Lieutenant Heise, 4 NCOs and 27 men. The unit's total strength, including support and medical personnel and walking wounded, was 90 men.[54] 'An organised return to Germany was no longer possible as the Allies controlled the sea and the air, but many succeeded in escaping,' reported Witzig. 'I received instructions to embark myself and my officers on a motorboat of the Navy and reached Trapani in Sicily on 10 May 1943.'[55]

On 7 May the Allies captured Bizerta and Tunis. That same day Goebbels faithfully recorded in his diary that Hitler considered the situation in Tunis 'pretty hopeless'. 'It is simply impossible to transport reinforcements there,' he admitted. 'If we could regularly deliver supplies to Tunis we might possibly hold on for a long time. But this is prevented by the watchfulness of the English, who won't let our ships get through.'[56] Five days later Generaloberst Jürgen von Arnim, commanding Army Group Afrika, sent his final message to Berlin: 'We have fired our last cartridge. We are closing down forever.' On 12 May Arnim surrendered with his staff to the 4th Indian Division and was brought to General ~~LT. GEN.~~ Anderson at First Army Headquarters. The next day all Axis forces ~~LT. GEN.~~ in North Africa capitulated. On hearing of the surrender of German and Italian forces, Hitler commented: 'The North African ... hymn of heroism ... has retarded [Allied] developments for half a year, thereby enabling us to complete the construction of the Atlantic Wall and to prepare ourselves all over Europe so that invasion is out of the question.'[57]

> The scenes in the Cap Bon peninsula area and to the south-west during the last three days were amazing [reported General Anderson]. The rout of the German army was complete; prisoners swamped their captors and drove in their own transport looking for cages. Thousands surrendered without attempt to resist further, while others fired their remaining stocks of ammunition at any target before giving themselves up ... The disaster was complete ... The booty was immense. Dunkirk had been avenged.[58]

According to Anderson, the total of prisoners eventually reached over a quarter of a million. Also captured were over 1,000 artillery pieces, 250 tanks and 'many thousands of motor vehicles', many of which were serviceable.[59] 'We must realise that our losses are enormous,' admitted Goebbels. 'We are indeed experiencing a sort of second Stalingrad, although under quite different psychological and material conditions.'[60]

As a result of their heavy personnel and equipment losses on the Eastern Front and in North Africa, the Italians had effectively been knocked out of the war and had no other option but to seek an armistice with the Allies at the first possible opportunity. Contrary to Hitler's assertions, the Allies had succeeded in knocking Italy out of the war military, in spite of the Wehrmacht's sacrifices. As a result, to strengthen Italy the Germans were forced to transfer three newly formed infantry divisions, two panzer divisions and two panzergrenadier divisions from the West to Italy in June, despite the fact that all were lacking in both equipment and training.[61] And this was only the beginning of a steady stream of units that would eventually reach a total of sixteen hand-picked German divisions deployed to dominate northern and central Italy by early September. Hitler's paratroopers were among those elite formations called upon to defend first Sicily and then the Italian boot in a campaign which would become every bit as gruelling as that on the Eastern Front. The 1st, 2nd, and 4th Parachute

Divisions, along with the *Hermann Göring* Parachute Panzer Division, an airborne division in name only, would all eventually be committed to the defence of Italy, as would I Parachute Corps Headquarters. Once again, the shortage of infantry condemned the Fallschirmjäger to decimation as ground troops in some of the bitterest fighting of the war.

The morale of the German and Italian soldiers captured in North Africa was good, though most had been eager to surrender as soon as ordered. 'The atmosphere in the cages was of relief that the campaign was over,' notes the official British history of the campaign, 'although the German troops were anxious that their country should judge that they, as soldiers, had done their whole duty. Physique and health of the troops seemed excellent, and German equipment was of very good quality. There was no doubt that ammunition and fuel were very scarce.'[62] The prisoners included Lieutenant Tietjen, commander of Witzig's 2nd Company, who was captured while serving with the *Ramcke* Brigade. He would not be released until February 1947, following an odyssey which would take him through Egypt, Canada and England. Others, like Matthias Scheurer, briefly escaped North Africa, only to find themselves forced back to its shores, where they were captured. 'Gentlemen,' Scheurer remembers a British officer telling him and his boatload of German paratroopers, 'you are prisoners of the Eighth Army. Follow me please.' After a long voyage to the United States, Scheurer spent two years in captivity at various camps in the American South. He was among the first to be returned to Germany after the war, arriving there in October 1945. His decorations from the war included the Iron Cross 2nd Class, the Luftwaffe Ground Combat Badge, and the Wound Badge.[63]

Scheurer provides some interesting insights into his commander in North Africa, noting that Witzig never wore a steel helmet in battle. Instead, he always wore his regulation officer's cap, which distinguished him on the battlefield. This is supported by the many surviving photographs of Rudolf Witzig in North Africa, showing him wearing his distinctive officer's cap, crushed and battered. According to Scheurer, Witzig was never a member of the Nazi Party and never had a political officer attached to his battalion, as was the norm in many other units. The reason for this was because he had been personally decorated by Hitler with the Knight's Cross early in the war, Witzig was deemed trustworthy and was never required nor pressured to join the Nazi Party.[64]

Counting replacements, few though they were, Witzig's battalion in North Africa suffered more than 100 per cent casualties. Especially hard-hit were the officers. In the 1st Company, Lieutenant Hünichen and Second Lieutenant Kubillus had been wounded and Sergeant Wenzel taken prisoner. In the 2nd Company, Lieutenant Braun had been wounded and Lieutenant Tietjen taken prisoner. In the 3rd Company, Second Lieutenant von Albert had been wounded and Lieutenant Friedrich had fallen ill by the end of the campaign. And in the 4th Company Lieutenant Hardt had been killed by a land mine. Captain Elbert of the battalion staff, who joined the battalion in February 1943, had died of wounds in hospital in Mateur.[65] In total, the parachute forces suffered some 10,000 casualties, or the equivalent of an entire parachute division, in North Africa.[66]

'Compared to our opponents we were more experienced in war,' wrote Witzig after the war about the North African campaign, adding: 'They moved frequently, while we remained in the same area.' He goes on to point out that reconnaissance patrols and Arab scouts brought the Germans sufficient information about enemy forces. On the other hand, Witzig notes that the British had a far better manpower situation than the Germans. He also writes that the British possessed good intelligence on their adversaries. 'Often we came across British prisoners who knew our battalion and even our commanders, surely something of an advantage,' remembered Witzig, who went on to counter that the lack of officers in his battalion was balanced by the presence of 'very good NCOs' and 'outstanding sergeants' who served as platoon leaders. Indeed, Witzig had high praise for his soldiers, highlighting their good training, motivation, mission-oriented tactics and superior quality over the British. Witzig singles out for special recognition his signals and communications troops, who ensured that he could talk from his defensive position near Djebel Abiod all the way to Field Marshal Kesselring's headquarters in Italy! He was also complimentary of his supply services, noting: 'We all accepted it as completely natural that food, clothing and the postal service were available. The timely arrival of military pay was less important as there was virtually nothing to buy.' And, despite shortages of motor vehicles, ammunition and fuel in North Africa, Witzig and his battalion remained relatively well supplied throughout the campaign.[67]

It says a great deal about Witzig that he was bothered by one incident in particular, which occurred on 1 December 1942 after a heavy night of combat in the southern portion of the Djefna position. 'I met a dying British soldier in front of the position,' he remembered. 'His last words were "Heil Hitler! Heil Hitler!" It was the product of Allied hate propaganda against Germany.' The biting sarcasm of the dying British soldier disturbed Witzig greatly. He respected his British enemies, calling them 'hard and persistent opponents who treated our prisoners decently'. After the war Witzig would say that the British were the best Allied soldiers of the war. And he wanted to believe that they, in turn, respected him and his soldiers. 'One of our opponents, Lieutenant-Colonel John Frost, commander of the British 2nd Parachute Battalion, later became a major general,' recalled Witzig. 'We – and the *Barenthin* Regiment – made a great impression on him, although the Corps Parachute Engineer Battalion had been weakened at Sedjenane immediately before our encounter with the 2nd Parachute Battalion. It was a surprise for us to meet such decent soldiers and human beings and it reduced our feelings of hate for them.'[68]

That Hitler's paratroopers had done their duty well in North Africa and elsewhere, but especially Russia, is reflected by the fact that a systemic activation of parachute divisions was begun in 1943, when these elite units were given the official title of Fallschirmjägerdivision. That year their number rose to four and by 1944 the Wehrmacht would have eight parachute divisions in its order of battle. This was done at a time when the shortage of ground forces in the German Army and the Luftwaffe was becoming more and more acute. An additional measure was the conversion, early in 1944, of the *Hermann Göring* Division into a 'parachute panzer division'. By the end of the year this division would be transformed into a 'parachute panzer corps' of two divisions – a parachute division and a parachute panzergrenadier division. However, the *Hermann Göring* Parachute Panzer Corps was never really an airborne formation, but merely given the title as an honorific, a further tribute to the fighting qualities of Hitler's Fallschirmjäger. To oversee the training of these new airborne formations and supervise their formation the First Parachute Army headquarters was established in the spring of 1944.[69]

But the formation of all these new units was more than a compliment to the fighting qualities of the German paratrooper. It was also an indication that a great deal of very hard fighting lay ahead.

Chapter 8

FROM PARTISANS TO THE RED ARMY

By the summer of 1943 Witzig had returned to Germany. As he prepared himself for a new command the Third Reich's military prospects continued to crumble. In July Hitler launched Army Groups Centre and North against the Soviet salient at Kursk in an attempt to eliminate it and shorten the Wehrmacht's defensive line, while at the same time inflicting such heavy casualties on the Red Army as to regain the strategic initiative on the Eastern Front. The Kursk offensive sought to encircle and annihilate the Soviet troops in the salient, end German fears of a flank attack and set the conditions for a follow-on offensive east of Kursk towards Moscow, and to the south-east towards the Don and Volga.

After the battle's opening on 5 July there followed a slugging match between German and Soviet tanks, artillery and infantry of unprecedented proportions and intensity. By 12 July the German advance had stalled against intense Soviet resistance. The following day Hitler called off the offensive to send German reinforcements to deal with the Allied landings in Sicily on 10 July and the imminent collapse of Italian resistance. Losses on both sides were heavy. Between 12 July and 23 August, the Red Army lashed back with a series of stinging counter-offensives against Army Group Centre that hurled the Wehrmacht back almost 150 km and liberated the city of Kharkov. As a result of their defeat at Kursk, Hitler and the Wehrmacht had lost the initiative on the Eastern Front forever.[1] 'With the Kursk offensive I wanted to reverse fate,' Hitler bemoaned afterwards to one of his long-time personal aides, SS Sturmbannführer Otto Günsche. 'I would never have believed the Russians were so strong.'[2] Stalin followed the battle of Kursk by launching new offensive operations in August and September, throwing the Germans back in the south an average of 240 km over a 1,000-km front and inflicting heavy casualties.

In October 1943 Witzig temporarily took command of the newly reconstituted Corps 21st Parachute Engineer Regiment, which was in the process of being formed, and of the regiment's fully formed 1st Battalion, which had been formed around his Corps 11th Parachute Engineer Battalion:

> I gathered what remained of my battalion once again in Wittenberg. There we reconstituted the battalion once more and, soon afterwards, were deployed to the centre of France. During the training phase we had to deal with French partisans and maquis, who were gaining in strength. They received their equipment and weapons from British agents, who also supported and led them.[3]

Predominantly rural guerrilla bands of the French Resistance, the Maquis were primarily composed of men who had escaped into the mountains to avoid being conscripted by Vichy France into working as forced labourers in Germany. What began as loose groups of individuals became increasingly organised, initially fighting the Vichy French and the Germans to remain free. They evolved, however, into active resistance groups.

The spring of 1944 found Witzig's Corps 11th Parachute Engineer Battalion deployed around Moulins in central France, conducting training of new personnel as well as engaging in anti-partisan operations. The Parachute Engineer Replacement Battalion in Decize had been subordinated to Witzig's regiment. According to Witzig there were no other strong German formations in the area. The widespread presence of the Maquis had become a continuing source of irritation and frustration to the Vichy and German authorities and in the third week of March the Wehrmacht launched large-scale operations with massive air support against one group on the plateau of Glières after an attack by French Vichy militia had failed.

> The fight with the partisans demanded [our] attention [wrote Witzig in his postwar history of the regiment], but was, however, limited to small engagements, which were conducted by individual companies. But at the beginning of the [Allied] invasion battle along the Channel coast, strong partisan formations made themselves felt in our area, which was under the control of the Vichy Government – tied to Germany by treaty

– but which only the German military had the power to confront.[4]

According to Karl–Heinz Hammerschlag, who served with Witzig in France, the two formations that formed the core of the battalion's anti-partisan operations were the 1st and the 4th Companies.[5] A particularly strong group of French Maquis had established themselves at St-Amand, located approximately 60 km west of Moulins. St-Amand had previously been under the control of a Vichy French battalion. Witzig's battalion received orders to quell the partisan force and ensure security and stability in the area. Using wood–burning buses with French drivers, Witzig prepared to deploy his battalion, but was certain the partisans had been tipped off to the operation. On 16 June 1944 the battalion deployed to St-Amand and advanced against the town on two sides in a double envelopment with orders to link up in the market-place. Most of the partisans, though caught unprepared, managed to escape the trap, however, leaving some equipment behind, including a rucksack, which Witzig appropriated and later used for hiking trips after the war. After the operation, while Witzig was speaking to the chief of police in front of the police station in St-Amand near the market square, a shot rang out, killing the Frenchman standing next to him: 'A partisan probably shot from one of the houses around the marketplace. Perhaps the shot was aimed at me.'[6]

According to Hammerschlag, another noteworthy incident took place at about the same time. A group of suspected partisans had been captured by Witzig's men and these were brought to the market square to be presented to him. Before this could be done, however, the paratroopers, wearing Wehrmacht uniforms due to a shortage of their unique airborne smocks, came under fire and the prisoners bolted. Witzig's men began firing at the escaping prisoners and, after they disappeared, into the bushes and trees close to the edge of town.[7] After the firing died out, Witzig and his men laid out the dead policeman in the police station. 'It remained only for me to visit the Vichy battalion and warn its commander to prevent such occurrences in the future,' wrote Witzig. 'Then we left St-Amand. As long as we remained in Moulins the peace in St-Amand held.'[8] As the battalion received notice to prepare to deploy to Lithuania and East Prussia the incident was quickly forgotten. Nonetheless, it would have serious repercussions for Witzig and haunt him long after the war.

In the meantime, the much-awaited Allied invasion of France, Operation Overlord, began just after midnight on 6 June 1944, when paratroopers of the American 82nd and 101st and the British 6th Airborne Divisions landed on the flanks of five invasion beaches in Normandy. The paratroopers were followed by assault landing forces totalling eight divisions on five beaches. By the end of the day those divisions were firmly established on the European continent. And by the end of June the Allies had landed more than 850,000 men in France.[9] At the beginning of the invasion the newly formed II Parachute Corps had been ordered to move to the St-Lô area. The corps had been formed at the end of 1943 and placed under the command of General-leutnant Eugen Meindl. At the time of the invasion, Meindl commanded the 2nd, 3rd, and 5th Parachute Divisions, in addition to various support units, including intelligence, reconnaissance and assault-gun detachments and a parachute training depot of battalion size. Meindl positioned the 3rd and 5th Parachute Divisions to the north-east and west of St-Lô, respectively, while the understrength 2nd Parachute Division was ordered by General Student to defend Brest in Britanny.[10]

Shortly after the Allied landings in Normandy, the German situation on the Eastern Front turned even more desperate. In June Stalin had unleashed his summer offensive in Belorussia, Operation Bagration, catching Army Group Centre and the entire German High Command by surprise. On the morning of 22 June, the third anniversary of the German invasion of the Soviet Union, some 2·4 million Red Army soldiers, supported by 36,400 artillery pieces and mortars, 5,200 tanks and assault guns, and 5,300 aircraft, opened an attack aimed at nothing less than the encirclement and complete annihilation of Army Group Centre. Stalin's marshals expected to encounter some 1·2 million German soliders, supported by 9,500 artillery pieces, 900 tanks and assault guns, and 1,350 Luftwaffe aircraft. The Red Army thus outnumbered the Wehrmacht by at least six-to-one in tanks, four-to-one in artillery pieces and combat aircraft, and two-to-one in personnel.[11]

Within days the Soviets had hurled the Germans back and by the end of July Hitler's armies were in headlong retreat, fighting desperately to avoid encirclement and complete annihilation. Bagration had torn a 400-km gap in the German front and only the wings of the reeling Army Group Centre, in the southern Baltic States, were still able to resist the Russian onslaught. In the north, the Third Panzer Army and the Second Army were all that remained between the Russians and East Prussia.

In a frantic attempt to shore up faltering German resistance, Hitler sent out Field Marshal Model to take command of the remnants of Army Group Centre. At the same time, Model retained command of Army Group North Ukraine. Model, the Wehrmacht's youngest field marshal, was known as 'The Führer's Fireman' for his ingenuity in salvaging apparently hopeless situations. He was one of the few officers remaining who enjoyed the complete trust of Hitler. Colonel–General Heinz Guderian praised Model as 'a bold inexhaustible soldier ... the best man possible to perform the fantastically difficult task of reconstructing a line in the centre of the Eastern Front'.[12]

Hitler also directed all available German forces northward. The Führer and his commanders assessed the situation on the Eastern Front, where the Red Army was advancing as fast as its logistics allowed, as much more threatening than the Allied force trying to break out from Normandy. Hitler had hoped to concentrate Germany's newly mobilised formations and manufactured weapons on defending Western Europe against an Allied assault, while the Eastern Front took care of itself. 'The threat from the East remains, but an even greater danger looms in the West: the Anglo-American landing! In the East, the vastness of the space will, as a last resort, permit a loss of territory even on a major scale, without suffering a mortal blow to Germany's chances for survival!' he had proclaimed, in Führer Directive 51 of 3 November 1943. 'Not so in the West! If the enemy succeeded in penetrating our defences on a wide front, consequences of staggering proportions will follow within a short time.'[13] But Hitler's policy of concentrating his forces in the West was now in shambles.[14] Thus, even as the Allies were fighting to break out of the lodgement they had established, the Germans were transferring elite formations eastwards towards the Baltic states.

While three of Student's elite Fallschirmjäger divisions had been committed to containing the Allies in Normandy, other paratrooper formations were diverted to the Eastern Front in an attempt to stop the Soviet advance. These included Rudolf Witzig's battalion:

> After the start of the Anglo–American invasion we were not transferred to Normandy, but to Lithuania. The Russians had succeeded in breaking through there and separating Army Group North in the Baltics from [Army Group Centre] in East Prussia. This problem had to be solved quickly; therefore, once again, units were moved and transferred to get it done.[15]

Witzig's command would fight as part of Lieutenant-Colonel Gerhard Schirmer's 16th Parachute Regiment, which had been virtually annihilated near Kiev earlier in the year and then reconstituted. Schirmer had commanded a parachute company as part of the German airborne assault on the Corinth Canal in Greece. Afterwards he commanded the 2nd Battalion of the 2nd Parachute Regiment in the Peloponnese and on Crete, landing near Heraklion as the strategic reserve. For capturing Hill 296, a piece of key terrain in the battle, Schirmer was awarded the Knight's Cross. In Tunisia he commanded the 5th Parachute Regiment's 3rd Battalion in heavy fighting and later assumed command of the regiment after Colonel Koch had been put out of action.[16] On 1 January 1944 Schirmer had been appointed to command the 16th Parachute Regiment. The regiment, deployed around Abbeville in France, had been brought up to full strength with four battalions in May and then received parachute training in June, with special emphasis on night drops.

The 954 soldiers[17] of the 16th Parachute Regiment entrained for Vilnius, in the south-eastern corner of modern Lithuania, in July. The German High Command considered the defence of Vilnius imperative. If the city fell, it would be impossible to maintain contact between the two German army groups in the Baltic States and to stop the Red Army's advance towards East Prussia. It had thus been declared a 'fortress' city by Hitler and was to be held to the last man.[18] Schirmer's regiment was subordinated to Field Marshal Model's Army Group Centre and the Third Panzer Army. Under the direct control of Major-General Stahel, an air-defence officer and commander of Vilnius, the 16th Parachute Regiment joined a hotch-potch of units in defence of the city, including the 399th and 1067th Panzergrenadier Regiments, an independent panzergrenadier brigade, the 16th SS Police Regiment, the 2nd Battalion, 240th Field Artillery Regiment, the 256th Anti-Tank Battalion and the 296th Flak Battalion.[19] In addition, elements of the 731st Anti-Tank Detachment, with 25 Hetzer tank destroyers were also available, as well as the 103rd Panzer Brigade with 21 Panther tanks, the 8th Assault Gun Detachment and the 6th Panzer Division with 23 Panzer IV tanks and 26 Panthers.[20]

Poised to advance on the Lithuanian capital were elements of the Soviet 5th and 5th Guards Armies of the Third Belorussian Front.[21] The Soviet attack on the city began on 8 July, with Russian tanks and infantry attacking across Lake Narocz towards the airfield, which was defended by the paratroopers. After bitter fighting, the Soviet 35th Tank Brigade took the airfield. Intense street fighting then commenced as the Soviets attempted to reduce German defences. By midday the Red Army had fought its way into the city, overrunning the initial line of anti-tank obstacles and destroying a number of the ad hoc German battle groups. The following day the Germans reported 500 dead and another 500 wounded. By 9 July Vilnius was encircled. Two days later the German High Command ordered a break-out. The following night the defenders broke contact with the enemy and crossed the Vilnia River. Some 2,000 *Landsers* made it across.[22] With the fall of Vilnius the Wehrmacht's position in the Baltic States became untenable.

In the meantime, the 16th Parachute Regiment had been followed to the Baltics by Witzig's 1st Battalion of the 21st Parachute Engineer Regiment, which arrived from France. The battalion, which had an authorised strength of 21 officers and 1,011 other ranks, had been conducting night parachute training at the Salzwedel airbase when it was alerted for movement to Lithuania. 'By means of a railway movement of several days duration via Berlin and through the peaceful and marvellously sunny summer countryside of Brandenburg and West Prussia and then through East Prussia the battalion reached the border with Lithuania,' wrote Witzig. 'The first deployment took place in the Kaunas area.' Witzig's battalion reached their planned defensive positions between Schescuppe and Wilkowischen, located only 10 km from the East Prussian border, at the end of July and began to entrench. Within a few days of arriving the unit was reinforced with an artillery detachment and elements of an assault gun brigade.

> Due to the length of the front we were deployed from right to left as follows: Parachute Engineer Battalion, 2nd Battalion, 1st Battalion, and the 3rd Battalion with the 13th Company in reserve and an assault gun brigade [recorded Witzig]. After a while the regiment, which was only equipped with its infantry weapons, received four 75-mm anti-tank guns, which were distributed among the frontline battalions. This position was held the whole of August and September 1944.[23]

Initially the Russians were nowhere in sight. Instead the men of Witzig's battalion witnessed the massive westward exodus of Nazi civilian leaders and their families fleeing for their lives to escape the advancing Red Army. The German population in the path of the

Russians was thus left leaderless. 'This was the beginning of the breakdown of law and order,' remembered Witzig.

After changing positions several times the battalion finally made contact with the Russians. Witzig's 3rd Company relieved the 500th SS. Parachute Battalion, a punishment battalion:

> Only the commander and a few members of the staff had the required rank. All of the company, platoon, and squad leaders were demoted SS officers and NCOs, who wore only an arm badge with their official position. These men had conducted a jump in a coup de main against the headquarters of Yugoslav partisan commander Marshal Tito, only a few weeks earlier. Only with great effort and at the very last moment had he managed to escape.

On the day of their relief the SS paratroopers bloodily repulsed a Russian tank attack.[24]

On 20 July 1944 a bomb planted at Hitler's East Prussian headquarters barely missed killing the leader of the Third Reich. In the confusion that followed the attempt, the vast majority of the Wehrmacht's leaders swore their loyalty to the Führer, while those opposed to the regime were hunted down, cruelly tortured and brutally murdered. A small number committed suicide; only a few survived. Hearing the news at an impromptu parade complete with loudspeakers, Witzig and his men were stunned and felt betrayed. 'Can you imagine how you would feel if you learned, fighting in the middle of a war, that someone had tried to kill your president?' one veteran asked the author, when recounting the incident.[25]

But the war went on. According to Witzig the Red Army attacked his positions about once a week, usually in division strength. Twice Soviet armour, in regimental strength, broke through the German positions:

> The majority of tanks, and especially the accompanying infantry, were destroyed by our forward companies in close combat, while the tanks which penetrated deeper were shot by our assault gun brigade. The position was reformed after each attack.

Witzig noted that the Soviets had a large superiority in artillery, which they used liberally. As a result the terrain surrounding the German defensive positions 'looked liked the World War I Verdun battlefield'. From time to time the artillery detachment attached to the regiment neutralised a Soviet battery, but it was a losing battle. Nonetheless, Witzig's battalion, which was deployed as infantry, fought with great determination.[26]

In one particulary hard-fought battle Witzig's battalion was mentioned in communiqués for destroying 27 Soviet tanks and stopping the advance of an entire Red Army tank division. On 25 July the battalion covered a movement to first the Kaunas–Daugavpils road and, later in the evening, still further to the north-east to Jonava and entrenched there. 'A few days ago a strong concentration of enemy tanks was observed and reported in this area,' reported Witzig, 'so it was assumed a major attack was imminent.' The 1st Battalion, 21st Parachute Engineer Regiment, was attached to a battle group commanded by a Colonel Theodor von Tolstorff for this deployment. Tolstorff was, according to Witzig, an excellent officer, and he would win the Swords and Diamonds to the Knight's Cross the following year as commander of the 340th Volksgrenadier Division.[27]

As had been so often the case, one of Witzig's companies was detached from the battalion and Witzig was forced to defend with his three remaining companies. The ground on which the battle was fought was open, although the battalion's flanks were covered by a large forest. The 1st Company, commanded by Lieutenant Kubillus, deployed on the left of the Kaunas–Daugavpils road, while the 2nd Company, commanded by Lieutenant Walther, deployed on the right as it was clear that the Soviets would focus their attacks on this road. Elements of Lieutenant Schürmann's understrength 4th Company were attached to the 2nd Company, while the remainder served as a battalion reserve. The 3rd Company, commanded by Lieutenant von Albert, was detached from the battalion to serve as a corps reserve in the rear. According to Witzig, several assault and anti-tank guns were deployed with the battalion, located at the edge of a wood and in battle positions in a cornfield, but were not attached to it. The battalions own T–mines, stored in stacks of a hundred, had been left in the woods in forward positions. Witzig notes that every squad was equipped with anti-tank weapons of some sort, including at least one Panzerschreck and three to five Panzerfausts.[28]

The Panzerschreck ('Tank Terror') or *Ofenrohr* ('Stovepipe') was similar to the American Bazooka rocket-launcher. More than 1·5 metres long and weighing more than 11 kg it was a handful for any soldier to carry, much less use effectively. However, its 88-mm, 3-kg, anti-tank rocket was capable of stopping any Allied tank at ranges of up to 120 metres. The Panzerfaust, on the other hand, was the world's first truly disposable anti-tank recoilless launcher. Weighing only 6 kg and easy to use, this shoulder-fired launcher shot a hollow-charge anti-tank grenade, which could pierce 200 mm at ranges of 30–80 metres. This was literally point-blank range against a tank and it took a great deal of raw courage, steady nerves and patience to use the weapon effectively.[29] By 1944 both weapons had acquired a fearsome reputation. In the last year of the war the Allies would find themselves losing hundreds of vehicles a week to the Panzerschreck and Panzerfaust.[30]

During the night of 25/26 July Witzig's companies entrenched in fighting positions optimised for anti-tank defence, with two to three men in each position. To defend against surprise attacks a string of forward outposts had been established, especially in the 1st Company sector. These preparations all took place against a backdrop of the constant sound of Russian tanks moving into place just forward of the battalion's positions. 'The defensive position was too exposed,' complained Witzig, who was convinced that the Russians would attack in strength. The battle began that night, with a combat patrol by the 4th Company, which surprised and captured a Soviet tank crew and a commissar. A short time later a Russian patrol evened the odds by capturing two outposts of the 2nd Company. Shortly afterwards a third outpost disappeared. 'Another outpost was gone,' remembered Witzig. 'Only the soldier's rifle was left in his foxhole.' The sound of tanks massing continued throughout the night and at the crack of dawn the next day they were visible across a wide front some 1,200 metres from the battalion's positions.[31]

> At the break of dawn on July 26, 1944 the men of the battalion were aware that a day was starting that would demand the greatest efforts from them. With a provoking directness an armada of steel and iron, aware of its superiority, deployed so that even the bravest individual felt depressed. Countless T–34 tanks, artillery pieces and the dreaded 'Stalin Organ' [multiple rocket launcher] and assault guns were deployed to break through the defensive positions of the parachute engineers. Yet not one round was fired. There was an uncanny silence on both sides, the calm before the storm.

Rudolf Witzig, the Eagle of Eben Emael, wearing the Knight's Cross presented to him by Adolf Hitler. Witzig is wearing the distinctive field-grey paratrooper's helmet and olive green jump smock. His helmet has been smeared with mud as camouflage.

Rudolf Witzig and companions marching in a 16th Engineer Battalion sports competition in Höxter in 1935. The battalion was part of III Motorised Corps.

Rudolf Witzig (second from the right) and fellow soldiers from the 16th Engineer Battalion, III Motorised Corps, performing physical exercises with their rifles in Höxter in 1935.

Rudolf Witzig (front left) and friends enjoying themselves on a rowing boat in 1936.

Cadet Rudolf Witzig studying in his barracks room while at the Kreigsschule in Dresden in 1936. The soldiers of Hitler's new Wehrmacht were housed in modern stone barracks.

Both above: German Airborne School, Stendal, 1938. Practice jumps from a Ju-52.

Rudolf Witzig with one of his soldiers in the field. Both are from the Engineer Platoon, Parachute Battalion, 1st Parachute Regiment, 7th Airborne Division. Witzig served with the unit from November 1938 to May 1940.

An aerial view of Fort Eben Emael with all the major works and objectives marked.

Hitler with the conquerors of Eben Emael. Rudolf Witzig is on the left in the back row.

Witzig briefing Hermann Göring in May 1940. Witzig served briefly as Göring's aide. Although he found Göring to be an interesting individual, Witzig believed the Reichsmarschall was a 'salon soldier' in self-designed uniforms of white and powder blue.

General Rudolf Schmundt and Nicolaus von Below, Hitler's aides, with Captain Koch and Lieutenant Witzig.

Hermann Göring with Rudolf Witzig, May 1940.

Göring with General Milch and Rudolf Witzig, May 1940.

itler walking with Hermann Göring,
he Commander of the Luftwaffe. The
ührer's valet, Heinz Linge, follows
ehind.

aptain Rudolf Witzig with Göring's
hief aide, Erich Gritzbach. Gritzbach
as chief of Göring's personal staff
nd in charge of all business
onnected with his art purchases. As
hief of the Prussian Press Bureau,
ritzbach became Göring's official
iographer in 1939. Göring used
ritzbach as an intermediary to seize
orks of art from Jews and others,
us distancing himself from illegal
ansactions.

An overworked Rudolf Witzig, aide to Reichsmarschall Hermann Göring, asleep in Göring's Ju-52 some time between May and August 1940.

Captain Rudolf Witzig relaxing outside
Göring's train near Dinant, Belgium
in August 1940.

Rudolf Witzig with Göring's chief aide,
Erich Gritzback, August 1940.

Left: Rudolf Witzig standing in front o one of one of the fortifications at Ebe Emael some time after the end of the Wehrmacht's campaign in the West. Witzig would repeatedly visit Eben Emael, the site of his greatest victory

Right: Major Rudolf Witzig briefing a group of young German students on 25 March 1941 on the assault on Eben Emael. Witzig was frequently called upon to inspire students and soldiers alike with his exploits.

Below: Rudolf Witzig in battle dress back in Düsseldorf following the successful attack on Eben Emael.

Above: Witzig's airborne engineers tearing up railway track in Jefna. They used the materials to strengthen their defensive positions, digging them deep and with strong overhead cover as protection against the accurate British guns.

Left: Witzig at Jefna, in his soft cap. Witzig seldom wore a helmet, even in combat. On his left breast can be seen his Iron Cross and below that the Screaming Eagle emblem of the Fallschirmjäger.

Right: A German propaganda photo showing German paratroopers under their parachute canopies in the air and on the ground with their weapons. Above them fly the Luftwaffe's ubiquitous Ju-52, the workhorse of Hitler's airborne forces.

Witzig and one of his lieutenants in North Africa.

The silence, however did not last long. 'And then, flashes from the other side, from thousands of barrels simultaneously', and shells were pounding the German positions unmercifully: 'Again and again, pounding, hammering, shattering, pulsating, bursting and cracking,' recorded Witzig. The incessant barrage lasted for an hour without any reduction in intensity, inflicting numerous casualties on the battalion. As it began to lift, Witzig's men noticed that the German assault guns had abandoned their battle positions and were nowhere to be seen. But there was nothing that could be done, for the Russian tanks, heavily laden with foot soldiers, were already advancing on the paratroopers through the smoke and the dust with more infantry running alongside the tanks.[32]

Witzig's men held their fire until the first line of enemy tanks were only twenty metres away, then unleashed a devastating barrage of anti–tank rounds. At this range, nothing, not even the thickly armoured Josef Stalin tank, was immune from the deadly German volley:

> The men of the 1st [Company] took heart and set themselves against this colossus. It came to furious fighting directly on the highway. Lieutenant Fromme fired his Panzerfaust at a T–34 which ground to a halt, engulfed in flames. He himself was wounded. Then Lieutenant Kubillus, the company commander, who had hastened to the highway after realising the focal point of the attack, went down seriously wounded. Sergeant Weber took command of the company. He himself blew apart three tanks, which stood burning and shattered in front of the company foxholes. Then he saw Sergeants Scheuring, Hüchering and a few other engineers, whom he could not recognise because of the dust and smoke, obliterate another three tanks. Within a short period, the men of the 1st Company, using Panzerfausts and *Ofenrohr*, had turned fifteen tanks into burning, smouldering iron.[33]

As the enemy tank attack was broken up, leaving dozens of T–34s and Soviet assault guns engulfed in flames, the Russian infantry sprang from their carriers to the ground, intent on making the paratroopers pay. Instead, they were mown down at close range by MG. 42s. Caught in the open and without their tanks to suppress the machine guns, the Red Army soldiers were slaughtered. Within minutes the first Russian attack had collapsed under the massed and accurate anti-tank and machine-gun fire of Witzig's parachute engineers. But the battalion, in turn, suffered heavy losses, with the 1st Company reduced to thirty men.[34]

In the meantime, to the south of the Kaunas–Daugavpils road the 2nd Company, reinforced with the understrength 4th Company, was having a more difficult time containing the Russian assault. A group of some fifty T–34s succeeded in fighting their way through the company positions and cutting off the road behind the two companies. 'The mounted infantry were taken under fire first and forced to jump off,' wrote Witzig. 'Engineer Stauss engaged a tank with his *Ofenrohr* and suddenly a second tank was also on fire. But the remainder rolled westward without bothering about their infantrymen left behind.' The German assault guns, which might have defeated the Russian tanks, had already left the battlefield and these had been followed by the surviving anti–tank guns, leaving the paratroopers to fight unsupported. 'I engaged the tanks which were passing close by my right as the Russians did not attack head on,' remembered Sergeant Hans–Ulrich Schmidt, from Hamburg, relating his escape in the midst of the advancing Red Army:

> After the first echelon passed by, I discovered about five Russian soldiers on every T–34. At the same moment another T–34 showed up about 100 metres to the right of me. I fired one shot with my *Ofenrohr* and hit it, but after two minutes it began moving and firing again. I charged my *Ofenrohr* with a second shell immediately as I heard the noise of battle behind me. I tried to establish contact to the right and left of me, but no one had remained in their positions. So I left the position and ran back into the cornfield behind me. Here I found myself between several Russian tanks, which surrounded me. I raised my *Ofenrohr*, aimed and fired, but the electrical firing trigger failed. One of the tanks discovered me and fired with its gun. I was knocked to the ground by the blast of the shell and hit my forehead against the *Ofenrohr*. That was my salvation. I pretended to be dead and the tanks moved on. After they were out of sight I ran as fast as I could to the rear, concealed by the cornfield.[35]

By this point in the battle there were Russian soldiers to the front, on the right flank and behind the battalion's position. Now it was only a matter of breaking contact with the Soviets as quickly as possible, withdrawing before the battalion could be encircled and annihilated, and regrouping on defensive positions to the west. But the Soviet tanks which had broken through had been followed by masses of Russian infantry, which attacked the German paratroopers as they sought to cross the 2 km. of open ground to reach the safety of the forest and cover. Now it was the Russian machine guns which fired unremittingly, mowing down the German paratroopers as they sought to escape. Few made it. Only twelve unwounded survivors of the 1st Company made it to the battalion rally point, along with only ten men from the 2nd Company. Major Witzig led the remnants of his battalion through the forests, bypassing the Soviets and avoiding battle until the survivors reached the German lines.

> We set out towards the north under heavy fire along a small trail [remembered Private Anzenhofer]. For some time we strayed through the forest in column formation led by Major Witzig, meeting remnants of the battalion. The commander led us, through Russian tank and crowded troop formations, back to our own lines without further losses. To this day, everyone who survived still gives him credit.[36]

Witzig himself had only praise for his men, especially his medical personnel, as he wrote after the war:

> Their sense of duty saved the lives of hundreds of German and Russian soldiers. Only someone who has been in the inferno of death and destruction can measure how these men fought. Selfless and fearless, animated by the thought of helping their wounded comrades, no matter which uniform they were wearing and bringing them back safely as quickly as possible.[37]

Many of the German medics were killed or seriously wounded, while others disappeared, never to be seen again.

Over the course of the next several days, other paratroopers rejoined the battalion, which, according to Witzig's account, numbered sixty-five men. Witzig used these to establish blocking positions and prevent the Russians from breaking through. This remnant of Witzig's battalion was committed again and again in a futile attempt to stop the Red Army.[38] By the end of August, the 1st Battalion, 21st Parachute Engineer Regiment, had a total strength of 8 officers and 274 men. Of these, however, only 4 officers and 184 men were frontline soldiers.[39] Karl-Heinz Hammerschlag, who fought under Witzig in Lithuania, remembered that from a battalion of more than 1,000 men in the summer of 1944, only 30 remained by September. 'We had no tanks, no field artillery, no anti-tank artillery and no Luftwaffe,' he told the author. 'We fought mostly with Panzerfausts and anti-tank mines.'[40]

Still, other intense battles followed near Memel and elsewhere in October. In the end, the unit's losses were so heavy it had to be pulled out of the line. Its few surviving officers were sent to fight on the Western Front, while the surviving rank and file were dispersed among the other parachute battalions. Witzig bade farewell to his men in order to take command of the newly formed 18th Parachute Regiment of the 6th Parachute Division. Lieutenant Tiemens, Witzig's adjutant for many years and the commander of the intelligence platoon, departed with Witzig, as did Lieutenant Heise, the medical officer and other officers, NCOs and soldiers who had served with Witzig. At the same time, Lieutenant von Albert departed to take command of the 2nd Replacement and Training Battalion in Güstrow. Others, including Lieutenants Fromme and Ackermann and Officer Candidate Wehnart, were sent to form the core of the newly reconstituted 2nd Parachute Engineer Battalion, to be commanded by Captain Siegfried Gerstner. The remainder, including the bulk of Witzig's 3rd Company, formed the core of the new 6th Parachute Engineer Battalion, commanded by Major Stipschütz:

> This was the end of the battalion, which endured along with the 1st Parachute Engineer Battalion, as the Corps Parachute Engineer Battalion, then as the 1st Battalion, 21st Parachute Engineer Regiment, for the longest time of all. Elements deployed to El Alamein under Ramcke and Rommel and it was one of the strongest and most reliable units during the long-lasting defence in Tunisia and on the Eastern Front in Lithuania.[41]

In another account Witzig recalled that:

> Schirmer stayed there [in the Baltics] with his battalion until the very end, when he was attached to the Fallschirmpanzer-korps *Hermann Göring* ... while I and the rest of my battalion were detached in the late autumn of 1944. My battalion, the pieces of it, was dissolved. They used it to build three new

battalions that were necessary for the Fallschirmjäger divisions in Holland.[42]

Witzig's elite parachute engineers had fought their last battle and learned that raw courage and skill were simply not enough in the face of the massive firepower and numbers the Red Army was hurling at the Germans. Even the Führer's elite Fallschirmjäger had proven unable to stop the relentless westward onslaught of Stalin's legions.

Nor was the damage confined to Army Group Centre's front. On 20 August, while Witzig and his battalion were defending against the Red Army in the north, two German and two Romanian armies of Army Group South Ukraine disintegrated almost totally between the Black Sea and the Carpathian Mountains in the face of another overwhelming Russian attack. Romania now lay open to an advance by the Red Army, while German troops in Greece were cut off altogether from the Reich. The collapse of Army Group Centre and Army Group South Ukraine made August 1944 the Wehrmacht's worst month of the entire war in terms of losses, with almost 278,000 German soldiers killed on the Eastern Front. Almost 170,000 more had been killed in July. And the number of Wehrmacht soldiers killed on the Eastern Front from July through September 1944 totalled almost 518,000, or 5,750 dead a day, the highest daily loss rate of the war.[43]

Now Hitler's network of alliances, from Scandinavia to the Balkans, began to unravel. On 25 August the Romanian people overthrew Marshal Antonescu, renounced their alliance with Germany and declared war upon Hitler and the Reich. This meant the loss of the desperately needed Ploesti oilfields to the Wehrmacht at a time when the German oil industry was being obliterated by the Allied air forces. To make matters even worse, on 25 August Bulgaria began negotiations with the Russians for an armistice and demanded the withdrawal of all German military personnel from its territory. At about the same time, a serious insurrection broke out in Slovakia, while Finland prepared to declare its alliance with Germany at an end, as it too sought an armistice with the Soviet Union.[44]

Soviet casualties have been equally horrendous. The Red Army and 1st Polish Army had lost 180,000 men killed and suffered another almost 600,000 sick and wounded in Operation Bagration alone. But they had succeeded in shattering the Wehrmacht on the Eastern Front and that success, in turn, forced the German High Command to transfer some 40–45 divisions to stem the Soviet onslaught and defend the Reich's increasingly vulnerable eastern borders.[45] In the meantime, the Western Allies were racing through France and into the Low Countries. On 25 August they moved into Paris; by 4 September they were in Antwerp, capturing the vital port undamaged. More ominously, Bagration also uncovered the roads to East Prussia and Berlin to an army fed on hate for the Germans and bent on vengeance. 'Murder, arson, rape and devastation marked the trail of the Russian armies, excited as the latter had been by an unimaginable propaganda of hate,' wrote Walter Goerlitz, in his authoritative history of the German General Staff:

> Huge columns of refugees were moving westward. Often they were overtaken by Russian tanks, in which case they were massacred or crushed beneath their tracks. Ships carrying thousands of refugees were sunk by Russian submarines. All the horrors perpetuated in Russia by the S.S., all the deeds of shame committed in this 'degenerate war' of *Weltanschauungen* which Hitler had so impiously declared, were now revenged a hundred and a thousand fold, the innocent population of the German East being the victims. The culture which had taken centuries to build was buried within a matter of days.[46]

But it was much more than 'an unimaginable propaganda of hate' that drove the Red Army soldier. It was unadulterated rage for the tremendous scale of death and destruction Germany and the Wehrmacht had inflicted on the Soviet Union and its people. 'Everything, from the deaths of beloved friends to the burning of cities, from the hunger of the children back at home to the fear of facing yet another hail of shells,' writes Catherine Merridale, in her masterful and uniquely insightful book on the Red Army soldier at war, 'everything . . . was blamed on the Germans.' One Russian soldier summed up what awaited the inhabitants of Hitler's Third Reich: 'We will take revenge, revenge for all our sufferings.' Another wrote home: 'We are clenching our fists and moving unrelentingly towards the west.'[47] With the Americans and British advancing in the west and the Russians pressing forward virtually unhindered in the east, the German people were about to reap the hate-filled whirlwind Hitler and his Wehrmacht had sown.

Chapter 9

HOLLAND: 'NO LONGER WAR'

From October 1944 until the end of the war on 10 May 1945 Witzig fought as the commander of the 6th Parachute Division's 18th Parachute Regiment in Holland against the Western Allies, following the ill-fated Market–Garden operation in September. Unlike the remainder of his military career, for which there is a wealth of material available, Witzig recorded nothing about his battles in Holland. Indeed, after the war, when he was asked to travel to Emmerich in the Netherlands to brief a Bundeswehr engineer battalion on his Second World War battles in Holland, Witzig absolutely refused, stating that by late 1944 it was no longer a war and there was absolutely nothing to be learned from it. He and his soldiers fought simply to survive.

There were indeed many German commanders and soldiers who spent most of their time simply trying to survive the last months of the war and who would have agreed wholeheartedly. Generalmajor Carl Wagener, Chief of Staff of Army Group "B" from February to April 1945, for example, wrote that there were no lessons that could be learned from the last period of the war: first, because of the poor performance of the German High Command during this period and the series of strategic mistakes made by Hitler and his generals; second, because the troops were fighting in 'an abnormal, unnatural condition [so] that even their experiences had no general or valid application'; third, because the Army Group was not really conducting operations but, instead, improvised, emergency 'first aid' measures for lower echelons, 'which they themselves were doing for the lower levels'. 'Strategy, of course, is always based on improvisations,' observed Wagener. 'However, there is a limit; and it must be appreciated that, beyond this limit, improvisation becomes ineffective and strategy and military "leadership" futile.'[1] Wagener's comments provide a great deal of insight into what Witzig experienced in the final year of the war. Thus Witzig's story in Holland must be told by other participants, most notably, his army, corps, and division commanders, as well as others who participated in the brutal fighting in Holland.

By early September 1944, the German armies in the West had been shattered. On paper, the German order of battle at the beginning of September included an impressive 327 divisions and brigades. Of these, 31 divisions and 13 brigades were armoured. However, most were significantly below strength. According to the High Command War Diary for the period, only 13 German infantry divisions and 3 panzer divisions in the West, along with 2 panzer brigades, were considered fully combat-capable, while the combat capabilities of another 12 infantry divisions, 2 panzer divisions, and 2 panzer brigades were described as 'shaky'. Altogether some 28 German infantry and panzer divisions in the West had been decimated or disbanded since D–Day, with only 11 of those regenerated. To stem the Allied onslaught, Hitler and his generals began diverting a steady stream of formations to O.B. West. Equipment losses had been equally disastrous and, according to Major Schramm, the keeper of the High Command's War Diary, Hitler's Western Front was defended by no more than a hundred German panzers.[2]

Following the Allied breakthrough towards Antwerp and the fall of that city on 4 September 1944, Hitler also directed the restoration of the First Parachute Army destroyed in Normandy. With an initial strength of 20,000 men, its mission was to defend from the North Sea to Maastricht, contain the Allied bridgehead at Antwerp and hold the Albert Canal. Initially, First Parachute Army was placed under Field Marshal Walter Model's Army Group B for operations along the Antwerp–Albert Canal line. Subordinate units initially included the 3rd, 5th and 6th Parachute Divisions, which were reorganising and refitting in northern Holland and Germany; LXXXVIII Corps from Holland with the bulk of the 719th and 347th Infantry Divisions; training groups from the Waffen SS and the *Hermann Göring* Depot Regiment (also from Holland); assorted security units from Belgium, northern France, and Germany; and thirty heavy and ten light anti-aircraft batteries.[3] While the reorganised First Parachute Army was no doubt born of necessity, the reputation for dogged tenacity bordering on fanaticism won by the I Parachute Corps at Monte Cassino, which held up the Allies for six months and resulted in more than 35,000 casualties, and the II Parachute Corps in Normandy, which was instrumental in holding up the U.S. advance on St-Lô, no doubt convinced Hitler to gather his few remaining paratroopers in north-west Europe into a single formation and reinforce them in a desperate bid to stem the American and British onslaught and win enough time for him to rebuild the German defences in the West.

By the beginning of September 1944 the situation for the Third Reich was grim. Hitler's armies were being forced back by the relentless Allied advance from the North Sea to the Mediterranean. In the northern coastal sector the Fifteenth Army was falling back before the First Canadian Army towards the line of the Scheldt from Antwerp to the sea and across it to Walcheren and the Dutch mainland. To the south of the Fifteenth Army the broken elements of the Seventh Army were escaping before the British Second and the American First Armies towards Aachen and the Ardennes. South of the Ardennes, the German First Army, having come from south of the Loire and the Biscay coast, was moving east and making for the Siegfried Line. Finally, the Nineteenth Army was retreating through Dijon towards the Belfort Gap, driven by the American and French armies which had landed on the Mediterranean coast. Most of the armoured divisions of the Fifth Panzer Army were being withdrawn for rehabilitation to the Saar and further south with a view to counter-attack; the rest of the Fifth Panzer Army was now under Seventh Army. As the German armies fell back towards the prepared positions of the Siegfried Line and its extensions, reinforcements were being sent forward from the Reich and from occupied Holland, notably from the First Parachute Army. A firmer front was soon to take shape, but in September the situation was changing daily. German units found themselves chronically short of personnel, weapons, ammunition and fuel; without reserves, artillery, or signals equipment; and facing absolute Allied superiority in the air, which not only hindered troop movements but also precluded reconnaissance. On paper the Führer still had ten million men in his armed forces, seven and a half million of them in the Army. Most of these, however, were scattered across Europe, in the Baltic States, Poland, the Balkans, Scandinavia, the Netherlands and northern Italy and were thus not available for the immediate defence of Nazi Germany.

To stem the Allied onslaught Hitler ordered the German armies facing the Allies to 'contest every foot of ground in a stubborn delaying action' in order to gain time to move up new forces to reinforce the western defences from the Zuider Zee to the Swiss frontier and to assemble a mobile combat force west of the Vosges mountains with which to attack the American flank and safeguard construction of the frontier defences.[4] 'The battle in the West has largely moved onto German soil,' Hitler proclaimed, in a Führer Order dated 17 September 1944. 'German cities and villages will be battlegrounds. This fact must make our fighting more fanatical and harden every available man in the battle zone to turn every bunker, every apartment block in a German city, every German village into a fortress.'[5] So desperate was Hitler for additional manpower that, on 25 September 1944, as the Allies pressed towards Germany's western and eastern borders, the Führer ordered the creation of the Deutscher Volkssturm, a last-ditch defence force comprised of boys and older men up to sixty years old. Placing it under Nazi Party control, in the form of Martin Bormann, his personal secretary, Hitler dreamed of a large, ideologically committed militia that would help rouse the entire German population to a fanatical resistance that would halt the Allied advance. The Führer's mistrust of his generals at this critical stage of the war was such that he believed the Nazi Party, rather than the military, would mount the final defence of Germany.

By September of 1944 Hitler's Total War effort had, according to senior Wehrmacht officers, almost completely exhausted the country's personnel and material resources. Allied air forces had partially or fully destroyed the majority of Germany's vital industries and the railway net, which was indispensable for continuing the war. Indeed, Allied strategic bombing was seen as such a threat that, by August 1944, there were more than one million men manning some 39,000 anti-aircraft batteries attempting to defend Germany's skies.[6] Pending a miracle, some senior Wehrmacht officers believed that the collapse of the Third Reich would take place in the spring of 1945 at the latest.[7]

The German soldier, however, continued to fight well. 'He no longer had any great ideals; however, in most cases, he still retained a remnant of faith in Hitler,' remembered Colonel Günther Reichhelm, Chief of Operations for Army Group 'B', after having visited almost all corps and division headquarters as well as several regimental and battalion staffs. According to Reichhelm, the German soldier was fighting for a last chance. By autumn 1944, there was hardly a German family which had not lost one of its close kin, or which had not been bombed out and thereby lost everything. In addition to this, there was the reluctance of the German soldier to take second place in the events regarding his own country. Last, but not least, there was the ever-increasing propaganda, announcement of new weapons, imminent large-scale actions by German fighter-bombers and new U-boats on all oceans, and too-favourable predictions by the highest German authorities regarding industrial capability.'[8]

According to General der Infanterie Hermann Foertsch, last commander of the German First Army, the German soldier continued to fight we well as he did in the final year of the war due to obedience and the fear of harming his comrades should he be forced back; the hope of winning time for an early end to the war by political measures; the hope that, as a consequence of a political decision, easier conditions as a prisoner of war would be granted to the surrendering troops, and the hope that delaying actions might reduce the number of troops eventually captured by the Soviets. For all these reasons, notes Foertsch: 'German troops performed more than one could have expected by sober comparison of the strength of the opposing forces. Whenever they were able to continue fighting, by having the necessary technical equipment, they were fighting successfully up to the very last moment.'[9]

It is not surprising that both Reichhelm and Foertsch fail to touch upon two other important factors, which played an increasing role in the continuing cohesion of the German armed forces late in the war. The first was the enormous programme of systemic bribery of the highest-ranking generals and admirals, implemented by Hitler to ensure the continuing loyalty of those at the top. Such inducements began with generous cash payments. Early in the war Hitler had instituted a programme in which those officers promoted to field marshal and colonel-general received a tax-free 'gratuity' of 4,000 and 2,000 Reichsmarks a month, a small fortune at the time.[10] He believed that such payments made it easier for his generals, especially the many who were not Nazi Party members, to subordinate themselves to his leadership and execute blindly whatever he demanded of them. According to Major Gerhard Engel, the Führer's Army adjutant, the process would be accomplished more easily, even against their inner convictions, if they were the recipients of honours awarded by the head of state.[11]

Another incentive that Hitler used to maintain the continued loyalty of his generals was the presentation of large and valuable estates. He gave General Heinz Guderian, for example, the Deipenhof estate valued at almost 1·25 million Reichsmarks. 'Previously a critic of Hitler's conduct of the war,' writes Richard Evans, in the final volume of his new history of the Third Reich in the Second World War, 'Guderian returned from enforced retirement towards the end of the conflict as one of the most determined supporters of a fight to the finish.' These were not just isolated cases, but generally representative of the benefits Hitler bestowed upon his generals to buy their service. Major Engel also recorded that the Führer made it clear to his generals that when the war was finally won, he would not be miserly in the distribution of land.[12]

For those in the lower ranks, there was, in addition to all other incentives, which included promotions, awards, and even fame, the terror of the German system of military justice, with an average of 5,000 soldiers executed every year for a wartime total of some 30,000 personnel or the equivalent of about three divisions.[13] This was a pittance, however, compared with the 158,000 Red Army soldiers formally sentenced and executed during the war or the almost 423,000 who died fighting in punishment units.[14] Still, the real German figure is probably much higher. Nor were generals exempt from summary execution. More than 7,000 people were arrested following the attempt on Hitler's life on 20 July 1944 and almost 5,000 of them were executed over the next few months, including sixty officers of the Army and Armed Forces High Commands and the General Staff. Twenty generals were executed and another thirty-six were condemned to death for opposition to the regime, while forty-nine committed suicide to escape the verdict of the courts. And at the front another 700 soldiers were executed.[15]

While the execution of Wehrmacht officers on this scale was an abnormality, even for Hitler's Third Reich, for the ordinary German soldier, summary executions would only accelerate in the last months of the war, with both the Wehrmacht and the SS hanging any soldier even suspected of deserting from the nearest tree or lamppost. Assigned the job of raising a replacement army, SS chief Heinrich Himmler posted an order soon after assuming his new responsibilities: 'Certain unreliable elements seem to believe that the war will be over for them as soon as they surrender,' he wrote. 'Every deserter will find his just punishment. His family will be summarily shot.' Nor was this an idle threat. Field Marshal Friedrich Schörner, Commander of Army Group Centre, dealt with stragglers by hanging them from the nearest tree with a poster tied to their bodies reading: 'I am a deserter and I refused to protect German women and children.'[16] And in the last months of the war, Hitler himself would threaten his soldiers from his bunker in Berlin with action against their families if they allowed themselves to be taken prisoner unwounded.[17] And so the German soldier continued the unequal struggle.

By November 1944 the First Parachute Army had been placed, together with the Twenty-Fifth Army, under Generaloberst Johannes Blaskowitz's Army Group 'H'. Blaskowitz was a staunch admirer of Adolf Hitler and had been the former commander of Army Group 'G', which had been sacrificed in southern France following the Allied invasion and break-out. On 25 April 1945 he would be awarded the Swords to the Knight's Cross, making him one of the last recipients of that award. He was the only officer holding the rank of Generaloberst commanding an army group.[18] Army Group 'H' was one of three army groups commanded by Field Marshal Karl Rudolf Gerd von Rundstedt, Commander-in-Chief West. At sixty-nine, Rundstedt was one of the Wehrmacht's oldest, most durable and most highly respected commanders.[19]

Leadership of the First Parachute Army, whose mission it was to stem the Allied advance in the north, was vested in Generaloberst Alfred Schlemm, who assumed command on 20 November 1944. A First World War artillery officer and winner of the Iron Class First and Second Classes, Schlemm had transferred to the Luftwaffe in 1938 and won the German Cross in Gold as commander of Combat Unit *Schlemm*, part of VIII Fliegerkorps. This was followed by assignments as commander of 1st Air Division and then II Luftwaffe Field Corps. Schlemm had also been Student's chief of staff in Crete. Afterwards, he left the paratroopers to command a regular army corps, fighting first at Vitebsk and then Smolensk in 1943. In January 1944 he was named commander of the I Parachute Corps in Italy, where his paratroopers fought with distinction, earning him the Knight's Cross on 11 June 1944 for its achievements near Velletri. Small and with a somewhat dark complexion, Schlemm was a man of strong personality and high intelligence, not afraid to hold his own with those who outranked him.[20] His Allied opponents would later dub him 'a fighting man of undoubted military ability'.[21] Now fifty years old, he was a highly skilled combat commander with a great deal of experience in fighting rearguard actions.

In November, Schlemm's new command consisted of two corps: II Parachute Corps, commanded by General Eugen Meindl, and

LXXXVI Infantry Corps, commanded by General Erich Straube. After commanding the Air–Landing Assault Regiment during the invasion of Crete, Meindl had gone on to command the 21st Luftwaffe Field Division, XIII Fliegerkorps and then I Luftwaffe Field Corps, providing him with a wealth of combat experience.[22] His three divisions, now the 6th, 7th, and 8th Parachute Divisions, each numbering some 10,000–12,000 fighting men, would serve as the defensive backbone of the First Parachute Army. These were supported by some 80 artillery pieces along with 60 dual-purpose 88–mm anti–aircraft guns.[23] Meindl was well–known among his British and Canadian opponents, who reported that his reputation had been enhanced by words of praise from both his seniors and subordinates.[24] Two additional corps would later join the First Parachute Army: General der Panzertruppen Heinrich von Lüttwitz's XLVII Panzer Corps, on 12 February 1945; and General der Infanterie Erich Abraham's LXV Infantry Corps, on 18 February 1945. Army reserves consisted of two battalions of the Armeewaffenschule (Army Weapons School), while each corps had local reserves of its own with varying strengths.[25] The immediate mission of the First Parachute Army when Schlemm took command in November 1944 was to hold its positions in the Reichswald Forest and on the Maas. The West Wall, extending along the German border, was the rear position of the army. The position was strongly constructed south of Geldern, while to the north it consisted only of field fortifications. Another line was under construction along the east bank of the Niers River. Adjacent units included the Twenty-Fifth Army to the north, commanded by General Blumentritt, and the Fifteenth Army to the south, commanded by General von Zangen.[26]

Schlemm's newly formed parachute divisions were airborne in name only. According to General Student, only parts of the six airborne divisions existing in 1944 were trained for airborne operations. Indeed, Student gives a figure of 30,000 trained parachutists in the summer of 1944. Most of these were in the 1st and 2nd Parachute Divisions, of whose personnel 50 and 30 per cent respectively were trained parachutists. Commitment of these divisions in ground combat continually decreased these figures so that parachutists from all units had to be recruited for a major airborne operation. Overall, the training of these troops was described as 'inadequate' and only about 20 per cent were capable of jumping fully equipped with weapons.[27] Nonetheless, much was expected of Schlemm's 'paratroopers'.

The vast majority of the Wehrmacht's parachute divisions had, in fact, been manned with any troops that were available, but especially remnants of Luftwaffe field divisions and fortress battalions, along with a small core of veteran paratroopers. It was with these 'paratroopers' that Schlemm was expected to resist the Allied advance. And yet they would fight as well and as desperately as any elite Fallschirmjäger, not so much because they were paratroopers but because they wanted to survive the war and there was no other option available to them.

The 6th Parachute Division was one of three parachute divisions assigned to the First Parachute Army. Originally formed in June 1944 at Amiens, France, elements of Generalleutnant Rüdiger von Heyking's 6th Parachute Division had entered combat as a regimental-size battle group formed around the Parachute Lehr (Demonstration) 21st Regiment. The battle group fought on the Normandy front in August 1944, along the Le Mans–Alençon axis as part of the German LXXXI Corps and the Fifth Panzer Army. After the withdrawal across the Seine, the remnants of the division sought refuge with the remainder of the Fifth Panzer and Seventh Armies in the Pas de Calais area. By early September the battle group, which had been reduced to two infantry battalions and a few heavy calibre weapons, had been pushed back to Mons, Belgium, by the First U.S. Army. Harassed from the air, ambushed by resistance groups, attacked by Allied spearheads and finally encircled near Mons, the Germans, with little ammunition, fuel, or communications, blundered repeatedly into American roadblocks and were thrown into confusion. Only a few escaped the Allied encirclement and Heyking was taken prisoner.[28] 'The 6th Parachute Division engaged in Normandy at the beginning of the invasion had been completely annihilated by the end of August 1944 during the heavy fighting which took place in the area roughly between the Seine and Amiens,' recorded Generalmajor Rudolf Langhaüser in a history of the unit. 'No remnants of any consequence were left of these fighting units which would, later on, be used as seasoned cadre for a subsequent reorganisation. The new organisation was effected in October 1944 in Holland in the area of Assen–Mepel–Coevorden.'[29]

The reorganised 6th Parachute Division was classified as an 'Infantry Division, Two Regiment Type' consisting of two infantry regiments with three battalions each and having a total strength of approximately 10,000 personnel.[30] The soldiers were far from the highly trained

Fallschirmjäger ideal one would expect in a parachute division, as Langhaüser remembered.

> The men of the outfit, all of them of the younger and youngest age groups and full of the highest initiative but without any experience in ground warfare, were furnished from units of the Luftwaffe ground crews, signal units, anti-aircraft artillery and pilot cadets. They had received no more than the private's basic infantry training and had never before taken part in any, not even the smallest-scale, exercises with combat teams. On the whole they were excellent replacements, who, however, first required a thorough training to bring out their true value.[31]

According to Langhaüser, the unit's leadership was equally deficient. The NCQs, who came from the same replacement sources, were poorly trained in infantry warfare and were much harder to retrain due to their many years of service in their specialised fields and their seniority. 'Their value in battle only rose later,' wrote Langhaüser, 'after they had gained more experience and when better trained elements of the battle-tested 1st, 4th, and 5th Parachute Divisions were incorporated into their ranks.' As for the junior officers, the bulk came from the anti-aircraft and signals troops and consisted of young, active men, ready for action, but weak in ground tactics. 'About 25 per cent of the commanders of battalions and regiments could be considered as very good,' assessed Langhaüser, '50 per cent as good and 25 per cent as weak in their ground warfare training. At the time of the newly formed division's first action, its commander, Generalleutnant Plocher, reported its aggregate battle value to the High Command as being "conditionally suited for defensive action".'[32]

Still, the Allies did not underestimate their opponents. A First Canadian Army intelligence report noted that the men of the parachute divisions gave the impression of high morale and intended on fighting to the end:

> They are proud of belonging to an elite branch, however exterminated it may become in the meantime. They are, as a rule, younger and physically better qualified than other troops. Their relations to the Army are without a stigma, in contrast to the notorious SS gang. They like to consider themselves the successors of the crack troops which invaded Holland in 1940,

Crete in 1941, and made a last-ditch stand in Cassino. Actually, only a handful have survived these 'memorable' days and, considering the quality and length of Para training now given, only very few would equal these accomplishments . . .

Practically all of them have been made to believe that Hitler has restored law and order, greatness and equality to the German people. The Hitler myth has taken so strong a hold on them that many refuse to consider even the possibility of a German defeat. Hitler's promise of a victory and of secret weapons to achieve it with is accepted by many like a guarantee from a higher being. Others think that Nazi Germany was a good thing until the war but that Hitler should never have challenged the entire world as he did.[33]

The reorganised 6th Parachute Division was composed of the 17th and 18th Parachute Regiments. Each regiment was authorised 3,206 personnel and, according to Allied intelligence reports, the 6th Parachute Division's total strength was approximately 6,000–7,000 men.[34] The division was commanded by Generalleutnant Hermann Plocher, a prewar infantry officer turned pilot prior to the beginning of the Second World War. Plocher had served as the chief of staff of Germany's Condor Legion for fourteen months during the Spanish Civil War and then on the Luftwaffe General Staff, the staff of V Fliegerkorps and that of Luftwaffe Command East during the first four years of the war. In 1943 he was rewarded with command of the 19th Luftwaffe Field Division followed by command of the 4th Fliegerdivision. Prior to serving as commander of the 6th Parachute Division he had been the Chief of Staff of Third Air Fleet. He had been awarded the German Cross in Gold in April 1942 and the Knight's Cross on 22 November 1943.[35] Plocher's Canadian adversaries would quickly learn to respect him and would later write about him: 'In the forceful personality of this sound professional soldier is a clue to the fierce, skillful fighting of his paratroopers.'[36]

Major Rudolf Witzig commanded the 18th Parachute Regiment. On paper the regiment would have consisted of a regimental headquarters, regimental headquarters company, three parachute infantry battalions, a 120-mm mortar or light artillery company, and an anti-tank company. Its authorised strength was 96 officers and 3,110 other ranks. At full strength, each of the three battalions was authorised 853 men and each of the parachute infantry companies 170. On paper the regiment's armaments included a high proportion of automatic and heavy weapons, giving it tremendous firepower and making it the ideal formation for defensive operations.

On 19 November 1944 the 6th Parachute Division was incorporated into the LXXXVIII Infantry Corps and took over the combat sector of II SS Panzer Corps on both sides of the Arnhem front running from Grebbedann to the bend of the Waal River near Nijmegen. The division command post was located in Velpe, east of Arnhem. The division was reinforced by four companies of the 30th Machine-Gun Battalion and, for a short period, by the 46th or 49th Machine-Gun Battalion. The fighting qualities of the machine-gun battalions was assessed as 'good', in comparison to most garrison battalions, which were considered 'weak', consisting of men of old age classes without combat experience and lacking initiative. As well as the normal artillery units the division's artillery consisted of a heavy artillery battalion with a battery of 170-mm guns, a battery of 150-mm guns, and several other medium-calibre guns. Artillery was thus not in short supply. Forces were deployed along the front so as to provide depth to the defence, while at the same time allowing necessary training. Available to the 6th Parachute Division for training purposes and as a reserve were another parachute regiment, a parachute tank company, and a parachute mortar company. In a series of minor engagements the men of the division were able to gain battle experience and confidence and improve their training. At the time it occupied its sector, defensive positions were weak and needing reinforcement. Lack of building material complicated improvements and the lack of mines precluded the desired depth of minefields in the outpost area. Although a fallback position was also under construction, this too suffered from the lack of building material. The strategic importance of the 6th Parachute Division's combat sector on both sides of Arnhem made it almost certain that the Allies would launch an attack there. 'A breakthrough at Arnhem could have folded up the whole lower Dutch defence and severed communications,' wrote Rudolf Langhaüser, 'as well as destroying the lower Rhine defences, opening up routes in the direction Bremen–Hamburg.'[37]

Around 10 December 1944 the 6th Parachute Division was relieved by the newly reconstituted 2nd Parachute Division and withdrawn from its first position. The following night it took over the sector then held by the 711th Infantry Division, extending from the recent western divisional boundary to the Waal bend at Hesselt. Subsequently, the division also took over in quick succession the sectors of the 712th and 719th Infantry Divisions so that by 20 December it was responsible for the defence of an 80–km front, extending from the beginning of the Holland Diep River, the right–hand boundary, to Schedrecht and then to the area east of Rhenen. A wide estuary of the Rhine and Meuse rivers, the Holland Diep runs between Rotterdam in the north and Breda in the south with a bridge spanning it at Moerdijk. The reason that the 6th Parachute Division assumed this tremendous frontage was the withdrawal of the 711th, 712th, and 719th Infantry Divisions for an attack in conjuction with the planned Ardennes offensive. The 6th Parachute Division was also scheduled to be detached in order to join the attack on the left wing and to ensure the security of the east flank. This plan, however, was later rejected as the forces available were thought to be too weak for the intended attack and its far–reaching aims. In the end the three infantry divisions were held in reserve for the Ardennes offensive.[38]

But in accordance with the High Command's earlier intent, the 6th Parachute Division had been reinforced with 30th Machine–Gun Battalion, the 800th Russian Battalion, and Kampfgruppe *Fuchs*, a mixed regimental size battle group, consisting of one Luftwaffe and one Army battalion commanded by a Luftwaffe Colonel Fuchs. In addition, the division was reinforced with a heavy artillery battalion and the division's 6th Artillery Regiment, consisting of three batteries, each with four 122–mm Russian medium howitzers. 'These howitzers were very good guns capable of great firing accuracy and small dispersion,' recorded Langhaueser, 'very mobile; sufficient ammunition was available.' In spite of the tremendous frontage and his force's relative weakness, General Plocher aimed to deploy as few troops as possible in the front lines and instead sought to keep strong and mobile reserves in high readiness. These reserves were also responsible for planned training and increasing the combat efficiency of the division.[39]

Apart from a short spell, during which Witzig's 18th Parachute Regiment was drafted out of the division to work on the construction of field fortifications in the Reichswald, south-west of Cleve, during the Christmas season of 1944, the division had, besides its local regiment reserves, two battalions of the 16th Parachute Regiment, one battalion of the 17th Parachute Regiment, and a motorised reserve group consisting of one parachute company, one parachute mortar platoon, one anti-tank company, and one engineer company. Appropriate steps had been taken by the division to ensure that these reserves, which were at the disposal of both division and the corps, were fully mobile. By this point, General Plocher had reported the division's fighting abilities to higher headquarters as 'fit for defensive action' and 'conditionally fit for offensive operations'.[40]

Opposite Plocher's 6th Parachute Division was the First Canadian Army commanded by Lieutenant–General Henry Crerar. Crerar was a First World War veteran, graduate of the Canadian Royal Military College and former Chief of the Canadian General Staff. According to historian Mark Zuehlke, the leading authority on the Canadian Army in the Second World War, Crerar was a fervent nationalist who wanted Canada to play a significant role in the Allied war effort. The title 'First Canadian Army' was somewhat of a misnomer, however. In reality, the Canadian contingent consisted of little more than a single corps – II Canadian Corps – supported by ancillary units attached to the army headquarters. The corps consisted of three divisions and one armoured brigade under the command of Lieutenant–General Guy Simonds, one of Canada's brightest military leaders and the youngest corps commander in the Allied army. On 23 July 1944 I British Corps, commanded by Lieutenant–General John Crocker, was attached to the First Canadian Army. It comprised the British 3rd, 49th, 51st (Highland), and 6th Airborne Divisions. Three days later the newly arrived Polish 6th Armoured Division joined II Canadian Corps – the beginning of a long relationship between the Canadians and the Poles. Arrayed against the Germans, from east to west, were the Dutch Princess Irene Brigade, the Canadian 4th Armoured Division, the Polish 1st Armoured Division, approximately two battalions of UK Royal Marine Commandos, and a regiment of paratroopers.

Witzig and the men of the 6th Parachute Division thus faced a combination of British, Canadian, Dutch and Polish soldiers and paratroopers. 'The 4th Canadian Armoured Division and the Polish Armoured Division were often mixed,' reported Langhaueser, 'from which it could be gathered that the Canadians did not rate the fighting qualities of the Poles very highly.' This was not so, although some of the Allied commanders did consider the Poles to be impetuous. It was with these superior Allied forces that the 6th Parachute Division engaged in a series of engagements, characterised by patrol actions, in difficult terrain, including largely flooded marshes and canals, and in extremely cold weather. Larger scale and more protracted fighting arose over possession of the small bridgehead at Kapellsche-Veer.[41]

In early December the 6th Parachute Division assaulted a small Allied bridgehead about 5 km upstream from Nijmegen across the Waal River, losing sixty men killed and more than a hundred captured to a British counter-attack. Afterwards the Germans were content with shelling enemy positions and floating mines and explosives down the river to damage British pontoon bridges. The 6th Parachute Division was also tasked to attack across the Maas as part of a planned three-division assault in support of the Ardennes offensive in December. These three divisions were to be ready to cross the Maas when ordered and seize the Wilhelmina Canal from Oosterhout to Dongen on the way to Breda. The outpost at Kapellsche-Veer, established by the 711th Infantry Division and later taken over by the 6th Parachute Division, was immediately increased in strength to one company. As a result, the Canadians decided to eliminate it.[42]

In the early morning of 16 December 1944 the Germans launched their Ardennes Offensive, code-named Operation Herbstnebel (Autumn Mist). Hitler's final great attack of the war sought to drive apart the two major Allied formations, Montgomery's Twenty-First Army Group from Bradley's Twelfth Army Group, by striking along the seam separating the two formations and then thrusting eastward towards the Meuse. From there German forces would drive towards Antwerp to recapture the Allies' most vital supply port. Hitler hoped to inflict a major defeat on the Allies and force a peace settlement on them that would end the war on the Western Front.

For the attack the Wehrmacht massed three armies against Lieutenant General Courtney Hodges First U.S. Army, part of Twelfth Army Group. Taking advantage of the heavy cloud cover and winter weather, which grounded the Allied air forces and both concealed and muffled the concentration of troops and equipment, the Germans managed to achieve total surprise on the first day. Once confusion subsided, however, General Eisenhower responded by directing a steady flow of reinforcements into the threatened sector. At the same time, the American defenders of first St-Vith and then Bastogne managed to hold their positions long enough to derail the entire German offensive timetable. Fierce fighting ensued, as the Germans struggled to break out eastward, while the Americans did everything in their power to prevent them from doing so. By 22 December the skies had cleared sufficiently for the Allied air forces to take to the air and begin savaging the attackers. In the end, this massive intervention proved crucial to the failure of the offensive, which was plagued from the beginning by fuel shortages, heavy snows, reliance on a poor road network, the narrowness of the front, and lack of manoeuvre space for the panzers.

By 16 January the Allies had pinched off the bulge caused by the German attack in the Ardennes and what remained of the attack force retreated to the east. Casualties on both sides were heavy, with the Germans suffering more than 100,000 casualties, including 80,000 killed, and the Allies suffering 70,000 killed, wounded, and missing. More importantly, the Germans lost some 600 tanks and 1,000 aircraft. While the Allies could replace their equipment losses in a matter of weeks, the losses to the Wehrmacht were irreplaceable.

As for the performance of the once vaunted Fallschirmjäger, the airborne operation during the Ardennes offensive, the last of the war, was assessed by the Germans themselves as a complete failure, demonstrating the low standards of training in both the parachute forces and supporting transport units. 'The number of parachute troops committed in the Ardennes was so small that a decisive influence on the overall offensive could not have been expected,' wrote a group of German airborne specialists after the war. 'Since most of the parachute divisions were committed in regular ground combat, only a battalion of inadequately trained parachutists was literally "scraped" together for this operation. Its strength would have been sufficient at the most to attain a small tactical success.'[43] The necessity of having well-trained, specialised troops available for airborne operations was adequately proven.

In the meantime, Plocher and the men of the 6th Parachute Division had been attempting to hold their ground against a Canadian attack on 26 December led by the Polish 1st Armoured Division and British Royal Marine Commandos. Well supported by artillery, the German paratroopers defended tenaciously and then counter-attacked fiercely, inflicting more than 200 casualties on the attackers. A deliberate assault at the end of the month, preceded by all the firepower of I Canadian Corps shattered the German defences, however, throwing the paratroopers back and allowing a Canadian infantry brigade, supported by an armoured regiment, to cross the river. The 6th Parachute Division suffered 300–400 casualties during this period, including almost 150 killed and another 100 who succumbed to frostbite. The Germans gave almost as good as they got, inflicting 234 casualties on their opponents. As a result of these heavy losses, however, the Kapellsche-Veer bridgehead was abandoned by the Germans in mid-January.[44] During this entire period numerous reconnaissance patrols were operating against the Allies furnishing excellent intelligence. On one occasion the 16th Parachute Regiment was transferred to the area of the 2nd Parachute Division, but then withdrawn again immediately.[45]

The beginning of 1945 brought no respite for Witzig, the men of the First Parachute Army, or the Third Reich. Instead, the Wehrmacht's strategic situation worsened drastically. On 10 January the Red Army launched its offensive against East Prussia, one of the springboards for the invasion of the Soviet Union in the summer of 1941. More than 130 Soviet divisions, consisting of more some 1·6 million men and supported by 25,000 artillery pieces and mortars, almost 4,000 tanks and assault guns and more than 3,000 aircraft, hurled themselves at what remained of Army Group North along a 500-km front. Caught in an annihilating encirclement were three German armies consisting of 40 divisions and numbering almost 800,000 men, 8,200 artillery pieces and mortars, 700 tanks and assault guns, and almost 800 combat aircraft.[46]

The battle for East Prussia would last until April, but the end was never in doubt. Two days later, on 12 January the Red Army launched its greatest offensive of the war aimed at destroying German forces between the Vistula and Oder Rivers, conquering Polish territory still under German occupation and plunging into the heart of the Third Reich to establish a bridgehead for the final assault on Berlin.

The two offensives succeeded in shattering German defences in East Prussia and Poland. By 27 January Soviet troops were 150 km from Berlin, having overrun the strategic Silesian industrial basin. Pondering the loss of the coal mines alone, Albert Speer, Hitler's armaments minister, told the Führer in a memorandum that the war was lost. Together, the two offensives stripped the Army and Luftwaffe of more than a million defenders as well as the vast bulk of their remaining tanks, artillery pieces, and combat aircraft. Few illusions now remained either among the military or the German population as to the ultimate outcome of the war. And yet, like German soldiers everywhere, the men of the First Parachute Army continued to defend desperately, true to their oath. But every day that Rudolf Witzig and his Fallschirmjäger fought to keep the Americans and British at bay saw the loss of huge swathes of the Reich's territory to the much-hated and feared Russians in the East, a fact that could not have been lost on the German soldiers in the West.

In the meantime, the 6th Parachute Division had launched a series of counter-attacks on 18 January 1945 against the British 49th Division near Zetten, about 15 km south-west of Arnhem. Although they initially gave way before the German onslaught, the British regrouped and then counter-attacked fiercely, regaining the town and their original defensive positions after bitter fighting, killing and wounding some 500 German paratroopers and capturing another 340. Allied casualties totalled 220 men.[47]

Incredible as it seems, somehow, in the midst of all that was happening, Rudolf Witzig found the time to get engaged and married. In December he had taken a day of leave to ask Hanna to marry him. She accepted and he returned to the front almost immediately. And then in January, he returned to Höxter for the wedding. It was a major event for the city. After all, Rudolf Witzig was not only still a major celebrity; he was also an adopted son of the city. Furthermore, with little money available for entertainment of any kind, the wedding, attended by the German press, offered the population a temporary diversion from the grim reality of the war and the Third Reich's declining prospects. The wedding took place in the church which Hanna and her family had attended for so many years. Dr Remmers, her father, was there, along with the hospital sisters and all the patients capable of attending. 'It was a beautiful wedding at the Kiliani Church in Höxter,' Hanna remembered later. 'The unforgettable Pastor Schloemann conducted the ceremony.'[48] The couple arrived and departed in a horse-drawn buggy and spent three days honeymooning in the city. They then departed for Austria and the Brenner Pass, where they spent eight days at Steinach in the Tyrol on the property of Dr Hans Holzmeister, Witzig's surgeon from his 21st Parachute Engineer Regiment days. Two and a half days were spent travelling to and from their destination aboard 'Front Holiday' trains, reserved for the those serving in an official capacity, with Witzig in his Luftwaffe uniform and Hanna in her German Red Cross uniform. There the couple enjoyed a short but peaceful respite from the war, which ended all too soon when Rudolf returned to his regiment.[49] Knowing what he was fighting for no doubt hardened his resolve to do his best to stop the Allied advance.

At the end of January 1945 the British and Americans launched a series of attacks against the boundary between the First Parachute and Fifteenth Armies, south and south-east of Roermond. German forces south of the Roer were pushed back to the north, but elements of Generalmajor Walter Wadehn's 8th Parachute Division succeeded in holding a small bridgehead on the south bank of the river. 'This enemy attack was believed to be more than a secondary effort,' recorded Alfred Schlemm, in a postwar monograph on the First Parachute Army.[50] On 2 February Plocher received welcomed reinforcements in the form of elements of six fortress battalions redesignated as paratroop units. The additional troops were welcome as his paratroopers found themselves alongside their comrades of the 7th and 8th Parachute Divisions resisting the II Canadian Corps near Cleve, some 24 km south-east of Nijmegen, during Operation Veritable. Generalmajor Hans Erdmann commanded the 7th Parachute Division.[51]

The Allies sought to clear the defenders from the west bank of the Rhine in order to facilitate a crossing of the river and an advance on the heart of Germany along a northern route. The German defence consisted of three belts, each made up of two to three lines of trenches, reinforced with wire and mines and anchored on village strong-points, farmhouses, and anti-tank ditches. Extensive flooding in the sector forced the Allies to attack along a narrow front to the north and south of the Reichswald, a heavily wooded area stretching from Nijmegen to Cleve.[52]

The Reichswald was ideal defensive terrain. The thick woodland was almost impenetrable to tanks and the heavy foliage prevented them from traversing their turrets. Additionally, the dense cover made them extremely vulnerable to Panzerfaust and Panzerschreck ambushes. A British lieutenant would later remember: 'The Reichswald was the nastiest battle we had fought since Normandy.'[53] Leading the Allied attack was the British XXX Corps, which had been transferred to the First Canadian Army.

The British–Canadian attack south-east of Nijmegen against the northern wing of the First Parachute Army began on 8 February. 'The enemy had great numerical superiority; their strength was estimated at six or seven full corps,' recorded Schlemm. 'They could relieve their divisions for reconstitution after three or four days of combat. First Parachute Army could not relieve its divisions at all.'[54] In fact, the Canadian First Army disposed of two corps, while the U.S. Ninth Army disposed of another three plus ten more divisions. These would be supported by more than a thousand artillery pieces. The Allies unleashed an artillery bombardment reminiscent of the First World War at five in the morning and, after five hours of unmerciful pounding, the ground forces began their advance. Confident that the opening artillery bombardment heralded the much-awaited Allied offensive, General Schlemm requested and received permission to move the 7th Parachute Division from below Geldern into the line on the left of the 84th Infantry Division.

By early evening the 84th Division had lost over 1,200 men taken prisoner and had five or six battalions shattered. The commander of the LXXXVI Corps believed that, if the British pushed on through the night, they would secure Cleve and achieve a break-through. This, in fact, is what they were trying to achieve and what Schlemm was trying to prevent. But low-hanging clouds and heavy rain persisted, curtailing air support and slowing ground movement. Still, the Siegfried Line defences were breached astride the northern boundary of the Reichswald and the Allies made good progress on the extreme right, although strong German resistance in the Reichswald halted their progress. But weather remained the greatest enemy and, after several days, water and mud put the brakes on ground movement, while low clouds and rain halted close air support.[55]

On about 10 February 1945 the 6th Parachute Division headquarters was withdrawn and transferred to a combat sector east of the Reichswald, south of Emmerich. There it relieved the staff of the 84th Infantry Division and took command of several composite battle groups, which had been subordinate to the 84th Division. In its new sector, the division was at first under the command of the XLVII Panzer Corps, commanded by General von Lüttwitz, and later under Meindl's II Parachute Corps.[56]

The men of the 6th Parachute Division found themselves facing the Canadian 2nd and 3rd Infantry Divisions, both of which the Germans assessed as 'excellent'. These two divisions were supported by armoured formations, including the 4th Canadian Armoured Division. 'These divisions relieved each other in their assaults and were thus able to return to the attack fresh and rested,' recorded Langhaüser, 'while facing the heavily battered but firmly resisting troops of the division.'[57] Still, in his monograph on the 6th Parachute Division in Holland, Langhaüser called the Allied conduct of battle 'highly schematic':

Every assault would be recognized in good time by its long term moving into positions and the careful adjustment of fires of the artillery. From these it was also possible – in most cases – to determine the direction of an assault and the point of main effort beforehand. Any infantry assault would be preceded by a heavy artillery barrage, lasting up to eight hours. Thus, it was often possible to withdraw our infantry from the danger zone at the beginning of the preparation fire, and return it to the front before the enemy attack was launched.[58]

Casualties in this phase of the fighting were still 'bearable', according to Langhaüser, with the 6th Parachute Division managing to repel the enemy's assaults, despite his 'crushing superiority' or clear up any penetrations with immediate counter-attacks:

After an attack had been repelled a pause of three days usually followed, used by the enemy for the relief of assault troops and their replacement with new formations for the next assault. The division used these pauses for planned withdrawals and preparation of the new main line of resistance. The disengagement was always voluntary and only executed on higher orders; also, great care was taken to maintain integral contact within the division, whose strength was steadily diminishing as a result of the severe fighting.[59]

When the men of the 6th Parachute Division were not defending in place, they were launching frequent counter-attacks, aimed at stealing the initiative from the Allies, inflicting casualties, and winning enough time either to prepare for the next series of attacks or to withdraw to another prepared defensive line. Supported by German artillery from across the Rhine, the German paratroopers desperately counter-attacked the Canadian thrusts on 19 February and continued their attacks on the 20th, when they were brought to a halt barely fifty metres from the forward Canadian positions. The Allies drove the Germans back on the following day in a well-coordinated attack backed by artillery, armour, flamethrowers and supported by rocket-firing Typhoons. 'The fighting, often in close combat, was hard and bitter on both sides,' remembered Langhaüser.[60]

Indeed, Allied losses since the opening of their offensive totalled more than 6,000 men, while the Allies believed the Germans had suffered

20,000 men 'put out of action'. 'Our troops had buried "a very great number" of their dead and had taken well over 11,000 prisoners,' reported General Crerar.[61]

In General Schlemm the Allies had come up against an opponent with experience fighting rear-guard actions in Russia and Italy [notes the official British history of the battle]. But in addition to his practical experience, Schlemm, in the Rhineland battle, had both ground and weather on his side; ground which drew from General Eisenhower the comment: 'Probably no assault in this war had been conducted under more appalling conditions of terrain than was that one'; and weather so unfit for air operations that it was only on the 28th of February that the Second Tactical Air Force, with 1,117 sorties, could give support on any large scale during the last fortnight.[62]

By 24 February the First Parachute Army's northern wing had been driven back to the general line of Rees–Udem–Weeze–Bergen–Maas River. Plocher's 6th Parachute Division, with Witzig's 18th Parachute Regiment, was located in the area of Marienbaum as part of XLVII Panzer Corps.[63] The 7th Parachute, 15th Panzergrenadier and 116th Panzer Divisions had already sustained heavy losses in the fighting in Lorraine and the Ardennes and were under–strength and by 24 February most of their regiments were reduced to battalion size.[64] Indeed, according to General von Lüttwitz of XLVII Panzer Corps, the 15th Panzergrenadier and 116th Panzer Divisions were at less than a third of their authorised strength and possessed only thirty-five tanks between them.[65]

'The enemy artillery fired, on an average, 80,000–100,000 rounds a day,' recorded Schlemm. 'First Parachute Army could expend only 8,000–10,000 rounds. The enemy had about 500 tanks; we usually had 40 or 50. However, morale was high and the performance of the troops excellent.' It is to their credit that, after sixteen days of heavy combat, the First Parachute Army had been thrown back 20 km on the northern flank but had prevented a breakthrough on its front and never lost control of a critical situation. 'Discipline and order behind the front were good,' boasted Schlemm after the war. 'The vast air superiority of the enemy had little effect on the fighting at the outset, since the weather made flying very difficult in early February 45.'[66] As usual at this late stage in the war, there was no air support on the

German side. Still, the Allied air forces had not succeeded in destroying or seriously damaging the two Rhine bridges at Wesel and the supply lines of the army across the river remained intact, even when ferrying was no longer possible because of high water. And Schlemm believed that the British and Canadians had also suffered heavy losses, which slowed their advance.[67]

Nonetheless, the end seemed near for the First Parachute Army. 'If you have a map before you, you will take in the situation at a glance,' Schlemm reported to Field Marshal von Rundstedt on 3 March. 'My divisions are surrounded with the Rhine at their back.'[68] Schlemm received permission to withdraw a number of formations to the east bank of the Rhine. These included large numbers of administrative staffs, supply units, and unit trains for both the First Parachute and Fifteenth Armies. There were also large numbers of trucks carrying machinery from the German factories on the west bank of the Rhine. 'There were, all told, about 50,000 vehicles of all types,' records Schlemm. 'Because of enemy air activity they could only move at night. The crossing of the Rhine was made on available bridges and ferries, which I had arranged for as early as January and February 1945.' Schlemm placed staff and numerous other personnel at the crossing points 'to maintain order and ensure that personnel and weapons no longer suitable for combat [would] be carried over to the east bank'. By 6 March all workshops, supply depots and material, ammunition dumps, excess hospitals, unit trains, and even veterinary equipment, as the German Army of 1945 was moved principally by horses, had been transferred to the east bank of the Rhine. 'The movement offered large and worthwhile targets because of congestion lasting until late in the day,' remembered the First Parachute Army commander, 'But they were little disturbed by enemy air attacks, in spite of good flying weather.'[69] This move allowed continued command, control, and supply of the German forces for weeks to come, further delaying the Allied advance and the end of the war.

Still, the final outcome of this uneven battle was never in doubt. 'It became clear as early as 3 March 1945 that First Parachute Army could not continue to hold the west bank of the Rhine against the overwhelming superiority of the Allied forces which were brought closer and closer together in concentric attacks,' wrote Schlemm, assessing the correlation of forces. 'Against our ten or eleven divisions, now reduced to regimental size and possessing about 20 tanks, stood nine or ten enemy corps with about 3,000 armoured vehicles.' Short on everything else, the First Parachute Army had an abundance of artillery, which proved to be the Wehrmacht's saving grace in the final months of the war:

> I succeeded in evacuating promptly large elements of the artillery employed in the West Wall [continued Schlemm] about 40 batteries, in spite of the lack of transport. The divisional artillery had lost few pieces despite the large number of shells the enemy had expended. In addition, First Parachute Army had two artillery corps with five battalions each. These were brought up from OB West in February 1945.

Full use of these heavy artillery assets for effective shelling of enemy concentrations of tanks and infantry, however, proved impossible. The increasing destruction of the German railway net by Allied air attacks prevented the supply of sufficient ammunition. 'I informed army group of this situation,' reported Schlemm. 'As an answer I received an order from OB West for the First Parachute Army to hold the west bank of the Rhine. This was necessary to prevent the Allied forces fighting against the Army from disengaging units for new operations.'[70]

The decision to hold on the west bank caused Schlemm great trouble: 'How could I defend the east bank of the Rhine if my army were completely destroyed on the west bank? The enemy could divert strong forces to carry out a crossing of the Rhine, perhaps between Emmerich and Xanten. The east bank had not been fortified for defence.' Aside from a few Volkssturm battalions with little combat value, there were no other units for the defence of the east bank of the Rhine. Schlemm believed that an Allied attack across the Rhine in his sector would have been immediately successful, even if carried out with only weak forces. He therefore asked army group to permit the withdrawal of the staff of LXXXVI Infantry Corps, commanded by General Straube, to prepare a defensive line on the east bank of the Rhine between Emmerich and Ürdingen followed by a transfer to the east bank of large elements of the artillery, for which there were neither positions nor ammunition in the narrow bridgehead. Once across the river, Schlemm planned on positioning these in such a way that, with a new supply of ammunition, they could support the army from the east bank. Both requests were granted on 3 March and by 9 March almost seventy batteries of artillery had been transferred across at night, most of them on ferries. Losses from Allied air attacks and artillery fire were slight. These batteries joined the Rhine defences, which were to be rebuilt, and later supported the fighting in the German bridgehead with great success, using flanking fire against the wings of the attacking Allied forces.[71] The extraction of the fighting formations themselves, along with numerous other units, followed. 'On the east bank were numerous *ersatz* [replacement] and *marsch* [personnel replacement transfer] battalions from Germany,' recorded Schlemm. 'They totalled about 40,000–50,000 men, but were of no use since they had no leaders, combat experienced cadres, or weapons.'[72]

Using the under-strength but still hard-fighting parachute divisions of the II Parachute Corps as a rearguard, Schlemm's First Parachute Army managed to retreat across the Wesel on 10 March, destroying the bridges at 0700 hours as they reached the east bank. The Allies did not follow up at first and later cautiously felt their way to the weak rearguard troops, who remained on the left bank of the Rhine for approximately twenty-four hours. Their retirement across the Rhine took place without any disturbance.[73] Rudolf Witzig's 18th Parachute Regiment was one of the last units to cross the Rhine. 'Thanks to the valiant resistance of the infantry and the Fallschirmjäger,' recorded Schlemm, 'heavy weapons and other troops could be brought over to the east bank.'[74]

'It is fairly clear that First Parachute Army crossed the Rhine reasonably well according to plan and in fairly good order,' noted a Canadian First Army intelligence report. 'It is also certain that the bulk of the equipment of this Army was transferred across the Rhine.'

British and Canadian casualties in the month's fighting totalled some 15,500 personnel. The Allies estimated that they had, in turn, killed or seriously wounded 22,000 Germans and taken another 22,000 prisoner. On 10 March Hitler replaced Field Marshal Gerd von Rundstedt with Field Marshal Kesselring as Commander-in-Chief West.[75]

Chapter 10

HOLLAND: LAST BATTLES

Although U.S. forces had seized two bridgeheads on the eastern side of the Rhine in early March, it was not until the third week of the month that the Allies crossed the last major barrier into Germany on a broad front. On 23 March, more than one million British, Canadian and American soldiers under the command of Field Marshal Montgomery began Operation Plunder. Supported by massive air strikes and the last large-scale airborne operation of the war, employing two airborne divisions and more than 20,000 paratroopers, the men of the Twenty-First Army Group succeeded in quickly crossing the river and within days the Allied armies were over in great strength. In accordance with earlier plans, the First Canadian Army on the northern flank was tasked with driving into northern Holland and the adjacent part of Germany, in the process cutting off the German garrison in western Holland. To the south and east of the Canadians, the Second British Army headed for Bremen and Hamburg. And farther south the U.S. Ninth Army, in addition to providing the northern pincer to cut off the Ruhr, also advanced across the Weser towards the Elbe.

During their final battles of the war, Witzig and the men of the 18th Parachute Regiment and the 6th Parachute Division found themselves increasingly battling their old foes, the soldiers of the First Canadian Army, whose mission was to clear the main supply route to the north through Arnhem, and then to clear the north-western Netherlands, the coastal belt of Germany eastward to the Elbe, and western Holland. General Crerar's First Canadian Army, however, had been reinforced and was far more completely Canadian than ever before as I Canadian Corps, which had fought so long and hard in Italy, had been transferred to North-West Europe. It brought with it 1st Canadian Infantry Division, 1st Canadian Armoured Brigade, 5th Canadian Armoured Division, and the usual complement of corps troops. Two Canadian corps would fight side-by-side for the first time in history: I Canadian Corps, commanded by Lieutenant-General Charles Foulkes, would deal with the Germans remaining in the western Netherlands north of the Maas; II Canadian

Corps, commanded by Lieutenant-General Guy Simonds, would clear the north-western Netherlands and the German coast.

Its latest move found the 6th Parachute Division, much depleted in strength, defending near Emmerich, 32 km east of Nijmegen. II Parachute Corps was the right-hand corps of the First Parachute Army, with 6th Parachute Division on the right between Emmerich and Rees, 8th Parachute Division in the centre between Rees and Xanten, and 7th Parachute Division on the left from Xanten to Wesel. The retreat brought Plocher and his men to defensive positions behind the Twente Canal. The division was given ten days grace to reorganise and prepare for further defensive operations. During this period it received replacements from Germany. The 3rd Police Regiment joined 6th Parachute Division but, according to Plocher, did not raise the fighting power of the division noticeably. 'The members of this regiment, although fully ready for action, were not very tough as soldiers because of their advanced age,' recorded Plocher. 'The officers were over-aged and only inadequately trained for infantry tasks. Equipment with weapons was insufficient.'[1] Division artillery support consisted of one medium and two light artillery battalions, as well as a mixed artillery battalion with 88-, 75-, 37-, and 20-mm pieces, a substantial contribution to the unit's firepower. The Germans believed that facing them were 1st, 2nd, and 3rd Canadian Infantry Divisions, Canadian 5th Armoured division, one British armoured brigade, and either the 8th or 27th Hussars, equipped with special tanks for amphibious and engineering tasks.[2]

Schlemm was particularly impressed with the Allies' complete domination of the skies over Germany. 'It was not possible after January 1945 to bring up to the Western Front the weapons, spare parts, ammunition, and motor fuel which were still plentiful within the Reich,' he wrote, in a critique of Allied operations against the First Parachute Army.

> Thus, First Parachute Army could not fully utilise its strong artillery because of the lack of ammunition. Anti-tank mines and material were lacking. The scarcity of fuel cut down the employment of tanks and the movement of troops. For example, during its movement from the Ardennes to the First Parachute Army, XLVII Panzer Corps had to leave 80 tanks behind because there was no fuel for them. Most of these tanks were never recovered.

Only inclement weather hampered Allied air operations, although Schlemm was puzzled why Allied air units failed to attack lucrative targets, including German march columns containing thousands of vehicles crossing the Rhine, critical bridges or ferries so vital to the First Parachute Army's resupply and freedom of movement on the battlefield, or massed artillery formations, as it had done so effectively in Italy in 1944. 'The main effort probably lay elsewhere,' he reasoned. The First Parachute Army commander was also struck with the organisation of Allied artillery fire, which he called 'a very impressive technical achievement of the enemy'. However, he noted deficiencies in Allied infantry and tank attacks, especially the exploitation of favourable opportunities, swift pursuit of a retreating enemy, and surprise attacks at dusk or at night without the support of artillery. 'For these reasons German troops were able time after time to break out of almost complete encirclement and, thus, withdraw and organise further resistance.'[3]

It was only a matter of time before the Allies unleashed another attack and brought this preponderance in ground forces to bear. 'We assumed that the Anglo–American troops would now increase considerably the speed of their attack against Germany east of the Rhine either for military or political reasons or perhaps for reasons of prestige,' remembered General Günther Blumentritt in a monograph on the First Parachute Army. 'The mobility of their forces and the quality of their air force permitted them a greater display of audacity. Their counter–intelligence should have known that the resistance of [the] German Wehrmacht was broken. The situation was similar to ours in 1940, during the second half of the campaign in France.' Blumentritt went on to note that the Allies should have directed their main effort against Berlin and that the centre of gravity should have been north of the Thuringian Forest, 'considering that all our power resources were in Northern Germany. The resistance in the South was then bound to cease of its own accord.'[4]

On 27 March the commander of Army Group H, Colonel–General Blaskowitz, described the situation to Blumentritt as 'serious' and submitted this frank estimate to OB West and the High Command. Writing about the First Parachute Army's mission, Blumentritt recorded: 'It was a utopian notion to throw back the British and American forces, who had already crossed the Rhine, by any kind of counter-attack. Our chief task was to maintain the loose continuity of the front and to withdraw, engaging the enemy.' Blumentritt describes even the latter as 'difficult'.[5] General Meindl's II Parachute Corps held the right wing of the First Parachute Army sector with the 6th, 8th, and 7th Parachute Divisions arrayed in that order. 'These three divisions had been knocked about by heavy battles west of the Rhine,' recorded Blumentritt, 'but they still were the portion of the army with the best [MOST] fighting power.' Blumentritt described Meindl as 'a stern and tough [PROFICIENT] former inhabitant of Württemberg, experienced as a fighter and leader of troops, always frank in his judgement' and notes that he 'was held in high esteem by his troops'. Also still fighting as part of the corps, on the right wing, was the 15th Panzergrenadier Division. Blumentritt rated its fighting qualities as 'excellent'. The 245th Division was another formation attached to II Parachute Corps, but consisted only of rear service units. To the left of Meindl's corps was LXXXVI Army Corps, consisting of the remainder of the 84th, 180th and 190th Divisions and a training division.[6]

On 28 March 1945 Blumentritt assumed command of the First Parachute Army, replacing his ailing colleague, who had been wounded in an Allied air attack on his command post. 'General [COLONEL] Schlemm, almost unconscious with a temperature of 40 [°C] was lying ill in a farmer's [GENERAL] house and hardly recognised him,' recorded Blumentritt after the war. 'I knew him as a particularly energetic and able officer, whom I had met at an instruction course for generals. I could not bother him with many questions. Before he was carried away in an ambulance he was able to describe to me in a few words the situation as serious.'[7]

Terrain now worked against the Germans, as there were few obstacles capable of halting the Allies up to the Teutoburger Wald, a low range of mountains and forest-encircled swamps in Lower Saxony and Westphalia. The Roman historian Tacitus had written of its 'topographical vagueness' almost 2,000 years before, calling it 'a shadowy land of horror', while Julius Caesar had recorded the seemingly limitless extent of these gloomy forests noting that 'no one seems to know where it begins'.[8] To the soldiers who had to fight in it, the Teutoburger Wald was simply a dark, green hell. 'If, in any way, a continuous front was to be maintained, it could be done only by a withdrawal in good time and by avoiding long halts,' recorded Blumentritt. 'Only in the Teutoburger Wald could we expect to make a tactical halt for some days.'[9] But the high mobility of the Allied forces, as compared with the makeshift mobility of their German counterparts, made a timely withdrawal extremely problematic. To make matters worse, the German High Command transferred both the LXIII and the XLVII Corps to Army Group B to stem an American advance, which threatened the rear of the First Parachute Army. 'We lost our best troops, but helped our neighbouring formations in their precarious situation,' remembered Blumentritt. Still, on 29 March, First Parachute Army's request to withdraw was approved and the movement began the following day with the speedy extraction of II Parachute Corps and the heavily battered XCI Corps towards the Teutoburger Wald, General Meindl's men carried out their movement successfully, but the LXXXVI Corps failed to maintain a continuous front. The First Parachute Army was now deployed with II Parachute Corps on the right, LXXXVI Corps in the middle, and XLVII Panzer Corps and LXIII Corps on the left. Opposing them were the Second British Army facing the German right and the Ninth U.S. Army facing the German left. Both were part of 21st Army Group. After surrendering the XLVII Panzer Corps and LXIII Corps to Army Group B, the two remaining corps (II Parachute and LXXXVI) were opposed by only British formations.[10]

In response to the unrelenting Allied attacks, Hitler ordered a counter-attack in the hopes of cutting off the two Allied armies, which had penetrated the Teutoburger Wald. 'We definitely had no forces for such a large-scale operation,' recorded Blumentritt. Hitler sent General-oberst Student to Army Group H with the mission of leading the counter-attack. Student arrived at the beginning of April to acquaint himself with the situation. He quickly came to the conclusion that Hitler had completely misunderstood the circumstances on the ground and the condition of the troops. Student reported his impressions and, surprisingly, Hitler's demand for a major counter-attack was soon dropped, one of the few times late in the war that the German leader actually took the advice of his generals. Instead, Wehrmacht units were ordered to launch local attacks wherever and whenever possible. These, however, were quickly defeated, though they no doubt served to win the First Parachute Army some breathing space from the relentless Allied offensives. Army Group B was soon afterwards transformed into Army Group Student, to which II Parachute Corps was subordinated.[11]

On 2 and 3 April Second British and First Canadian Armies renewed its attacks. A Canadian thrust northward on the German right flank quickly threw General Meindl and his II Parachute Corps into great confusion. By 2 April, leading elements of the Canadian II Corps had

Rudolf Witzig, as commander of the 18th Parachute Regiment, receiving orders from Generalleutnant Hermann Plocher of 6th Parachute Division in Holland. By March 1945, Hitler's First Parachute Army in the Netherlands, consisting of ten under-strength divisions, faced some ten Allied corps supported by 3,000 armoured vehicles.

reached the Twente Canal and quickly established bridgeheads across it, pushing the Germans back further. According to Plocher, the Allied force made good use of amphibious tanks. 'Thanks to his crushing superiority on the ground and in the air, the enemy soon succeeded ... in establishing a small bridgehead and expanded it in most vigorous battles that were extremely costly to both sides,' remembered the parachute division commander. 'Under the cover of this bridgehead, the enemy immediately started to construct a bridge and, since there was no Luftwaffe operating any longer in the area and since the German artillery had only a minimum amount of ammunition at its disposal, he could move up strong forces in rapid succession.'[12]

The bulk of the Allied force, in the meantime, pushed east of the division towards the east and north, eliminating light resistance from the area Feldkommanduren (military administration headquarters) near Amelo. To bolster its defences, the 6th Parachute Division moved up reinforcements to its eastern flank in the path of the advancing Canadians. As a result the Germans were able to repel a series of attacks on that flank. 'The terrain was rather favourable for that purpose,' remembered Plocher.[13] Two days later, however, the Canadians broke out to the north. A sharp thrust by the Canadian 4th Armoured Division, following its crossing of the Twente Canal, resulted in the Allied capture of Amelo, Hengelo and Nordhorn and split II Parachute Corps from LXXXVIII Corps to its right. The speed of the attack also cut off the 6th Parachute Division from the 7th. As a result, the 6th Parachute Division was taken from Meindl's command and placed under LXXXVIII Corps. This corps, part of the Twenty–Fifth Army, was then ordered to retire behind the Ijssel River and defend eastern Holland from attack. By 8 April the Canadians had captured Zutphen, along with elements of 6th Parachute Division, after a stiff fight.[14]

'Wherever we have met determined resistance during the past few days the enemy's fighting qualities have belied any suggestion that recent disasters have diminished the German Army's will to fight,' highlighted one Canadian intelligence summary for the period. 'The skill and fighting spirit of individual units has often been to the standard of elite troops,' it continued. 'Even though the soldiers are often youths from Training Centres, they are fanatical and brave. Officer instructors from Training Units have provided the highest standard of leadership.' The Canadians later learned that the German garrison commanders had been given explicit instructions to make all towns centres of resistance. An announcement by Heinrich Himmler (as chief of the Home Army) and Martin Bormann (as head of the Volkssturm), read over German radio on 12 April stated:

> Towns which are usually important communications centres must be defended at any price. The Battle Commanders appointed for each town are personally held responsible for compliance with this order. Neglect of duty on the part of the Battle Commander, or the attempt on the part of any civil servant to induce such neglect, are punishable by death.

'Tenacious fighting, as well as the crushing effect of the enemy weapons thereby used up the fighting power of the division to a great extent,' recorded Plocher in turn, during the same period.

> The division having a very few, weak, local reserves at its disposal owing to the unusual extension of its sector, coherence within it and contact with the unit adjoining to the west could,

as a rule, only be maintained by carrying out a further with-drawal at the point where the enemy had broken into German lines, thus preventing the final encirclement and annihilation of the division.[15]

Between 1 and 11 April, Meindl's subordinate commanders acted on their own initiative without reference to higher authority. According to Meindl there was no overarching strategic plan for the withdrawal north into Germany. The only order he received was the desperate and often repeated entreaty to 'Hold at all costs!' The boundary between the LXXXVIII Corps and his own II Parachute Corps was roughly the Dutch border. With Plocher's 6th Parachute Division on the right flank and the 7th and 8th Parachute Divisions taking over the rest of the corps front to the Ems River, II Parachute Corps began its slow retreat.[16]

At this stage Plocher received orders to swing his defensive line back into Holland. He now understood his task to be a withdrawal over the Ijssel River and the defence of the west bank of the river. Establishing a bridgehead position at Deventer and slowly falling back in a north-westerly direction he carried out a curious tactical move. Once back across the Ijssel, part of his division crossed over to the west bank at Weihe, while the balance of it took up another bridgehead at Zwolle. Plocher attributed his ability to carry out this rather complicated manoeuvre to the same slow and planned Allied tactics which had enabled him to fall back to the Reichswald. 'The [Allied] tactics', he told his interrogators after his capture, 'always followed the same pattern. First there was a reconnaissance, then a tank attack, the infantry widened the penetration and then there was a consolidation.' Each step took about three days and each time Plocher was able to regroup and consolidate his front.[17]

Interrogation of German prisoners at the time indicated that even the veterans in the ranks of the parachute divisions were beginning to lose heart. A Canadian report described German morale as 'not very good' as the paratroopers 'always have to fight against armour and because they never get their promised rest'. However, some German prisoners explained that they 'enjoyed' fighting the Canadian infantry, although this certainly did not hold true of all the paratroopers. One paratrooper prisoner admitted to being 'terrified' of the Allied flame-throwers, which broke his final defensive position. Almost a thousand Allied air sorties in support of the First Canadian Army between 2 and

7 April added to the German concerns. Nonetheless, according to the same report, it was still expected that most of the paratroopers would fight to the end 'for in the Nazi way of life there seemed to be no place for capitulation'.[18]

In the midst of all this fighting Hitler continued to reorganise his higher headquarters as there was little else he could do for his soldiers. On 6 April Army Group H was reconstituted as Commander–in–Chief North-West and placed under Field Marshal Ernst Busch. Busch's area of responsibility included over 300 km. of front, extending from the North Sea around Bremen to Magdeburg, after Blaskowitz's army was cut off in the Netherlands. With the First Parachute Army and the remnants of other formations, he was responsible for opposing Montgomery's final drive on Bremen and Hamburg.[19] At the same time Blaskowitz was appointed Commander–in–Chief in Holland, which had been cut off and which Hitler had declared a 'fortress'. Finally, on 9 April, Blumentritt was ordered to give up command of the First Parachute Army to Student and to assume command from Student of the troops between the Weser and Elbe, designated Army Group *Blumentritt*.[20]

By 14 April the 6th Parachute Division was holding a line running from Deventer to Holten and then to the hills north of Holten and as far south as Hellendoorn. But even this line could only be held temporarily. 'Once again, the division had to give way during continuous, tough battles with a greatly superior enemy and fall back to a line running from Olst to Raalte and from there to a point west of Lemelerveld, all the time being very careful not to lose contact with the Ijssel River,' remembered Plocher. During these battles the division command post was almost always located on the west wing close to the command post of the 17th Parachute Regiment. According to the division commander, the 17th, 18th, and 31st Parachute Regiments fought 'in a brilliant way' during the course of these battles. On the other hand, the combat efficiency of the 3rd Police Regiment 'caused the command quite some concern'. 'The necessity of shortening the front and moving the defence lines further back was', according to Plocher, 'also due to the dwindling fighting power of the 3rd Police Regiment.'[21]

In the meantime, elements of the Canadian 4th and 5th Armoured Divisions had begun a series of large–scale attacks against the eastern flank of the 6th Parachute Division. The sectors to the east and north of the division were held by one police regiment, which acquitted itself

Lieutenant-Colonel Rudolf Witzig and Generalleutnant Hermann Plocher in the last months of the war in Holland. Both would go on to serve with distinction in the postwar German armed forces.

well, and several Feldkommandanturen units, responsible for securing a vast open area. These units were not subordinate to Plocher. During the withdrawal to the next line of resistance near Zwolle, the defence put up by the 149th Training Division proved to be very effective, enabling the 6th Parachute Division to transfer major formations over to the west bank of the Ijssel by way of Weihe, from where they moved north to cross the river again near Zwolle and were once again committed on the east bank of the Ijssel. But even this line could not be held in the face of what Plocher describes as 'the most vigorous tank attacks' launched repeatedly from the south, east and north-west. As a result Zwolle, too, had to be surrendered and a new defence established on the western bank of the Ijssel.[22]

The division's new sector extended from Apeldoorn to north-west of Deventer and along the Ijssel as far as the road bridge west of Zwolle. Joining the unit was the Police Regiment of the Zwolle Police School, which was assigned as a reinforcement to the 3rd Police Regiment. Kampfgruppe *Fuchs*, the mixed Luftwaffe and Army combat group, guarded the division's northern flank. 'The combat morale and efficiency of this unit was remarkable,' recorded Plocher. Once the division had withdrawn to the western bank of the Ijssel, the so-called Fortress Holland was completely encircled and the division had to depend on its own means for the continuation of the battle. Allied attacks had become so dangerous that the commander of LXXXVIII Army Corps pulled the bulk of the 6th Parachute Division out of the Ijssel area and moved it by forced marches to a line running from Barneveld to Apeldoorn and then to Terwolde. The 17th and 18th Parachute Regiments were positioned between Barneveld and Apeldoorn, while the 3rd Police Regiment was left behind. At the same time, Kampfgruppe *Fuchs* remained subordinated to Plocher, who recorded: 'The division arrived just in time in the new combat sector to stop attacks launched by the greatly superior Canadian 5th Armoured Division against completely exhausted German troops and, thus, it managed to prevent a breakthrough in the direction of Putten.'[23]

Still, Plocher could not prevent the disintegration of his left wing under the relentless Canadian attacks. Fighting tenaciously, Rudolf Witzig and the paratroopers of the 18th Parachute Regiment clung desperately to a single stronghold on the eastern bank of the Ijssel. According to Plocher, Witzig's regiment suffered 'considerable' losses, many of them to tanks. Only a last-ditch effort by the division anti-aircraft battalion, equipped with 88-mm guns, which sacrificed themselves 'almost to the last gun' and the division's 6th Artillery Regiment managed to prevent an Allied breakthrough near Putten, which would have threatened the division with being cut off and would have led to its encirclement. Allied forces that had penetrated into Putten were thrown back and the village completely cleared.[24]

In the meantime Allied attacks resumed between Deventer and Zwolle, forcing the weak security detachments of the division still on the Ijssel River back to the west. This was followed by a very strong attack aimed at cutting off the largest possible number of German formations, especially the 6th Parachute Division, in the area by the Zuider Sea. But once again the Germans were a step ahead of the Allies.

> It was possible to lead the numerous rear service units of the formations that had been fighting in this area out through the narrow passage which was left between the front and the Zuider Sea and move the majority of them back to the west in proper time across the Zuider Sea in the direction of Hilversum. Some elements were shipped across the Zuider Sea to Amsterdam. It

was surprising that this could be accomplished without any losses, considering the crushing enemy air superiority.[25]

In rapid succession the 6th Parachute Division was withdrawn again and again, delaying at each position, according to Plocher, 'as much as the badly exhausted troops were able'. The paratroopers tried to prevent by any means possible an enemy breakthrough in the south in order to enable the remnants of German forces there to get back to the new line of resistance on the Grebbe Canal and restore a coherent front. At the end of April the division was ordered to occupy defensive positions behind the canal in a general line running from Woudenberg to Amersfoort to Barn (dubbed the Grebbe Line) and to maintain advanced security detachments around Hoevelaken and Nijkerk.

As it worked constructing new defensive positions, replacements flowed in and the strength of the division increased considerably thanks to reinforcements from the Parachute Training Division – which had been redesignated the 20th Parachute Division. 'Thus it was finally possible to bring the 16th Parachute Regiment up to standard strength again and send it in with three battalions,' wrote Plocher. 'The 17th and 18th Parachute Regiments now also had again three battalions, which were fit for combat action.' The remainder of the 31st Parachute Regiment was incorporated into the 16th, 17th, and 18th Parachute Regiments. 'Thus,' recorded Plocher, 'with the 3rd Police Regiment consisting of two battalions, the division had eleven infantry battalions at its disposal. Finally, Kampfgruppe *Fuchs*, which still had considerable combat strength, remained subordinated to the division.' Division artillery consisted of one medium battalion (containing a battery each of 150-mm and 100-mm guns) two light battalions and an anti-aircraft battalion that had been brought back up to full strength with two 88-mm batteries for ground support and one light battery.

Altogether the division had 11,000–12,000 men, with 8,000 serving in combat units. 'Once the division had been reconstituted its combat efficiency could be considered to be "good",' recorded Plocher.[26] Thus, the pause in Allied operations had, once again, allowed the Germans sufficient time to rest and reconstitute their badly depleted formations and ensured they were ready for the next phase of fighting.

On 15 April 1945, only two weeks before he took his own life deep in his bunker in Berlin, Hitler issued his last order to his soldiers on the Eastern Front: 'Anyone ordering you to retreat will, unless you know him personally, be immediately arrested and if necessary killed on the spot, no matter what rank he may hold.'[27] By it was to no avail. The following day, on 16 April, the Red Army launched its last major offensive of the war aimed at encircling and capturing Berlin and then advancing along a broad front to the Elbe to link up with American and British forces. Some 2.5 million Soviet soldiers, supported by almost 42,000 artillery pieces and mortars, 6,200 tanks and assault guns, and nearly 7,500 aircraft unleashed multiple attacks. Army Group Vistula, responsible for the defence of Berlin, was organised into three armies containing some thirty divisions and numbering approximately one million men supported by 10,400 artillery pieces and guns, 1,500 tanks and assault guns and nearly 3,300 aircraft. In a little more than two weeks the Red Army conquered the capital of the Third Reich, planting its banners atop the Reichstag on 30 April. On that same day Hitler committed suicide, after designating Grand Admiral Karl Dönitz as his successor. The Wehrmacht had fought its last major battle.[28]

The 6th Parachute Division too had fought its last battle. The new front was not subject to any further large-scale Allied attacks. 'On the other hand, vigorous individual battles developed around the advanced strongpoints near Hoevelaken and Bunschoten', remembered Plocher, 'until they eventually had to be given up to the far superior enemy.' Reinforced reconnaissance patrol activity and attacks by Allied fighter-bombers continued until a truce came into effect, to allow food to be dropped by the Allies for the Dutch population, which Hitler had ordered deliberately starved. By this time the enemy facing the division consisted of the bulk of I Canadian Corps. On 5 May 1945 German forces in Fortress Holland capitulated. 'The division was assembled in the Oesterberg internment area,'[29] concluded Plocher. In its short second lifespan the 6th Parachute Division had fought with great distinction and determination, a tribute to the division's excellent leadership and to the fighting ability of the German soldier until the very last days of the war.

At 0800 hours on 5 May 1945, the cease-fire between the Allied and German forces went into effect. The war's end found almost 300 Allied divisions, including approximately 180 Russian, 68 American, 16 British and 10 French, arrayed against the Germans.[30] Still, despite any claims to the contrary, the men of First Parachute Army, II Parachute Corps, and 6th Parachute Division had not been overwhelmed by numbers on the Canadian front. German forces in Holland and north-west Germany numbered approximately 213,000 men. General Crerar's Canadian First Army, on the other hand, had some 260,000 troops under command at the time of the Wehrmacht's capitulation.[31] This marginal superiority was offset by the terrain, which precluded their deployment in numbers large enough to swamp the defenders. Nor was there great validity to German claims that they had been defeated by the preponderance of Allied technology and equipment. This is yet another postwar myth created by the leaders of the Wehrmacht to explain their final defeat. It is true that the policy of II Canadian Corps had been to crush resistance 'by fire and steel and not by the blood of our soldiers' – which should be the aim of any army determined to defeat another. Unfortunately, the terrain in East Friesland made bringing this fire and steel to bear extremely difficult. 'General Simonds was not able to bring into play anything like the full force of his armour and artillery,' records an official Canadian report on the German surrender. 'Consequently, the burden fell heaviest upon the infantry and the engineers.'[32]

A review of the battles fought by First Parachute Army, II Parachute Corps and 6th Parachute Division between January and May 1945 shows conclusively that the Allies won through a combination of mass, agility, and flexibility, bringing to bear unrelenting offensive pressure all along the front, frequently changing the main effort, and making skilful use of flanking attacks, thus forcing the Germans to withdraw again and again before they could be encircled. Indeed, once the first Allied offensive kicked off, the British and Canadians never stopped moving forward for more than two or three days before launching their next attack. Firepower, in the form of relentless attacks from the air and well prepared and executed artillery plans, also played a key role. As a result, German defences were almost always overwhelmed.

And when the Germans did manage to stage a significant counter-attack of their own, they were inevitably stopped in their tracks by resolute Canadian and British soldiers still capable of fighting doggedly, though no less tired than their opponents. Indeed, recent historical scholarship depicts the British, Canadian and Polish armies of 1945 as much more fragile than previously thought, verging on exhaustion, and almost totally out of infantry replacements.[33] It is to their everlasting credit that they were able to impose their will on the Wehrmacht so effectively.

With the war finally over, the Wehrmacht simply disintegrated. II Canadian Corps found 4,106 German officers and 88,793 men in its sector. On 6 May the Canadians moved into the portions of East Friesland not occupied by Allied troops. By 7 May, they had completed the occupation of their allotted areas and the disarmament of the German forces began. 'The defeated Germans co-operated fully in the task,' notes the report on the German surrender.[34] II Canadian Corps was also responsible for the reception of Germans in the concentration areas north of the Ems–Jade Canal. By 15 June, when the Canadians handed over all their responsibilities in Germany to the British XXX Corps, all main German formations had arrived at their place of internment in East Friesland north of the canal. By 18 June there was a total of 192,099 internees concentrated in northern East Friesland, including 2,348 female auxiliaries.[35] These represented only a small fraction of the more than eleven million German soldiers held as prisoners of war by the Allies in the late spring of 1945. The Western Allies held almost 7,750,000, the majority with the Americans, while the Soviets held some 3,350,000.[36]

Among those interned in East Friesland was Rudolf Witzig, who had been taken prisoner, along with survivors of the 18th Parachute Regiment and the 6th Parachute Division. The internees were relatively free to live as they liked. But the entire length of the canal was blocked by barbed wire and other obstacles and access to all the crossing points was tightly restricted.[37] 'The establishment of the German concentration area north of the Ems–Jade Canal was one of the problems which demanded constant vigilance to prevent escapes and to maintain order while the process of disbandment was in process,' noted a Canadian report.[38] After a few months, however, the prisoners became restless, not having heard from their relatives and families for a great while. As a result, many attempted to cross the canal and return to their families. Some succeeded. In response, heavy guards had to be established all along the canal and the chief obstacles illuminated by searchlights.[39]

Hanna Witzig first learned of her husband's plight in July 1945. A German soldier approached her in the hospital in Höxter, where she had continued to work after her wedding assisting her father. The soldier passed on Rudolf Witzig's greetings and informed Hanna of his whereabouts. Obtaining all the necessary travel documents, complete with multiple stamps from the sympathetic British commander of the town, who wrote that she was travelling to East Friesland to pick up 'luggage', Hanna then spent the next three days hitch-hiking west and then north to Oldenburg and the Ems–Jade Canal. She walked and travelled on trucks, trailers, and wagons, as the opportunity arose. The last leg of her journey was aboard a horse-drawn wagon. As the wagon approached the British crossing point, the driver, for some unexplained reason, sped up and then flew across the checkpoint without slowing down. Hanna recalled later that she expected the British guards to open fire at any time and was surprised when they did not. Once across, she inquired at a central office, manned by a German soldier, as to the whereabouts of her husband. He informed her that her husband was in Norden on the coast. Traveling there, she found the members of his regiment living in a farmhouse, but no Rudolf Witzig. Major Witzig, she was told, was out on his daily horseback ride and swim! While waiting for her husband she learned that farmers in the area were feeding and billeting not only the many German soldiers interned there, but also a large number of refugees from East Prussia who had fled the approaching Red Army. Finally, Witzig arrived. 'He was very surprised to find me!' she remembered with a laugh almost sixty-five years later.[40]

The couple then spent three 'very happy' weeks together on the farm, where they were given the best room in the house by the owners. Hanna helped the farmer's wife and later Rudolf took her on a tour of East Friesland, in a wagon pulled by two horses, to visit relatives. All too soon, however, the second honeymoon came to an end. Rudolf became ill, developing first a severely sore throat, and then a fever, and finally a scarlet rash. He had scarlet fever, no doubt acquired by living with so many internees in such a confined space, and had to be quarantined for five weeks in the hospital in Norden. There was nothing for Hanna to do but return home.[41]

In the meantime, a large number of German soldiers had left the concentration area during July, August, and September without being properly documented and discharged. The British believed that in most cases they had returned to their homes and to work on the land. In some cases the escapees were men who had deserted from the Wehrmacht to escape arrest. The increased number of escapes was due in large part to the withdrawal of searchlights for use in other parts of the British zone. As a result a series of sweeps was instituted, consisting of sudden raids without warning in the dead of the night. All those who were unable to establish their identity satisfactorily, who were not in possession of the required discharge certificate, or who gave cause for suspicion were detained for interrogation. If they remained under suspicion after interrogation they were placed under the authority of the military governor, if they were civilians, or returned to the internment area if they were Wehrmacht deserters.[42]

Orders were received to step up the rate of discharge of German soldiers and soon afterwards the Canadians were moving some 3,000 Wehrmacht veterans every other day to various discharge locations in the British, French, and Russian zones. These discharges required increased guards for both train and truck convoys and considerable difficulty was experienced in these moves due to the condition of the German railways and highways, which had been heavily damaged during the war.[43] In October, Rudolf, now completely recovered, received his discharge certificate and was officially released. He was among the more fortunate German prisoners of war held by the Allies. The last of those held by the Soviets would not return home for more than another decade and those were the fortunate few who had survived the Russian concentration camps. Even those held by the Americans and British could not always be assured of a rapid repatriation back to Germany after the war. Rudolf Valentine, a German paratrooper who fought in Italy and was captured after the brutal battle for Monte Cassino in Italy, spent more than a year in U.S. prisoner of war camps in the States and was being repatriated to Bremerhaven, when the ship he was travelling in was diverted to England. There, all the German P.O.W.s on board were marched off by the British and held for three years, during which time they cleared rubble in bombed-out cities and worked the fields. Valentine and his comrades were only released and returned home in 1948, their hearts forever bitter against the British.[44]

After his release, Witzig hitch-hiked to the home of Hanna's parents, where he was reunited with his wife. He and Hanna were fortunate in that Höxter had never been bombed, despite the more than one and a half million tons of bombs dropped on the Third Reich by the British and Americans in the last year and a half of the war. After the war, Witzig would joke to his son, Jürgen, that, during the war he preferred to be with his unit at the front as the bombings made the cities too dangerous.[45] Unlike so many other homes still standing in the British sector of Germany, Hanna's parents' house had not been occupied because it lodged not only the Remmer family, but also refugees from other parts of the country.

The Russians were not the only ones exacting retribution against the German population. The home in Höxter of Amanda Witzig, Rudolf's mother, was occupied for two years by British soldiers. According to Jürgen Witzig, the British destroyed all the furniture in the house and treated her like 'a personal slave', making her do all the washing and cooking. Such behaviour, notes the younger Witzig, was common among the victors in the north and engendered hard feelings among the German population for many years to come. Colonel Witzig recounts how, even thirty years later when his engineer unit was conducting manoeuvres in the area, German farmers welcomed the Bundeswehr, but said quite emphatically: 'No British soldiers!'[46] Still, the British Army of the Second World War had left a powerful impression on Rudolf Witzig, who ranked the British Tommy as the best Allied soldier of the war. Witzig's son told the author that his father disliked the New Zealanders altogether (no doubt due to the massacre of his company and battalion in Crete), never spoke to his family about the Russians, and had had no contact with the U.S. Army until after the war.[47]

After ten years of service, Rudolf Witzig's career in the Wehrmacht and the Fallschirmjäger had come to an end. His parting from his airborne brethren must have been a sad one indeed, but he had a good deal to show for his sacrifices. He had participated in two of the greatest airborne operations in military history – Eben Emael and Crete – and had emerged from the war as a legendary figure and the Wehrmacht's most decorated parachute engineer. He had fought on the Western and Eastern Fronts and in almost every major theatre, including North-west Europe, the Mediterranean, North Africa, and Germany. His awards included the Parachute Qualification Badge, earned in 1938; the Knight's Cross and Iron Cross First and Second Classes, awarded in 1940; the Wound Badge in Gold and Crete Armband, awarded in 1941; the German Cross in Gold, Africa Armband, and German–Italian Africa Medal, awarded in 1943; the Oak Leaves to the Knight's Cross, awarded in 1944; and the Luftwaffe Close Combat Clasp in Gold, awarded in 1945. Only 134 Knight's Crosses were awarded to members of the German Airborne Forces during the Second World War. Of these 69 were awarded the German Cross in Gold and only 15 the Oak Leaves. Rudolf Witzig had truly been an elite soldier among the elite.[48]

Chapter 11

THE NEW GERMAN ARMY AND RETIREMENT

The Reich's military ambitions were ended, and the individuals who had cast their fortunes with the German war machine now found themselves facing a new reality. Many, Rudolf Witzig among them, managed to extricate themselves from the wreckage and move on with their lives. Some did not.

Hermann Göring, once Hitler's designated successor and commander of the Luftwaffe, surrendered to the U.S. Army in Bavaria on 9 May 1945. The highest-ranking Nazi official tried at Nuremberg, he was found guilty and sentenced to death. Cheating the hangman's noose, Göring committed suicide with a potassium cyanide capsule the night before he was to be hanged. His body was cremated, along with those of other executed Nazi leaders, and their ashes were scattered in the Conwentzbach River in Munich.

Richard Heidrich, the first commander of the Third Reich's parachute infantry battalion, was captured by the Americans on 2 May 1945 and later handed over to the British. He died in hospital in Hamburg-Bergedorf on 23 December 1947.[1] Gerhart Schirmer, Witzig's comrade in arms on Crete and in the Baltic States, was taken prisoner by the Soviets on 8 May 1945.[2] It would be almost eleven years before he was released. Bruno Brauer, who had commanded the *Hermann Göring* Regiment's 1st Battalion, the 1st Parachute Regiment, the East Group during the airborne invasion of Crete, Fortress Crete until March 1945, and finally the 9th Parachute Division until the end of the war, was taken prisoner by the British on 10 May 1945. He was delivered to Greece, tried for the atrocities committed by German soldiers on Crete and sentenced to death.[3] Ironically, Brauer had not only proven the most humane of the generals who commanded the German garrison on the island following the invasion, but also one of the few with the courage to dismiss stories of Cretan mutilation of German paratroopers. Such stories would have deadly repercussions for the island's population. Brauer's execution was delayed 'with distasteful symbolism' according to historian Antony Beevor, until 20 May 1947, the anniversary of the German airborne invasion of the island. 'His death shocked international opinion so much that . . . other senior officers who were far guiltier, escaped with prison sentences.'[4] One of those who escaped the full wrath of the Allies' justice was Kurt Student.

Captured by the British, Generaloberst Student, the father of Germany's Fallschirmjäger, ended the war as Commander–in–Chief of Army Group Vistula. He was tried by the Allies for war crimes that took place in Crete during and immediately following the German airborne invasion of the island. The ninth of his 'Parachutist's Ten Commandments', issued to each Fallschirmjäger before the invasion of the island, and another order issued soon after Crete had been conquered, now came back to haunt him with a vengeance. Prosecutors argued that it was this order, 'Fight chivalrously against an honest foe; armed irregulars deserve no quarter', that prompted his paratroopers and, more importantly, the German soldiers who later garrisoned the island, to commit wide–scale atrocities against the island's civilian population. 'The excessively high casualties of the Parachute Division were soon being explained away by outraged stories in which Cretan crones with kitchen knives cut the throats of paratroopers caught in trees, and roving bands of civilians tortured wounded German soldiers lying helpless on the field of battle,' writes Antony Beevor in his account of the German reprisals and Cretan resistance on the island. 'As soon as these accounts reached Berlin, Göring ordered Student to instigate an immediate judicial enquiry and carry out reprisals.'[5] Despite the fact that, after three months of gathering evidence, a panel of German military judges could only find twenty–five cases of mutilation on the entire island, and almost all of those had been inflicted after death, General Student had already issued an order on 31 May for reprisals to be taken against the Cretan population. According to that order:

> It is certain that the civilian population including women and boys have taken part in the fighting, committed sabotage, mutilated and killed wounded soldiers. It is therefore high time to combat all cases of this kind, to undertake reprisals and punitive expeditions which must be carried through with exemplary terror. The harshest measures must be taken and I order the following: shooting for all cases of proven cruelty, and

I wish this to be done by the same units who had suffered such atrocities. The following reprisals will be taken:
1. Shooting
2. Fines
3. Total destruction of villages by burning
4. Extermination of the male population of the territory in question.

My authority will be necessary for measures under 3 and 4. All these measures must, however, be taken rapidly and omitting all formalities. In view of these circumstances the troops have a right to this and there is no need for military tribunals to judge beasts and assassins.[6]

The reprisals began soon afterwards. By 9 September some 1,135 Cretans had been executed; only 224 of these had been sentenced by military tribunal. Despite overwhelming evidence showing his complicity in these atrocities, Student was sentenced to only five years imprisonment. Incredible as it seems he was released after only serving two years.[7] He was indeed among the privileged. Countless other paratroopers languished for many years in Soviet prisoner of war camps, with the vast majority dying in Russia. Those who survived did not return home for almost a decade.

Others enjoyed various degrees of fortune. General of Paratroopers Hermann Ramcke, the hero of Crete and North Africa and under whom Witzig's 2nd Company had served in Tunisia, was captured on 18 September 1944, after his forces completely destroyed the port facilities of Brest before surrendering to U.S. troops. Held as a prisoner of war at Camp Clinton, Mississippi, he broke out on New Year's Eve 1945 and spent the day in Jackson before returning to camp of his own accord. Transported back to France and held there, he escaped once again and returned to Germany, probably with the assistance of his old Fall-schirmjäger comrades. Fearful of trouble with the French, the German government promptly returned him to France, where he stood trial. Despite testimony on his behalf by his former adversaries, including General Middleton, to whom he had surrendered at Brest, Ramcke remained in French captivity until 1951.[8] Generalmajor Walter Barenthin, who had risen to command 3rd Parachute Division at the end of 1943 and later commanded 20th Parachute Division and was responsible for all of First Parachute Army's training and replacement units, was captured by the British in May 1945 and released in August 1947.[9] Generalleutnant Friedrich Freiherr von Broich, Witzig's division commander in North Africa, was captured by the British at Gombalia in Tunisia on 12 May 1943 and released on 2 October 1947.[10] Another of Witzig's division commanders in Tunisia, General der Panzertruppe Hasso von Manteuffel, later commanded Fifth Panzer Army on the Western Front and Third Panzer Army on the Eastern Front. After surrendering to the British on 3 May 1945, he was held as a prisoner of war by first the British and then the Americans until 1946. Wounded by a direct hit from a bomb on his command post in the last months of the war, General of Paratroopers Alfred Schlemm, Rudolf Witzig's First Parachute Army commander, was captured by the British on 8 May 1945 and spent until March 1948 as a prisoner of war.[11] General of Paratroopers Eugen Meindl, Witzig's II Parachute Corps commander in the last months of the war, was captured on 25 May 1945, again by the British, and released in September 1947.[12] Generalleutnant Hermann Plocher, Witzig's 6th Parachute Division commander, was also captured by the British on 8 May 1945. He was released in 1947. Plocher joined the postwar German Air Force in 1957 and finally retired from military service in December 1961 as acting Commander of the Luftwaffe's Group South.[13]

Colonel Friedrich August Freiherr von der Heydte was wounded and taken prisoner by the Americans on 24 December 1944, after having led Kampfgruppe *von der Heydte* into the Ardennes following the Fallschirmjäger's last parachute jump of the war, which opened the Ardennes offensive. Von der Heydte was released on 12 July 1947[14] and immediately flown over from the British prisoner of war camp at Colchester to appear as a witness for the prosecution, causing consternation when he testified that, along with British Field Marshal Alexander, General Kurt Student was the general he most admired.[15]

In the meantime, for the first two years following the end of the war Rudolf and Hanna Witzig lived with Hanna's parents in two rooms on the upper floor of their house. Between 1946 and 1955 Hanna gave birth to two sons, Jürgen and Hans, and two daughters, Elisabeth and Angela. Their decision to have children reflected the confidence he and Hanna had in their future and in Germany. After the war, the country was struck by extremely low birth rates, a testimony not only to the absence of millions of potential fathers, but also to the disinclination of German women to bear children in the midst of a devastated society.

'Many shared the conviction of one German woman in Berlin, who asserted after the birth of her younger son in 1947 that "it was irresponsible in this terrible time of need that I would put another child into this world",' notes historian Richard Bessel. 'It would take a long time for many Germans . . . to find a path back to "normal" life through the re-establishment of conventional, patriarchal family relationships.'[16] Unlike the majority of Germans, however, Rudolf and Hanna were committing themselves to building a 'normal' family life as quickly as possible. 'My parents were convinced that Germany had a chance after the war,' remembered Jürgen, 'especially with the help of the U.S. and the British.'[17] For the sake of his children, Rudolf Witzig also became 'reluctantly religious'.[18]

Still, life in postwar Germany was extremely harsh. At the beginning of January 1947 there were still almost 250,000 German soldiers interned by the Americans, British, French, and Soviets.[19] And even as late as 1950, the Federal Republic still held over 10 million expellees and refugees, roughly 2 million former Reich civil servants, Nazi Party officials and professional soldiers who had lost their jobs, 2.5 million war dependents, and 1.5 million war invalids and their dependents, 2 million late-returning German prisoners of war, and between 4 and 6 million people who had been bombed out of their homes. All of this was in addition to about 1.5 million unemployed.[20]

Yet, despite the challenges and the urgency of finding a job, Rudolf Witzig was looking ahead. He went back to school to study civil engineering for two and a half years, a prudent choice in a country desperately in need of rebuilding after the devastation of the war. The following years were spent working as a construction foreman and civil engineer in the British-occupied sector of Germany and then heading construction teams in Höxter, Hanover and Hamburg. In 1952 the Witzig family moved to Essen, where Rudolf worked for a water purification firm. The family lived there for the next four years. But, despite his best attempts and many achievements, his heart was not in the civil engineering business. According to Jürgen, Rudolf was a good civil engineer but the salary was very poor.[21] And so, on 16 January 1956, Rudolf Witzig joined the re-established German Army, the Bundeswehr. The decision to rejoin the military could not have been an easy one for Witzig and his wife. Still, both believed that he could use his knowledge and experience better to assist in the building of a new German Army within the framework of NATO.[22]

Nazi Germany's complete defeat in the Second World War meant the end of the Wehrmacht. The Potsdam Agreement stipulated its final abolition 'in such a manner as permanently to prevent the revival or reorganisation of German militarism and Nazism'. This included all German land, naval, and air forces, with all their organisations, staffs and institutions, including the General Staff, the officer corps, and all other military and semi-military organisations, including any clubs and associations which might serve to keep alive the military tradition in Germany.[23] Public opinion in West Germany five years after the war overwhelmingly believed it was not right to become a soldier again and most Germans did not want their husbands and sons to join the military. While a narrow majority of West Germans favoured the formation of a national army in 1951, nearly half the population, including more than half of former Wehrmacht soldiers, approved of conscientious objection.[24]

That is not to say that the German population had a negative image of the Wehrmacht. Indeed, according to Richard Bessel, 'a very positive image emerged as a counterpoint to a negative assessment of Nazism'.[25] On 5 April 1951 Konrad Adenauer, first Chancellor of the Federal Republic, who had previously declared that 'the proportion of those [German soldiers] who are really guilty is so extraordinarily modest and so extraordinarily small that no damage was done to the honour of the German Wehrmacht', rejected 'once and for all', in his famous Declaration of Honour for the ordinary Wehrmacht soldiers, the ideal of 'collective guilt' of former professional soldiers. Thus was born the myth of the 'clean Wehrmacht' in postwar Germany, a lie that would take more than forty years to correct.[26]

Rudolf Witzig's return to the ranks of the German military was probably also influenced by his experience with postwar Allied justice. In 1949, while working as a civil engineer on a road construction project, he was ordered to see the British commander in Clausthal Zellerfeld. There he was confronted by a French policeman, who began to ask him questions about his battalion's activities in St-Amand in 1944 and the death of the chief of police of the town. 'My description of the shooting . . . hardly interested him and he seemed to be suspicious of me,' remembered Witzig.

> Soon afterwards I learned that my presence in the French zone
> of occupation had been requested. Aware of other such similar
> incidents, for example the bad treatment General Ramcke had

experienced in France, I discussed the situation with Colonel–General Student, who lived at the time in a village near Hamburg. His war crimes trial had been decided in his favour and he had been acquitted due to the assistance of the New Zealand General Freyberg, his opponent in Crete. I knew the commander in the British zone and requested that he intervene on my behalf.

As a result of British intervention, the French attempt to bring Witzig to their zone of occupation was rejected.[27]

But Witzig's problems were far from over. Two years later he was ordered by the Federal Government's Centre for Legal Protection to report to Bonn, where he learned that he had been sentenced in France to a 'heavy punishment' and warned he should avoid that country in the future. By 1956 Witzig believed that incident 'nearly forgotten' and attributed that to the fact that he was a member of the German armed forces. But in 1979, thirty-five years after the event, he was cited in the Munich regional court for the same incident. 'Due to a new German–French agreement, the Federal Republic of Germany agreed to take over [responsibility] for all existing war crimes,' recalled Witzig. Soon after the hearing a preliminary investigation against him for murder, 'in accordance with Article 170/II of the Code of Criminal Procedure' was stopped. At that hearing he was accused of having arranged the shooting of captured partisans and found guilty. 'I did not give such an order!' wrote Witzig after the war, protesting he was unaware of any such shootings and that he had been condemned even before appearing in court. In 1981 the head of the National Union of Paratroopers in France intervened on Witzig's behalf, hoping to have the verdict overturned. Witzig was at the time the Chairman of the Federation of German Paratroopers. In 1983, however, the judgement against Witzig was repeated, despite the fact that Witzig was never requested to appear in court. Intervention by the Union of European Paratroopers on his behalf also failed to have any effect and, in fact, the UEP rejected a proposal by the Federation of German Paratroopers to replace Witzig as chairman if that would help bring better relations with the UEP.[28]

'Since that time I have been under that indictment, despite the fact that neither the judgment nor the basis for it were ever handed down to me personally,' protested Witzig, bitterly.

I was condemned to death in absentia for having arranged the execution on 18 June 1944 in St-Amand of 11 captured personnel and the burning of several houses. None of it is correct! What happened in combat I can no longer prove. No cross-examination of witnesses was allowed me and no other German soldier was connected with the incident.

Witzig believed that the responsibility and consequences of the large-scale battles between the French partisans and Vichy French soldiers were placed on his shoulders for simplicity's sake and to avoid embarrassment to members of the French government and the armed forces regarding collaboration with the Germans, which had resulted in the death of fellow Frenchmen.

'My battalion and I, as commander, acted without brutality, in accordance with the 3 February 1944 instructions of the Commander-in-Chief West, Field Marshal von Rundstedt,' remembered Witzig. According to Witzig, those instructions directed 'heavy' punishment for subordinate commanders and soldiers who took overly harsh measures against the French population and even the French resistance movement. Witzig admitted that this instruction ran counter to an OKW order of 8 June 1944 which directed that members of the French resistance movement were to be treated 'like partisans'. Still, Witzig accepted the inevitable: 'We lost the war. "*Vae Victis*" bows the defeated one . . . This still applies today.'

It is unlikely Witzig would have been unable to avert the consequences of the French condemnation, despite its injustice, had he not been a member of the Bundeswehr, which was needed by NATO to counter the huge Soviet preponderance in military power. The Bundeswehr and the German government protected and sheltered Witzig for almost fifty years, forcing the French government, in the end, to back down and accept the fact that it would never be allowed either to imprison or execute him. No rapprochement with the French ever took place over the matter and there is no evidence that one was ever solicited by Witzig.

Rudolf Witzig entered the new German Army as a lieutenant-colonel of Engineers. According to his son Jürgen, the Bundeswehr did not want Rudolf Witzig as a paratrooper, perhaps because his reputation and accomplishments as a former Fallschirmjäger would draw too much attention to an organisation that was viewed as highly

Lieutenant-Colonel Rudolf Witzig (left) commanded the 7th Engineer Battalion in Holtzwinden after the war. He was incensed that the postwar German Army ignored so many military traditions, especially among the airborne forces.

controversial. For the next year Witzig worked diligently on the staff of an engineer regiment in Düsseldorf, imparting his vast experience to a new generation of German soldiers. Between 1957 and 1959 Witzig commanded the 7th Engineer Battalion in Holtzwinden. Unfortunately, Witzig's command was abbreviated, ending on a dark note, when three soldiers were killed or injured, when their crane touched a high-voltage power line during a river crossing. As Witzig had been present to witness the training, he was held accountable and lost his command shortly thereafter. According to Jürgen Witzig, his father had conducted a map reconnaissance of the location prior to the training, but the maps used did not show the power lines involved in the accident.

The incident left Rudolf Witzig bitter as he felt he had been unjustly relieved of command. In the old Wehrmacht, a battalion commander would not have been held responsible for a training accident such as this one. Indeed, the German officers of the Second World War were expected to make combat training as realistic as possible and to suffer casualties, including deaths, during field exercises. But perhaps Germany's new leaders believed that, with the war long over and the more democratic Bundeswehr having replaced Hitler's Wehrmacht, there was no longer room in the German armed forces for officers who allowed the lives of their men to be lost in training, especially officers like Rudolf Witzig, who embodied the old Wehrmacht and the Fallschirmjäger. Germany had lost enough men during the war and could not afford to keep losing them in peacetime. Witzig's loss of command was followed by several years of staff assignments in Cologne.[29]

In 1963 Rudolf Witzig visited Eben Emael, still Belgian military property, for the first time since the war. Witzig and other surviving members of Sturmgruppe Granit had been invited by a private individual, a Dutchman, who was writing an article on the capture of the fort in the Second World War. 'We were living in Cologne at the time,' remembered Jürgen, who was then sixteen, 'and I drove to Eben Emael with my father. During the drive he told me the story of what had happened there during the war and also informed me about his life.' Still, his son admits that Witzig was never one to talk a great deal about the war. At the fort, Rudolf Witzig, in civilian clothes like all the other visitors, preferred to stay atop the superstructure, shying away from

Lieutenant-Colonel Rudolf Witzig of the German Bundeswehr.

going inside, saying there was little to be learned there. 'He would point to an area and say: "Here it was no problem. The Belgians made it easy for us,"' remembered his son. Also present at the fort was the former Sergeant Helmut Wenzel, who had commanded the actual storming of Eben Emael in Witzig's absence. Like Witzig, Wenzel had fought in Crete and after two years of combat had risen to the rank of captain. Captured in North Africa, he was shipped to the United States and spent the last three years of the war as a prisoner at Camp Crossville, Tennessee. 'He talked more than my father,' remembered Jürgen Witzig, 'and I found him more interesting. My father talked about grand strategy and tactics.

Wenzel talked about what actually took place. He would say things like: "My foxhole was over there!" and he would point. "The gliders came in from this direction!" Then "Boom! Boom!" It was really living history!' laughed the younger Witzig remembering the visit more than forty years later. Jürgen Witzig admits there was a great deal of tension between Wenzel and his father: 'He [Wenzel] felt his whole life had suffered

Witzig (right) and two other veterans of the Seūcond World War assault on Eben Emael visit the fort in May 1963.

because he did not get the Knight's Cross and my father did. He felt that by the time my father had shown up at Eben Emael, the whole show was over.' Witzig, his son, Wenzel, and their host spent the entire day at the fort, interrupted only by lunch at nearby Kanne. After the visit, Witzig asked his son to write an article for publication. Jürgen's article and the photos he had taken were later published in a German military journal as well as his school newspaper in Cologne.[30]

Other visits to the site of his greatest victory would follow. Jürgen Witzig noted that his father visited Eben Emael often, perhaps even every year, on 10 May, the anniversary of his seizure of the fort. 'He would meet with other veterans and their wives at the German military cemetery at Eysselstein near Venlo,' remembered Jürgen. 'The gatherings would last two or three days, with one day at Eben Emael, one day at the cemetery, and then a free day.' Rudolf Witzig's last visit to Eben Emael was in 2000, the year before his death, when his family was living in Mainz. 'He said: "They are getting old!"' recalled his son, discussing his father's last meeting with his remaining comrades and their wives. 'It was his sense of humour, you see!' laughed the younger Witzig, '"They are getting old!" Not: "We are getting old!"'[31]

In 1965 Rudolf Witzig was promoted to full colonel in the Bundeswehr, evidence that someone was looking out for him, especially in light of the incident six years earlier. Still, his years in the

Bundeswehr left him increasingly frustrated and bitter towards the new German government and the Army. 'We spent years making it the Army it is today,' he told Jürgen, referring to the old veterans of the Second World War, 'and now we are accused of having served a criminal regime and shunted aside.' The older Witzig was particularly incensed that the Bundeswehr had decided to ignore so many of the traditions built up prior to and during the Second World War, especially among the Fallschirmjäger. Furthermore, the older Witzig believed he was the target of petty jealousies from his superiors, which effectively blocked him from rising any higher. Nonetheless, he retired in 1974 as the head of the Engineer Policy and Equipment Office and the Engineer School near Munich.[32] Many years later when Jürgen told his father that he had been promoted to colonel of engineers in the Bundeswehr, Rudolf Witzig asked him angrily: 'Are you allowed to associate with a war criminal?'

In retirement Witzig occupied himself with gardening, sailing, skiing, and mountaineering, and spent several weeks a year in the mountains with his family and a few close friends. His old war

Rudolf Witzig visiting Eben Emael after the war. Witzig returned frequently to the site of his greatest triumph.

wound continued to give him problems, but failed to slow him down. He took up model shipbuilding when he reached his seventies, building a number of large and intricate nineteenth-century sailing ships. Model shipbuilding is a hobby requiring patience, attention to detail, a sharp eye and steady hands and suggests that Rudolf had aged well and that, even in his golden years, he possessed the energy and need to create. Jürgen remembers his father spending hours in the cellar of their home, working on his sailing ships. Rudolf also continued to read voraciously, devouring books in many genres and annotating their margins with copious notes and corrections, especially if they concerned Eben Emael or the German airborne forces in the Second World War. He even wrote a short history of his parachute engineers in the war.

Rudolf Witzig also travelled extensively and was very active with the 'Bund Deutscher Fallschirmjäger', the German Paratroop Association, serving as its head from 1980 to 1988. He was very involved with writing and teaching about the assault on Eben Emael and the German airborne forces in the Second World War. In 1960 and 1961 he published his own official account of the assault on Eben Emael, in three parts, for *Der Deutsche Fallschirmjäger*, the official magazine of the association. He also published a separate account for the German engineer school. He and Hanna even compiled a German Fallschirm-jäger songbook. And though he seldom spoke about the war with his family, he was always ready to discuss it at length with his old comrades. Witzig also wrote and discussed the attack on Eben Emael with officers of the new Bundeswehr. But not every request to speak was accepted. In 1987 Witzig received an invitation from the commander of the German 140th Engineer Battalion stationed in Emmerich, where Witzig's 6th Parachute Division had fought during the last months of the Second World War, to speak to the officers of the battalion about the war. According to his son, Witzig replied, emphatically: 'No! By then it was not a war any more! There's nothing for your officers to learn and I will not come!' 'Those [last months in Holland] were very hard days for him,' Jürgen Witzig told the author.[33]

In 1984 Witzig visited Monte Cassino in Italy, the site of a bitter series of battles, for a memorial service and tribute to the 20,000 Germans, many of them paratroopers, who had died fighting around the abbey. Afterwards, he continued on to Crete, 'the island of destiny for German paratroopers' as he called it, and visited the Maleme area, site of the greatest Fallschirmjäger victory and greatest tragedy. In all, he would visit the island six or seven times, assisting in the establishment and then rebuilding of the German cemetery there and the nearby monument.[34] The German military cemetery on Crete, located at Maleme, on Hill 107, the place where so many Fallschirmjäger lost their lives during their airborne assault of the island, was inaugurated on 6 October 1974. It contains the remains of 4,465 dead. To the west the olive groves slope down to the bed of the wild Tavrontis River, while in the distance there is a view of the deep blue sea. The arrangement of the cemetery is commensurate with the four main battle areas during the battle: Canea, Maleme, Rethymnon, and Heraklion. There are benches in the shade of the olive trees, many of which are old enough to have witnessed the battle. These invite the visitor to rest and ponder the fate of those who lie buried there. The path leads to an open hall, with a book of the names of the fallen, and then uphill to the graves enclosed by walls. Each stone table displays the name and dates of birth and death of two German soldiers – the Germans believing that comrades in battle should remain comrades for eternity. In the middle of the cemetery is a memorial square, where the names of 350 soldiers, who fell on Crete but whose remains have never been found, are recorded on metal plates.[35] Less known is a second memorial, devoted strictly to the Fallschirmjäger, a statue in the form of the 'storming eagle', situated on a hill some 3·5 km west of Canea on the left of the main road to Maleme. The condition of this memorial prompted Witzig to write an article for *Der Deutche Fallschirmjäger*. That article, the last he would write, was an obituary for the memorial.

Remembering his comrades who had fallen in Crete meant to great deal to Rudolf Witzig. 'You have read my opinion regarding the monument in the last issue of *Der Deutsche Fallschirmjäger*,' he told a German officer interviewing him only a month before his death, shortly after the memorial in Canea was closed. By then the storming eagle could not be reconstructed, the pedestal on which it stood had rotted and the lease on the property had expired. 'The architects had not thought about these things in 1941,' wrote Witzig. 'They wished to honour those killed in the battle of Crete with a large, attractive memorial and this wish was fulfilled by their successors despite resistance.'[36] The memorial was dedicated to the men of the 2nd Battalion of the Assault Regiment and inscribed with the words: 'Gratitude is due to the dead, those who gave their lives, loyal to their oath of allegiance to our Grea̖   Germany, far from home.'[37] After the war the memorial and the cemetery became run-down but it was restored by veterans of the Assault Regiment. Years later the remains of the dead were transferred to the monastery at Gournia and stored there before being transferred to the new cemetery in Maleme. Finally, in 1971, the German Paratrooper Association took responsibility for the site, leasing the land for thirty years and spending some DM 30,000, all of it private money, for the upkeep of the site. 'But soon the eagle became dilapidated, parts fell down,' lamented Witzig. 'It turned out it was not built for eternity.'[38] The German community on the island, however, answered the call, renovating the site and installing a new granite plaque inscribed in German, English, and Greek: 'This memorial was built in 1941 by German paratroopers for their comrades who were killed in the war.'[39]

But once again the Mediterranean weather attacked the new memorial and in the end it proved impossible to continue its upkeep. 'There are people who will not realise that the time for the monument has expired, that the location can no longer be kept,' Witzig told his interviewer.

> I think it is impossible to move it and set it up elsewhere. To set up a new monument in a new location is not possible either. We have neither the ground nor the permission of the owner, the mayor, the state government or the federal government to build a new war memorial ... Even if we had permission to do it, we would still need not DM 10,000 but DM 100,000 to build a solid memorial. Even this will not be enough. A new memorial needs maintenance, care, and oversight. We know exactly how people treat war memorials in Germany. What do we expect of a war memorial abroad?[40]

Only the old marble plaque remains on the original site. 'The people of Crete lovingly called our memorial "The German Bird",' concluded Witzig, sadly. 'In 1983 an engineer said that due to its historical importance it was forbidden to rearrange or change the memorial, the most beautiful in the Mediterranean area. But the time has passed for that.'[41] Then eighty-five years old, Rudolf Witzig probably recognised that his own time was coming to an end. In fighting for the further longevity of the memorial, a reminder of the many dear friends and comrades who had died fighting for Crete some sixty years before, he was fighting for his own longevity, fighting to be remembered, fighting to keep from slipping into decay and oblivion.

Witzig also spent more and more time organising his wartime papers and photos and filling in the gaps with documents and pictures he obtained from the Bundesarchiv as well as from other veterans. He collected articles, newspaper clippings, and books in German, English and French on Eben Emael and the German airborne forces in the Second World War. He compiled an authoritative history of the Corps 11th Parachute Engineer Battalion and 21st Parachute Engineer

The German war memorial on Crete. Witzig was an ardent advocate for the restoration and maintenance of the memorial.

Regiment from January 1942 to October 1944, complete with maps and photographs. 'This history of the battalion, which fought and suffered for nearly three years, is being compiled before the last documents are lost,' he began. That history was based on operation reports and personal experiences, as well as manning and other documents. He even included numerous references to sources he considered to be highly authoritative, especially Heintz Austermann's book, *Von Eben Emael bis Edewechter Damm. Fallschirmjäger Fallschirmpioniere.* Austermann had served with the parachute engineers and his book was based on reports and other documents of the parachute engineer formations, as well as personal experiences. Missing in both books were the unit war diaries, which had been lost or destroyed during the war. Witzig also published his own account of the assault on Eben Emael in English, which appeared in the British series *History of the Second World War*, published by Marshall Cavendish in the early 1970s.

One suspects, in light of his love of books and proclivity for writing and creating, that Witzig no doubt had another book in mind, one aimed at setting the record straight and correcting the many myths and mistakes surrounding the German assault on Eben Emael. However, Jürgen insists, very emphatically, that his father had no intention of writing a book about Eben Emael or the German airborne forces in the Second World War. 'Of that I am very sure,' the younger Witzig told the author. 'He said there were enough books on the subject.'[42] After going through all Rudolf's papers, photos and books, this author is not entirely convinced. But if Rudolf Witzig intended on writing a book, why didn't he write it? There are many good reasons. First, his immediate postwar years were extremely busy ones. He had a new career to build and a family to provide for. He spent almost forty years defending himself against French allegations of war crimes. And on top of all of that, he needed to prove to himself and to others that he was as good a 'new' German officer as he had been an old one. Also, postwar Germany society was not receptive to the memoirs of an officer who had served in Hitler's Wehrmacht. After his retirement, Witzig remained quite busy. Furthermore, he was certainly a stickler for detail and accuracy and this no doubt accounts somewhat for the delay. But in light of the tremendous sensitivity existing in Germany after the war and for many years to come regarding all aspects of Hitler's Third Reich, the timing for a book which attempted to set the record straight on the use of German forces in Belgium or Crete was never really quite right. And by the time it was, it was too late.

If he was not interested in writing a book, Witzig remained devoted to writing articles on Eben Emael and Crete for *Der Deutsche Fallschirmjäger* and staying in touch with his old comrades and their families through his many, many letters. When he was in his eighties he complained to Jürgen that his typewriter was 'too old' and his letters 'too ugly' compared to those he received from his friends, which were obviously written on a computer. So he asked his son to teach him how to use a computer. 'I tried, but it proved too difficult,' recounted Jürgen to the author. 'So I suggested to him that he take a computer course. And he did! Afterwards I gave him my old computer. And that's what he used to write with!'[43]

In retirement Rudolf also devoted more and more time to his ten grandchildren, six girls and four boys, taking them hiking in the mountains, skiing, and sailing. He became less reluctant, as old veterans do, to talk about the Second World War and his years in the military, sharing his stories and experiences with Jürgen's son, Heinrich. The last pages of his photo album show a tall, slender, suntanned, and still handsome and active man surrounded by close friends and family and engaged in living his life to the fullest. In the last photo of his album, Rudolf Witzig is sailing the high seas, his hands at the rudder of his boat.

Rudolf Witzig died on 3 October 2001, German Reunification Day. He was eighty-five years old. The funeral and burial took place at Ober-schleißheim, near Munich, and was presided over by Monseigneur Volck, an individual every bit as unique as Rudolf Witzig. Volck had fought as a young German paratrooper at Monte Cassino in Italy. When the fighting was at its worst, he had promised God that if he survived he would become a Catholic priest, a testimony to both the fierceness of the battle as well as to the inability of Hitler and the Nazi Party to wipe out religion in the Third Reich altogether. Volck survived and held true to his promise. Afterwards he presided at many German Fallschirmjäger functions. 'My father loved him!' remembered Jürgen Witzig, who described the elder Witzig's funeral as 'impressive'. It was attended by some 150 people, including former senior Fallschirmjäger officers, some who had risen to become generals in the Bundeswehr, including Hermann Plocher, Witzig's division commander in the last days of the war. Also present were the last remaining German survivors of Eben Emael, including Helmut Wenzel. The bond between the former paratroopers proved stronger than the tension over a Knight's Cross that divided them. After the funeral the participants went to the officers' mess of the Engineer School in Munich, Rudolf Witzig's last posting, for coffee.

> Eben Emael was a small part of his life [remembers Jürgen Witzig]. He was interested in many facets of life and was very involved. He read and wrote extensively, was an expert in many fields, and had a broad outlook of the world. He was my idol and I miss him very much.[44]

NOTES

Chapter 1: *A Child of War*

1. Rudolf Witzig, 'Rudolf Friedrich Witzig', *Ahnen-tafel Witzig mit Anlagen*.
2. Holger H. Herwig, *The First World War. Germany and Austria-Hungary 1914–1918*, pp. 295–6.
3. Rudolf Witzig, 'Rudolf Friedrich Witzig', *Ahnen-tafel Witzig mit Anlagen*.
4. Ibid.
5. Rudolf Witzig, 'Amanda Henriette Adolphine Ziehn', *Ahnen-tafel Witzig mit Anlagen*.
6. Rudolf Witzig, 'Rudolf Friedrich Witzig', *Ahnen-tafel Witzig mit Anlagen*.
7. Rudolf Witzig, 'Rudolf Witzig', *Ahnen-tafel Witzig mit Anlagen*.
8. Rudolf Witzig, 'Amanda Henriette Adolphine Ziehn', *Ahnen-tafel Witzig mit Anlagen*.
9. Ibid.
10. Ibid.
11. Ibid.
12. Evans, *The Coming of the Third Reich*, pp. 389–90.
13. Ibid., p. 83.
14. Kennedy, *The German Campaign in Poland (1939)*, p. 3.
15. Ibid., pp. 17–19.
16. Metelmann, *A Hitler Youth*, pp. 53–4.
17. Ibid., p. 54.
18. Ibid., p. 80.
19. Rudolf Witzig, 'Rudolf Witzig', *Ahnen-tafel Witzig mit Anlagen*.
20. 'Bündische Jugend', in Kirk, *Cassell's Dictionary of Modern German History*, p. 73; Kater, *Hitler Youth*, p. 16.
21. 'Deutsches Jungvolk', in Kirk, *Cassell's Dictionary of Modern German History*, p. 96.
22. Kater, *Hitler Youth*, p. 19.
23. Rudolf Witzig, 'Rudolf Witzig', *Ahnen-tafel Witzig mit Anlagen*.
24. Bessel, *Nazism and War*, p. 28. The Nazi Party also managed to attract workers, Catholics, women, urban dwellers and the older in greater numbers than any other political party in Germany had done previously.
25. Kater, *The Nazi Party. A Social Profile of Members and Leaders 1919–1945*, p. 44.
26. Jürgen Witzig to Gilberto Villahermosa, 'Rudolf Witzig', 23 August 2005.
27. Villahermosa, 'Interview with Colonel Jürgen Witzig', 31 March 2005; Villahermosa, 'Interview with Hanna and Jürgen Witzig', 14 May 2005.

Chapter 2: *Fallschirmjäger*

1. Müller-Hillebrand, *Das Heer 1933–1945*, Vol. 1, p. 253.
2. Parker, *Monte Cassino*, p. 46.
3. Kennedy, *The German Campaign in Poland (1939)*, p. 23.
4. *Technical Manual E 30-451 Handbook on German Military Forces*, p. I-4.
5. Kennedy, *The German Campaign in Poland (1939)*, p. 22.
6. Ibid., p. 75.
7. Showalter, *Patton and Rommel. Men of War in the Twentieth Century*, p. 159.

8. Hart, Hart and Hughes, *The German Soldier in World War II*, p. 8.
9. Ibid., p. 9.
10. *TM E 30-451 Handbook on German Military Forces*, p. I-75.
11. 'Rhineland, demilitarization of the', Tim Kirk, *Cassell's Dictionary of Modern German History*, pp. 287–8.
12. *TM E 30-451 Handbook on German Military Forces*, p. I-75.
13. Rudolf Witzig, 'Hanna Witzig', *Ahnen-tafel Witzig mit Anlagen*.
14. McNab, *German Paratroopers. The Illustrated History of the Fallschirmjäger in World War II*, p. 19.
15. 'Bruno Oswald Bräuer', in Kurowski, *Knights of the Wehrmacht: Knight's Cross Holders of the Fallschirmjäger*, p. 33.
16. *Gespräch mit Rudolf Witzig Am 14 September 2001*.
17. *Department of the Army Pamphlet No. 20-232 Airborne Operations. A German Appraisal*, p. 2.
18. 'Kurt Student', in Hildebrand, *Die Generale der Deutschen Luftwaffe*, Vol. 3, pp. 363-5; Farrar Hockley, *Student*.
19. Kuhn, *German Paratroopers in World War II*, p. 18.
20. *Airborne Operations. A German Appraisal*, p. 5.
21. Kuhn, *German Paratroopers in World War II*, p. 16
22. Otway, *The Second World War 1939–1945: Army Airborne Forces*, pp. 6–7.
23. Von der Heydte, *Daedalus Returned*, p. 25.
24. Ibid., p. 26.
25. Ibid.
26. McNab, *German Paratroopers*, p. 26.
27. Pöppel, *Heaven and Hell: The War Diary of a German Paratrooper*, p. 10.
28. Parker, *Monte Cassino*, p. 248.
29. Ibid.
30. McNab, *German Paratroopers*, p. 28.
31. Ibid., pp. 30–1.
32. McGuirl and Feist, *Fallschirmjäger*, pp. 12–13.
33. Forty, *Battle of Crete*, p. 47; Lagarde, *German Soldiers of World War II*, pp. 14–15.
34. 'Richard Heidrich', in Kurowski, *Knights of the Wehrmacht*, p. 83.
35. *Gespräch mit Rudolf Witzig Am 14 September 2001*.
36. Maier *et al.*, *German and the Second World War, Vol. II: Germany's Initial Conquests in Europe*, pp. 90, 101, 123; Kennedy, *The German Campaign in Poland (1939)*, pp. 88, 125.
37. Kuhn, *German Paratroopers in World War II*, p. 20.
38. *Gespräch mit Rudolf Witzig Am 14 September 2001*.
39. 'Walter Koch', in Kurowski, *Knights of the Wehrmacht*, p. 117.
40. Kuhn, *German Paratroopers in World War II*, p. 21.

Chapter 3: Eben Emael
1. *Department of the Army Publication No. 20-271 The German Northern Theater of Operations 1940–1945*, pp. 3–17.
2. Vliegen, *Fort Eben Emael*, p. 23.
3. Ibid., p. 23.
4. Le Comité de l'Amicale du Fort D'Eben-Emael, *Ceux du Fort D'Eben Emael*, pp. 9–11; Vliegen, *Fort Eben Emael*, pp. 29–30.
5. Vliegen, *Fort Eben Emael*, pp. 24, 46; *Ceux du Fort D'Eben Emael*, p. 19 3n.
6. *Ceux du Fort D'Eben Emael*, pp. 123–4.
7. Vliegen, *Fort Eben Emael*, pp. 29–30.
8. Ibid.
9. Kuhn, *German Paratroopers in World War II*, p. 21.
10. Kuhn, *German Paratroopers in World War II*, p. 21.
11. U.S. Army Center of Military History, *Attack on Eben Emael by Oberst a. D. Rudolf Witzig*, pp. 20–1.
12. U.S. Army Center of Military History, *Attack on Eben Emael*, pp. 2–3.
13. Ibid., p. 3.

14. Ibid., pp. 21–2.
15. Ibid., p. 4.
16. Ibid., p. 5.
17. Ibid., pp. 5–6.
18. War Diary, Sturmabteilung Koch der Flieger-Division 7, Witzig Collection.
19. Ibid.
20. Ibid.
21. Witzig, 'Coup from the air; the capture of Fort Eben Emael', *History of the Second World War*, Part 4, p. 109.
22. U.S. Army Center of Military History, *Attack on Eben Emael*, p. 8.
23. Ibid. pp. 23–4.
24. Ibid., p. 8.
25. Ibid., p. 23.
26. Ibid., p. 18
27. *Gespräch mit Rudolf Witzig Am 14 September 2001*
28. U.S. Army Center of Military History, *Attack on Eben Emael*, p. 9.
29. Ibid., pp. 9–10.
30. Ibid., pp. 10–11.
31. Ibid., p. 11.
32. Ibid., p. 12.
33. Ibid., pp. 14–15.
34. Witzig, 'Coup from the air,' p. 109.
35. *Gespräch mit Rudolf Witzig Am 14 September 2001.*
36. Ibid.
37. Witzig, 'Coup from the air', p. 109.
38. Ibid.
39. Nowarra, *German Gliders.*
40. War Diary, Sturmabteilung Koch der Flieger-Division 7, Witzig Collection
41. U.S. Army Center of Military History, *Attack on Eben Emael*, p. 17.
42. Witzig, 'Coup from the air', p. 109.
43. U.S. Army Center of Military History, *Attack on Eben Emael*, pp. 17–18.
44. Ibid., p. 18.
45. Below, *At Hitler's Side*, p. 57.
46. *Gespräch mit Rudolf Witzig Am 14 September 2001*
47. Kuhn, *German Paratroopers in World War II*, p. 33.
48. Ibid.
49. *Gespräch mit Rudolf Witzig Am 14 September 2001*
50. Witzig, 'Coup from the air', p. 109.
51. *Gespräch mit Rudolf Witzig Am 14 September 2001*
52. Witzig, 'Coup from the air', p. 109.
53. Ibid.
54. U.S. Army Center of Military History, *Attack on Eben Emael*, p. 50.
55. *Gespräch mit Rudolf Witzig Am 14 September 2001*
56. Witzig, 'Coup from the air', p. 109.
57. *Gespräch mit Rudolf Witzig Am 14 September 2001*
58. U.S. Army Center of Military History, *Attack on Eben Emael*, p. 46.
59. Witzig, 'Coup from the air', pp. 109–10.
60. Ibid., p. 110.
61. *Ceux du Fort D'Eben Emael*
62. Vliegen, *Fort Eben Emael*, p. 43.
63. U.S. Army Center of Military History, *Attack on Eben Emael*, p. 47.
64. Witzig, 'Coup from the air', p. 109.
65. U.S. Army Center of Military History, *Attack on Eben Emael*, pp. 49–50.
66. Witzig, 'Coup from the air: the capture of Fort Eben Emael', *History of the Second World War*, Second Edition, Part 4, p. 11.
67. Ibid., pp. 110–11.
68. Official Report of Captain Rudolf Witzig, 'Albert-Kanal und Eben-Emael', reprinted in *Der Deutsche Fallschirmjäger*, No. 1, January 1961, pp. 11–12.

69. Witzig, 'Coup from the air; the capture of Fort Eben-Emael', p. 111.
70. U.S. Army Center of Military History, *Attack on Eben Emael*, p. 46.
71. Villahermosa, 'Interview with Colonel Jürgen Witzig', 27 May 2004.
72. Witzig, 'Coup from the air', p. 110–11.
73. U.S. Army Center of Military History, *Attack on Eben Emael*, pp. 51–2.
74. De Vos, *La Belgique et la Seconde Guerre Mondiale*, p. 58–9.
75. Ibid.
76. Witzig, 'Coup from the air', p. 110–11.
77. Kuhn, *German Paratroopers in World War II*, p. 47.
78. See, for example, Mrazek, *The Fall of Eben Emael.*
79. *Airborne Operations. A German Appraisal*, p. 18.
80. Ibid., p. 17.
81. Brongers, *The Battle for the Hague, 1940*, pp. 267–8.
82. U.S. Department of the Army, *MS # P-105 Evaluation of German Airborne Operations by Hellmuth Reinhardt, Generalmajor a. D.*, p. 42.
83. Ibid., p. 48.
84. U.S. Army Center of Military History, *Attack on Eben Emael*, p. 43.
85. *Airborne Operations. A German Appraisal*, pp. 18–19.
86. Villahermosa, 'Interview with Hanna and Jürgen Witzig'.
87. Ibid.

Chapter 4: *Crete*

1. *MS # P-105 Evaluation of German Airborne Operations*, p. 87.
2. Weinberg, *A World at Arms*, p. 678n.
3. *MS # P-105 Evaluation of German Airborne Operations*, p. 21.
4. Ibid., p. 88 35n
5. *MS # P-105 Evaluation of German Airborne Operations*, p. 88 35n
6. Weinberg, *A World at Arms*, pp. 88–90.
7. Department of the Army, *ETHINT 31 – An Interview with Reichsmarshall Hermann Goering. German Military Strategy (1939–1941)*, pp. 9–10.
8. Villahermosa, 'Interview with Hanna and Jürgen Witzig'
9. Trevor Roper, *Hitler's War Directives 1939–1945*, pp. 82–3.
10. U.S. Department of the Army, *MS # C-065 Operation Felix by Helmuth Greiner*, p. 20
11. Harclerode, *Wings of War. Airborne Warfare 1918–1945*, p. 58; *MS # P-105 Evaluation of German Airborne Operations*, pp. 47–8.
12. 'Eugen Meindl', in Hildebrand, *Die Generale der deutschen Luftwaffe*, vol. 2, pp. 372–3; 'Eugen Meindl', in Kurowski, *Knights of the Wehrmacht*, p. 145.
13. Playfair., *History of the Second World War. The Mediterranean and Middle East*, Vol. 2: *The Germans Come to the Help of Their Ally (1941)*, p. 128.
14. *Gespräch mit Rudolf Witzig Am 14 September 2001*
15. Department of the Army, *Pamphlet 20-260 The German Campaigns in the Balkans (Spring 1941)*, p.121; Forty, *Battle of Crete*, p. 14.
16. Department of the Army, *MS # B-646 Capture of Crete (May 1941) by Julius Ringel, General der Gebirgstruppen a.D.*, p. 22.
17. 'Alexander Löhr', in Hildebrand, *Die Generale der deutschen Luftwaffe*, vol. 2, pp. 307–8.
18. Playfair, *The Germans Come to the Help of Their Ally*, p. 129.
19. Ibid., pp. 128–9.
20. Nasse, *Green Devils! German Paratroopers 1939–45*, p. 20.
21. *MS # B-646 Capture of Crete*, p. 29.
22. Kuhn, *German Paratroopers in World War II*, pp. 64–5.
23. Von der Heydte, 'Crete: The German Viewpoint', *History of the Second World War*, Part 18, p. 502.
24. Cunningham, Commander-in-Chief Mediterranean, 'The Battle of Crete', *Supplement to the London Gazette*, 24 May 1948, p. 3105.
25. MacDonald, *The Lost Battle*, p. 149.
26. Ibid, p. 153; Forty, *Battle of Crete*, p. 7.

27. Cunningham, 'The Battle of Crete', p. 3105.
28. U.S. Military Intelligence Service, 'Rations as a Factor in Parachute Efficiency', *Intelligence Bulletin*, June 1944.
29. U.S. Military Intelligence Service, 'Parachutists (German)', *Intelligence Bulletin*, September 1942.
30. *MS # B-646 Capture of Crete*, p. 30.
31. Kuhn, *German Paratroopers in World War II*, p. 70.
32. Ibid.
33. *Gespräch mit Rudolf Witzig Am 14 September 2001*
34. *MS # B-646 Capture of Crete*, p. 26.
35. Ibid., pp. 46–7.
36. Nasse, *Green Devils!* p. 44.
37. Lagarde, 'Paratrooper, Crete, 1941', in *German Soldiers of World War II*, pp. 14–15.
38. 'Parachutists (German)', *Intelligence Bulletin*, September 1942; 'Parachute Troops (German)'; U.S. Military Intelligence Service, *Intelligence Bulletin*, May 1943.
39. Ibid., p. 47.
40. Davin, Appendix IV: Summary Strength of All British and Greek Forces in Crete, 20 May 1941, *Official History of New Zealand in the Second World War 1939–45. Crete*, p. 480.
41. Davin, *Crete*, p. 123.
42. Beevor, *Crete*, p. 111.
43. Davin, 'Battle of Crete, Phase 1', *History of the Second World War*, Part 18, p. 486.
44. *Gespräch mit Rudolf Witzig Am 14 September 2001*
45. MacDonald, *The Lost Battle. Crete 1941*, p. 175
46. Forty, *Battle of Crete*, p. 9.
47. *The German Campaign in the Balkans*, p. 130.
48. Ibid., p. 132.
49. *MS # B-646 Capture of Crete*, p. 40.
50. 'Bernard Ramcke', in Hildebrand, *Die Generale der deutschen Luftwaffe*, vol. 3, pp. 76–7; 'Bernard Hermann Ramcke', in Kurowski, *Knights of the Wehrmacht*, p. 175.
51. *MS # B-646 Capture of Crete*, p. 44.
52. *Gespräch mit Rudolf Witzig Am 14 September 2001*
53. *MS # B-646 Capture of Crete*, p. 68.
54. Forty, 'Chronology of Major Events', *Battle of Crete*, pp. 9–10.
55. *MS # B-646 Capture of Crete*, p. 101.

Chapter 5: *The Spearhead Shattered*

1. Kuhn, *German Paratroopers*, p. 131.
2. *The German Campaign in the Balkans*, p. 147.
3. 'Wolfgang Lebrecht Graf Blücher', in Kurowski, *Knights of the Wehrmacht*, p. 27; Beevor, *Crete*, pp. 177–8.
4. *MS # B-646 Capture of Crete*, p. 105.
5. Department of the Army, *MS # C-100 Der Deutsche Feldzug in Griechenland und Auf Kreta by E. Mueller-Hillerbrand, Generalmajor a.D.*, p. 61.
6. *MS # B-646 Capture of Crete*, p. 104.
7. 'Eine Insel wird aus der Luft erobert', *Der Deutsche Fallschirmjäger*, No 5. May 1961, p. 7.
8. *MS # B-646 Capture of Crete*, p. 34.
9. Ibid., p. 103; The German authors of *MS # P-105 Evaluation of German Airborne Operations* cite a figure of 260 aircraft.
10. Department of the Army, *MS # B-250 Answers to the Questions Concerning Greece, Crete and Russia by General Warlimont*, p. 1.
11. *ETHINT 31 – An Interview with Reichsmarshall Hermann Goering*, p. 11.
12. Schrieber *et al.*, *Germany and the Second World War*, Vol. III:

The Mediterranean and South-east Europe, and North Africa 1939–1941, p. 552.

13. Pöppel, *Heaven and Hell*, p. 67
14. Churchill, *The Grand Alliance*, p. 301.
15. Ibid., p. 302.
16. Davin, Appendix V: Casualties, *Crete*, p. 486; *The German Campaign in the Balkans*, p. 139.
17. Ibid., Appendix VI: Summary of Strength of All British and Greek Forces in Crete, 20 May 1941, p. 480.
18. *Gespräch mit Rudolf Witzig Am 14 September 2001*
19. Ibid., p. 145.
20. *The German Campaign in the Balkans*, pp. 144–7.
21. *Gespräch mit Rudolf Witzig Am 14 September 2001*
22. *The German Campaign in the Balkans*, p. 147.
23. Von der Heydte, *Daedalus Returned*, pp. 180–1.
24. *Airborne Operations. A German Appraisal*, p. 19.
25. Von der Heydte, 'Crete: The German Viewpoint', p. 504.
26. Ibid.
27. *Gespräch mit Rudolf Witzig Am 14 September 2001*
28. *Airborne Operations. A German Appraisal*, p. 13.
29. Von der Heydte, 'Crete: The German Viewpoint', p. 504.
30. See Thomas Fleming, 'The Man Who Saved Korea', in Cowley, *The Cold War: A Military History*, p. 109.
31. *MS # B-646 Capture of Crete*, p. 101.
32. Schrieber *et al.*, *Germany and the Second World War*, Vol. III: *The Mediterranean and South-east Europe, and North Africa*, p. 552.
33. Villahermosa, 'Interview with Hanna and Jürgen Witzig',
34. See 'German Manpower. A Study of the Employment of German Manpower from 1933–1945', in *MS # P-105 Evaluation of German Airborne Operations*, p. 19.
35. Burdick and Jacobsen, eds., *The Halder War Diary 1939–1942*, entry for 3 July 1941, p. 446.
36. Ibid., entry for 29 August 1941, p. 521.
37. Weinberg, *A World at Arms*, p. 284.
38. 'Erich Petersen', in Hildebrand, *Die Generale der deutschen Luftwaffe*, Vol. 3, pp. 23–4.
39. Kuhn, *German Paratroopers*, pp. 133–8.
40. 'Richard Heidrich', in Hildebrand, *Die Generale der deutschen Luftwaffe*, Vol. 2, pp. 47–8.
41. *Ahnen-tafel Witzig mit Anlagen.*
42. Ibid.
43. 'RAD', in Kirk, *Cassell's Dictionary of Modern German History*, p. 272.
44. *Ahnen-tafel Witzig mit Anlagen.*
45. Ibid.
46. Villahermosa, 'Interview with Hanna and Jürgen Witzig'
47. Engel, *At the Heart of the Reich*, p. 82.
48. Witzig, *Das Korps Fallschirm-Pionierbataillon und I./Fallschirm-Pionierregiment 21.*

Chapter 6: *North Africa: First Battles*
1. *MS # P-105 Evaluation of German Airborne Operations*, p. 20.
2. Ibid., pp. 51–5.
3. *MS # P-105 Evaluation of German Airborne Operations*, pp. 90–1.
4. *MS # D-094 Preparations for the Capture of Malta by Conrad Seibt General Major*, p. 2; *Kesselring's Plan for the Invasion of Malta, 31 May 1942*, RG 549, NARA, pp. 2–7.
5. *MS # P-105 Evaluation of German Airborne Operations*, p. 91.
6. *MS # D-094 Preparations for the Capture of Malta*, p. 2; *Kesselring's Plan for the Invasion of Malta, 31 May 1942*, pp. 2–7.

7. Ibid.
8. *MS # P-105 Evaluation of German Airborne Operations*, pp. 92–4.
9. Holland, *Fortress Malta*, p. 265.
10. Ibid., pp. 280–1.
11. *The Future of German Paratrooper and Airborne Operations. A Report Addressed to Goering by General Student, 10 November 1942*, RG 549, NARA.
12. Ibid.
13. Witzig, *Das Korps Fallschirm-Pionierbataillon und I./Fallschirm-Pionierregiment 21*.
14. Ibid, p. 3.
15. 'El Alamein', in Dear and Foot, *The Oxford Companion to World War II*, pp. 326–8.
16. Witzig, *Das Korps Fallschirm-Pionierbataillon und I./Fallschirm-Pionierregiment 21*.
17. Howe, *United States Army in World War II. The Mediterranean Theater of Operations. Northwest Africa: Seizing the Initiative in the West*, pp. 3–4.
18. Ibid., p. 21.
19. Schrieber *et al.*, *Germany and the Second World War, Vol VI: The Global War*, pp. 792–3.
20. *ETHINT 31 – An Interview with Reichsmarshall Hermann Goering*, p. 8.
21. *MS # D-066 Situation in OKW (October–December 1942) by Generalmajor Christian Eckhard*, p. 4.
22. Ibid., p. 6.
23. Ibid., p. 7.
24. Schrieber *et al.*, *The Global War*, p. 794.
25. Playfair, *The Destruction of the Axis Forces in Africa*, pp. 170–1.
26. Schrieber *et al.*, *The Global War*, pp. 792–3; Farrar-Hockley, 'The Follow-Up to Torch', *History of the Second World War*, Vol. 3, No. 41, p. 1140.
27. *MS # P-105 Evaluation of German Airborne Operations*, p. 84.
28. Schrieber *et al.*, *The Global War*, pp. 792–3; Farrar-Hockley, 'The Follow-Up to Torch', p. 1140.
29. 'Walter Koch', in Kurowski, *Knights of the Wehrmacht*, p. 117.
30. Nasse, *Green Devils!*, p. 72.
31. *Gespräch mit Rudolf Witzig Am 14 September 2001*
32. War Office, 'Corps Parachute Engineer Company', *Pocket Book of the German Army 1943*, p. 104, Table 60.
33. Witzig, *F.Pi.11. Am Div. v. Broich E.O., 11 Januar 1943*, p. 1.
34. Witzig, *Das Korps Fallschirm-Pionierbataillon und I./Fallschirm-Pionierregiment 21*.
35. Nasse, *Green Devils!*, p. 72.
36. Ibid., p. 72.
37. Wenzel, *Auszug aus dem Kriegstagebuch von Helmut Wenzel Einsatz Tunesien, 16 November 1942 – 23 February 1943*, p. 1.
38. *MS # D-147 The First Phase of the Battle in Tunisia by Walter Nehring, General der Panzer-Truppe a. D.*, p. 1.
39. Ibid, pp. 1–2.
40. Ibid., p. 8.
41. Howe, *Northwest Africa: Seizing the Initiative in the West*, p. 286, 286n.
42. Nasse, *Green Devils!*, p. 72.
43. Anderson, 'Operations in North West Africa', p. 5463.
44. U.S. War Department, 'Germany's Replacement Army May be in Last Battle', *Tactical and Technical Trends*, No. 51, October 1944.
45. *MS # D-147 The First Phase of the Battle in Tunisia by Walter Nehring*, p. 3.
46. *MS # C-098 Recollections of Tunisia by General Hans Jürgen von Arnim*, p. 121.
47. Playfair, *The Destruction of the Axis Forces in Africa*, p. 172.
48. *MS # C-098 Recollections of Tunisia by General Hans Jürgen von Arnim*, p. 121.
49. Anderson, 'Operations in North West Africa', pp. 5453, 5463.
50. *MS # C-098 Recollections of Tunisia by General Hans Jürgen von Arnim*, p. 10.

51. Anderson, 'Operations in North West Africa', p. 5452.
52. Ibid., pp. 5450–1.
53. Witzig, *Das Korps Fallschirm-Pionierbataillon und I./Fallschirm-Pionierregiment 21.*
54. Witzig, *F.Pi.11. Am Div. v. Broich E.O., 11 Januar 1943.*
55. Villahermosa, 'Interview with Matthias Scheurer', 27 August, 2005.
56. Witzig, *Das Korps Fallschirm-Pionierbataillon und I./Fallschirm-Pionierregiment 21.*
57. Ibid.
58. Ferrar-Hockley, 'The Follow-Up to Torch'.
59. Wenzel, *Auszug aus dem Kriegstagebuch von Helmut Wenzel Einsatz Tunesien*, entry for 18 Nov. 1942.
60. Witzig, *F.Pi.11. Am Div. v. Broich E.O., 11 Januar 1943.*
61. Anderson, 'Operations in North West Africa', p. 5453.
62. Witzig, *F.Pi.11. Am Div. v. Broich E.O., 11 Januar 1943.*
63. Wenzel, *Auszug aus dem Kriegstagebuch von Helmut Wenzel Einsatz Tunesien*, entry for 19 Nov. 1942.
64. Witzig, *F.Pi.11. Am Div. v. Broich E.O., 11 Januar 1943.*
65. Harclerode, *Wings of War*, pp. 20–1.
66. Villahermosa, 'Interview with Matthias Scheurer'.
67. Witzig, *F.Pi.11. Am Div. v. Broich E.O., 11 Januar 1943.*
68. Witzig, *F.Pi.11. Am Div. v. Broich E.O., 11 Januar 1943*; Witzig, *Das Korps Fallschirm-Pionierbataillon und I./Fallschirm-Pionierregiment 21.*
69. Nasse, *Green Devils!*, p. 74.
70. 'S-Mine', *TM-E 30-451 Handbook on German Military Forces*, pp. 486–7.
71. Nasse, *Green Devils!*, p. 74.
72. Ibid., pp. 74, 76.
73. Witzig, *F.Pi.11. Am Div. v. Broich E.O., 11 Januar 1943*; Witzig, *Das Korps Fallschirm-Pionierbataillon und I./Fallschirm-Pionierregiment 21.*
74. Anderson, 'Operations in North West Africa', p. 5450.
75. Witzig, *F.Pi.11. Am Div. v. Broich E.O., 11 Januar 1943.*
76. Atkinson, *An Army at Dawn*, p. 213.

Chapter 7: *North Africa: To the Last Man*
1. Atkinson, *An Army at Dawn*, pp. 239–40.
2. Witzig, *Das Korps Fallschirm-Pionierbataillon und I./Fallschirm-Pionierregiment 21.*
3. Weinberg, *A World at Arms*, p. xvi.
4. Witzig, *Das Korps Fallschirm-Pionierbataillon und I./Fallschirm-Pionierregiment 21*, p. 4.
5. Nasse, *Green Devils!*, p. 75.
6. Witzig, *F.Pi.11. Am Div. v. Broich E.O., 11 Januar 1943.*
7. *MS # P-105 Evaluation of German Airborne Operations*, p. 83.
8. Nasse, *Green Devils!*, p. 78.
9. 'Tellermine', *TM-E 30-451 Handbook on German Military Forces*, pp. 491–2.
10. Witzig, *F.Pi.11. Am Div. v. Broich E.O., 11 Januar 1943*; *Handbook of the German Army 1940*, pp. 135–6.
11. Nasse, *Green Devils!*, p. 75.
12. Witzig, *F.Pi.11. Am Div. v. Broich E.O., 11 Januar 1943.*
13. Ibid.
14. Ibid.
15. Witzig, *Das Korps Fallschirm-Pionierbataillon und I./Fallschirm-Pionierregiment 21.*
16. Ibid.
17. Witzig, *F.Pi.11. Am Div. v. Broich E.O., 11 Januar 1943.*
18. Villahermosa, 'Interview with Hanna and Jürgen Witzig'.
19. Hart, Hart and Hughes, *The German Soldier in World War II*, p. 16.
20. Witzig, *F.Pi.11. Am Div. v. Broich E.O., 11 Januar 1943.*

21. Ibid.
22. Witzig, *Das Korps Fallschirm-Pionierbataillon und I./Fallschirm-Pionierregiment 21*.
23. Witzig, *F.Pi.11. Am Div. v. Broich E.O., 11 Januar 1943*.
24. Ibid.
25. Ibid.
26. Ibid.
27. *MS # C-098 Recollections of Tunisia by General Hans Jürgen von Arnim*, p. 19.
28. Anderson, 'Operations in North West Africa', pp. 5463–4.
29. *MS # P-105 Evaluation of German Airborne Operations*, p. 49.
30. Anderson, 'Operations in North West Africa', p. 5464.
31. *MS # C-098 Recollections of Tunisia*, p. 10.
32. Ibid.
33. Ibid, p. 6.
34. *MS # B-270 Questions Regarding the General Strategy During the Italian Campaign by Field Marshal Kesselring and General Westphal*, p. 49.
35. Ibid., p. 51.
36. Ibid., pp. 51–2.
37. Ibid., pp. 53–4.
38. Witzig, *F.Pi.11. Am Div. v. Broich E.O., 11 Januar 1943*.
39. Ibid.
40. Earl Ziemke, 'Stalingrad, Battle of', in Dear and Foot, *The Oxford Companion to World War II*, pp. 1057–9.
41. Ziemke and Bauer, *Moscow to Stalingrad. Decision in the East*, p. 501.
42. Beevor, *Stalingrad*, p. 398.
43. Trevor-Roper, *Final Entries 1945: The Diaries of Joseph Goebbels*, p. xxiii.
44. Warlimont, *Inside Hitler's Headquarters*, p. 267.
45. Schramm, *Hitler: The Man and Military Leader*, p. 27.
46. Macksey, *Kesselring*, p. 132.
47. Witzig, *F.Pi.11. Am Div. v. Broich E.O., 11 Januar 1943*.
48. Witzig, *Das Korps Fallschirm-Pionierbataillon und I./Fallschirm-Pionierregiment 21*.
49. Ibid., p. 6.
50. Ibid.
51. Ibid.
52. Witzig, 'Ernst-Georg Witzig', *Ahnen-tafel Witzig mit Anlagen*.
53. Witzig, *Das Korps Fallschirm-Pionierbataillon und I./Fallschirm-Pionierregiment 21*.
54. Ibid., pp. 6–7.
55. Ibid., p. 7.
56. Entry of 7 May 1943, in Lochner, *The Goebbels Diaries*, pp. 394–5.
57. Warlimont, *Inside Hitler's Headquarters*, p. 313.
58. Anderson, 'Operations in North West Africa', p. 5462.
59. Churchill, *The Second World War*, Vol. 4: *The Hinge of Fate*, p. 780.
60. 'May 9, 1943', in Lochner, *The Goebbels Diaries*, p. 405.
61. Warlimont, *Inside Hitler's Headquarters*, pp. 332–3.
62. Playfair, *The Destruction of the Axis Forces in Africa*, p. 460.
63. Villahermosa, 'Interview with Matthias Scheurer', 27 August 2005.
64. Rudolf Witzig's name is not found on a database of some 11 million Nazi Party members held at the U.S. National Archives and Records Administration.
65. Witzig, *Das Korps Fallschirm-Pionierbataillon und I./Fallschirm-Pionierregiment 21*.
66. Stimpel, *Die deutsche Fallschirmtruppe 1942–1945. Einsätze auf Kriegsschauplätzen im Süden*, p. 136. This includes the men of the *Hermann Göring* Division.
67. Witzig, *Das Korps Fallschirm-Pionierbataillon und I./Fallschirm-Pionierregiment 21*.
68. Ibid.

69. *MS # P-105 Evaluation of German Airborne Operations*, pp. 16–18.

Chapter 8: *From Partisans to the Red Army*

1. Weinberg, *A World at Arms*, pp. 602–3; Dupuy and Martell, *Great Battles of the Eastern Front*, pp. 79, 91–5; Krivosheev, *Soviet Casualties and Combat Losses in the Twentieth Century*, pp. 132–3.
2. Eberle and Uhl, *The Hitler Book*, p. 119.
3. *Gespräch mit Rudolf Witzig Am 14 September 2001*
4. Witzig, *Das Korps Fallschirm-Pionierbataillon und I./Fallschirm-Pionierregiment 21.*
5. Villahermosa, 'Interview with Karl-Heinz Hammerschlag', 27 August 2005.
6. Witzig, *Das Korps Fallschirm-Pionierbataillon und I./Fallschirm-Pionierregiment 21.*
7. Villahermosa, 'Interview with Karl-Heinz Hammerschlag', 27 August 2005.
8. Witzig, *Das Korps Fallschirm-Pionierbataillon und I./Fallschirm-Pionierregiment 21.*
9. 'Overlord', in Dear and Foot, *The Oxford Companion to World War II*, pp. 848–53; Man, *The D-Day Atlas*, p. 43.
10. Kuhn, *German Paratroopers*, pp. 208–9; Stimpel, *Die deutsche Fallschirmtruppe 1942–1945*, p. 586
11. Ustinov *et al.*, *Istoriya Vtoroi Mirovoi Boiny 1939–1945*, Vol. 10: *Osvobozhedenie Territorii SSSR I Evropeiskikh Stran. Voina na Tikhoi Okeane i v Azii*, pp. 42–7.
12. Carlo D'Este, 'Model', in Correlli Barnett ed., *Hitler's Generals*, p. 319.
13. Appendix D: Directive No. 51, Fuehrer Headquarters, 3 November 1943, Harrison, *United States Army in World War II. The European Theater of Operations. Cross Channel Attack*, p. 464.
14. Weinberg, *A World at Arms*, p. 667.
15. Witzig, *Das Korps Fallschirm-Pionierbataillon und I./Fallschirm-Pionierregiment 21*, p. 39.
16. 'Gerhart Schirmer', in Kurowski, *Knights of the Wehrmacht*, p. 203.
17. Stimpel, *Die deutsche Fallschirmtruppe 1942–1945*, p. 298.
18. Kuhn, *German Paratroopers in World War II*, p. 236; Witzig, *Das Korps Fallschirm-Pionierbataillon und I./Fallschirm-Pionierregiment 21*, p. 39.
19. Haupt, *Army Group Center: The Wehrmacht in Russia 1941–1945*, p. 205
20. Stimpel, *Die deutsche Fallschirmtruppe 1942–1945*, p. 299.
21. Ustinov, *Osvobozhedenie Territorii SSSR I Evropeiskikh Stran*, p. 57.
22. Haupt, *Army Group Center*, p. 205
23. Stimpel, *Die deutsche Fallschirmtruppe 1942–1945*, p. 303; Witzig, *Das Korps Fallschirm-Pionierbataillon und I./Fallschirm-Pionierregiment 21*, pp. 39–40.
24. Ibid.
25. Villahermosa, 'Interview with Karl-Heinz Hammerschlag', 27 August 2005.
26. Witzig, *Das Korps Fallschirm-Pionierbataillon und I./Fallschirm-Pionierregiment 21.*
27. Fellgiebel, *Elite of the Third Reich*, p. 34.
28. Witzig, *Das Korps Fallschirm-Pionierbataillon und I./Fallschirm-Pionierregiment 21*, p. 39.
29. 'Panzerfaust' and 'Panzerschreck', *TM-E 30-451 Handbook on German Military Forces*, pp. 318–19.
30. In three weeks of fighting in Middle Franconia some 300 American vehicles fell victim to German soldiers and Hitler Youth wielding Panzerfausts. See Fritz, *Endkampf: Soldiers, Civilians, and The Death of the Third Reich*, p. 94.
31. Witzig, *Das Korps Fallschirm-Pionierbataillon und I./Fallschirm-Pionierregiment 21.*
32. Ibid., pp. 40–1.
33. Ibid., p. 41.
34. Ibid., pp. 40–1.
35. Ibid., p. 43.

36. Ibid., p. 45.
37. Ibid.
38. Ibid., p. 47.
39. Witzig, *Das Korps Fallschirm-Pionierbataillon und I./Fallschirm-Pionierregiment 21*; Stimpel, *Die deutsche Fallschirmtruppe 1942–1945*, p. 305.
40. Villahermosa, 'Interview with Karl-Heinz Hammerschlag', 27 August 2005.
41. Witzig, *Das Korps Fallschirm-Pionierbataillon und I./Fallschirm-Pionierregiment 21*
42. *Gespräch mit Rudolf Witzig Am 14 September 2001*
43. Overmans, *Deutsche militärische Verluste im Zweiten Weltkrieg*, pp. 278–9.
44. Warlimont, *Inside Hitler's Headquarters*, p. 467.
45. Krivosheev, *Soviet Casualties and Combat Losses*, pp. 145–6.
46. Goerlitz, *History of the German General Staff 1657–1945*, p. 489.
47. Merridale, *Ivan's War*, p. 260.

Chapter 9: *Holland: 'No Longer War'*

1. *MS # A-964, MS # A-965 Report of the Chief of Staff Army Group B (25 January 1945 – 21 March 1945) by General Major Carl Wagener*, p. 53.
2. Schramm, *Kriegstagebuch des Oberkommandos der Wehrmacht 1940–1945*, Vol. 7, Part I, pp. 376–88; Weinberg, *A World at Arms*, p. 750.
3. Ellis, *History of the Second World War. Victory in the West*, Vol. II: *The Defeat of Germany*, p. 10, 10n.
4. Ibid, p. 11.
5. Yeide, *The Longest Battle*, p. 7.
6. Weinberg, *A World at Arms*, p. 578.
7. *MS # B-701 Summary of A Gp B Engagements From the Middle of Oct 44 Until the Middle of Apr 45*, p. 2.
8. Ibid., pp. 2–3.
9. *My Opinions with Regard to Reports 1 (MS # B-238) and 2 (MS # B-348) by General Major Heuser*, p. 1.
10. Engel, *At the Heart of the Reich*, p. 96.
11. Ibid.
12. Engel, *At the Heart of the Reich*, p. 96.
13. Weinberg, *A World at Arms*, p. 466.
14. For the figure of Red Army soldiers executed during the war, see Merridale, *Ivan's War*, p. 136. The final figure for Red Army soldiers executed by the state during the war is probably, like its German counterpart, considerably higher and awaits further research by scholars. For the figure of those who died in punishment units, see Beevor and Vinogradova, *A Writer at War: Vasily Grossman with the Red Army 1941–1945*, p. 73.
15. Eberle and Uhl, *The Hitler Book*, p. 161n.
16. Shirer, *The Rise and Fall of the Third Reich*, pp. 1411–13.
17. Dallas, *1945. The War That Never Ended*, p. 372.
18. 'Blaskowitz, Johannes', in Boatner, *The Biographical Dictionary of World War II*, pp. 45–6.
19. 'Rundstedt, Karl Rudolf Gerd von', in ibid., p. 476.
20. 'Alfred Schlemm', in Hildebrand, *Die Generale der deutschen Luftwaffe*, pp. 192–3; 'Alfred Schlemm', in Kurowski, *Knights of the Wehrmacht*, p. 205; Whiting, *Hunters from the Sky*, p. 218.
21. Canadian Army Headquarters, *Report No. 19 Operation 'PLUNDER'*, p. 23.
22. Hildebrand, *Die Generale der deutschen Luftwaffe*, pp. 372–3.
23. *MS # B-084 First Parachute Army (20 Nov 44 – 21 Mar 45) by Alfred Schlemm, General of Fallschirmtruppen a. D.*, pp. 1–2.
24. *Report No. 19 Operation 'PLUNDER'*, p. 24.
25. *MS # B-084 First Parachute Army*, pp. 1–2.
26. Ibid.
27. *Airborne Operations. A German Appraisal*, p. 13.
28. *MS # A-956 Kamfhandlungen Nordfrankreich 1944 Der 6. Fallschirmjaeger*

Division by Generalleutnant von Heyking; MS # A-898 Kampfhandlungen in Nordfrankreich 1944 der 6. Fallschirmjaeger Dviision. II. Teil. Kampf an der Seine und Rueckzugsbewegungen durch Nordfrankreich by Generalleutnant von Heyking; Blumenson, *United States Army in World War II. The European Theater of Operations. Breakout and Pursuit,* pp. 498–500, 503, 575–8, 671, 683.

29. *MS # B-368 6th Parachute Division (19 Nov 44 – 10 May 45) by Rudolf Langhaeuser, Generalmajor a. D.,* p. 1.
30. *TM-E 30-451 Handbook on German Military Forces,* p. 86.
31. *MS # B-368 6th Parachute Division (19 Nov 44 – 10 May 45),* p. 1.
32. Ibid., p. 2.
33. *Report No. 19 Operation 'PLUNDER',* pp. 24–5.
34. Ibid.
35. 'Hermann Plocher', in Hildebrand, *Die Generale der deutschen Luftwaffe,* Vol. 3, pp. 46–7.
36. *Report No. 19 Operation 'PLUNDER',* p. 24.
37. *MS # B-368 6th Parachute Division (19 Nov 44 – 10 May 45),* pp. 3–5.
38. Ibid., pp. 5–6.
39. Ibid., pp. 6–7.
40. Ibid., pp. 7–8.
41. Ibid., pp. 8–9.
42. Ellis and Warhurst, *History of the Second World War, Victory in the West,* Vol. II: *The Defeat of Germany,* pp. 237–9.
43. *MS # P-105 Evaluation of German Airborne Operations,* pp. 82–3.
44. Weinberg, *A World at Arms,* pp. 239–40.
45. *MS # B-368 6th Parachute Division (19 Nov 44 – 10 May 45),* pp. 8–9.
46. Dupuy and Martell, *Great Battles of the Eastern Front,* pp. 193–209.
47. Ellis and Warhurst, *The Defeat of Germany,* p. 241.
48. *Ahnen-tafel Witzig mit Anlagen.*
49. Villahermosa, 'Interview with Hanna and Jürgen Witzig'.
50. *MS # B-084 First Parachute Army (20 Nov 44 – 21 Mar 45),* pp. 1–2.
51. Ellis and Warhurst, *The Defeat of Germany,* p. 254.
52. Ibid.
53. Hastings, *Armageddon,* p. 349.
54. *MS # B-084 First Parachute Army (20 Nov 44 – 21 Mar 45),* p. 4.
55. Ellis and Warhurst, *The Defeat of Germany,* pp. 257–63.
56. *MS # B-084 First Parachute Army (20 Nov 44 – 21 Mar 45),* pp. 9–10
57. *MS # B-368 6th Parachute Division (19 Nov 44 – 10 May 45),* pp. 12–13.
58. Ibid., p. 13.
59. Ibid.
60. Ibid.
61. Ellis and Warhurst, *The Defeat of Germany,* p. 271.
62. Ibid., pp. 275–6.
63. *MS # B-084 First Parachute Army (20 Nov 44 – 21 Mar 45),* pp. 2–3.
64. Ibid., p. 4.
65. *Report No. 19 Operation 'PLUNDER',* p. 25.
66. Ibid.
67. Ibid, p. 5.
68. Whiting, *Hunters from the Sky,* p. 215.
69. *MS # B-084 First Parachute Army (20 Nov 44 – 21 Mar 45),* pp. 10–11.
70. Ibid., pp. 12–13.
71. Ibid., pp. 13–14.
72. Ibid., p. 16.
73. *MS # B-368 6th Parachute Division (19 Nov 44 – 10 May 45),* pp. 13–14.
74. *MS # B-084 First Parachute Army (20 Nov 44 – 21 Mar 45),* p. 16.
75. *Report No. 19 Operation 'PLUNDER',* p. 21.

Chapter 10: *Holland: Last Battles*

1. *MS # B-580 6th Parachute Division*, p. 1.
2. *Report No. 19 Operation 'PLUNDER'*, p. 21; *MS # B-580 6th Parachute Division*, p. 2.
3. *MS # B-580 6th Parachute Division*, pp. 17–19.
4. *MS # B-354 First Parachute Army (28 Mar – 9 Apr 45) by Guenther Blumentritt, General der Infanterie a.D.*, p. 8.
5. Ibid., p. 9.
6. Ibid., pp. 10–12.
7. Ibid., p. 12.
8. Morelock, 'Walk Where They Fought: Teutoburger Wald. Arminius vs. Varus, 9 AD', *Armchair General*, November 2005, p. 82.
9. *MS # B-354 First Parachute Army*, p. 15.
10. Ibid., pp. 15–17.
11. Ibid., pp. 21–22.
12. *MS # B-580 6th Parachute Division*, p. 3.
13. Ibid.
14. Canadian Army Headquarters, *Report No. 32: The Concluding Phase of Operations by the First Canadian Army. Part I: The Operations of First Canadian Army, 2–11 April 1945*, pp. 53–4.
15. *MS # B-580 6th Parachute Division*, p. 4.
16. *Report No. 32: The Concluding Phase of Operations by the First Canadian Army*, p. 54.
17. Ibid., p. 54.
18. *Report No. 32: The Concluding Phase of Operations by the First Canadian Army*, pp. 55–6.
19. 'Busch, Ernst', in Boatner, *The Biographical Dictionary of World War II*, pp. 70–1.
20. *MS # B-354 First Parachute Army*, p. 8.
21. *MS # B-580 6th Parachute Division*, pp. 4–5.
22. Ibid., pp. 5–6.
23. Ibid., pp. 6–7.
24. Ibid., p. 8.
25. Ibid., p. 9.
26. Ibid., pp. 9–10.
27. Warlimont, *Inside Hitler's Headquarters*, p. 497.
28. Dupuy and Martell, *Great Battles of the Eastern Front*, pp. 219–22.
29. *MS # B-580 6th Parachute Division*, pp. 10–11.
30. Stacey, *Report No. 56. The German Surrender, May 1945*, p. 126.
31. Ibid., pp. 126, 128.
32. Ibid.
33. See for example Hart, *Montgomery and 'Colossal Cracks'*, and Buckley, *British Armour in the Normandy Campaign*.
34. *Report No. 174: The Canadian Army Occupation Force in Germany May 1945 to June 1946*, p. 88.
35. Ibid., pp. 89–90.
36. Bessel, *Nazism and War*, p. 156.
37. Villahermosa, 'Interview with Hanna and Jürgen Witzig'.
38. *The Canadian Army Occupation Force in Germany*, p. 40.
39. Ibid.
40. Villahermosa, 'Interview with Hanna and Jürgen Witzig'.
41. Ibid.
42. *The Canadian Army Occupation Force in Germany*, p. 41.
43. Ibid.
44. Villahermosa, 'Interview with Rudi Valentine', 27 August 2005.
45. Jürgen Witzig to Gilberto Villahermosa, 'Rudolf Witzig', 23 August 2005.
46. Ibid.
47. Ibid.

48. Witzig, 'Rudolf Witzig', *Ahnen-tafel Witzig mit Anlagen.*

Chapter 11: *The New German Army and Retirement*
1. 'Richard Heidrich', in Kurowski, *Knights of the Wehrmacht*, p. 83.
2. 'Gerhart Schirmer', in Kurowski, *Knights of the Wehrmacht*, p. 203.
3. 'Bruno Oswald Bräuer', in Kurowski, *Knights of the Wehrmacht*, p. 33.
4. Beevor, *Crete*, p. 342.
5. Ibid., p. 235.
6. Ibid., p. 236.
7. 'Kurt Student' in Hildebrand, *Die Generale der Deutschen Luftwaffe*, Vol. 3, pp. 363–5.
8. 'Hermann Bernhard Ramcke', in Hildebrand, *Die Generale der Deutschen Luftwaffe*, Vol. 3, pp. 76–7; Boatner, *The Biographical Dictionary of World War II*, p. 444; Whiting, *Hunters from the Sky*, p. 175n.
9. 'Walter Barenthin', in Hildebrand, *Die Generale der Deutschen Luftwaffe*, vol. 1, pp. 45–6.
10. 'Friedrich Freiherr von Broich', in Hildebrand, *Die Generale des Heeres 1921–1945*, vol. 2, pp. 279–80.
11. 'Alfred Schlemm', in Hildebrand, *Die Generale der Deutschen Luftwaffe*, vol. 3, pp. 192–3.
12. 'Eugen Meindl', in Hildebrand, *Die Generale der Deutschen Luftwaffe*, vol. 2, pp. 372–3.
13. 'Hermann Plocher', in Hildebrand, *Die Generale der Deutschen Luftwaffe*, Band, pp. 46–46
14. 'Friedrich August Freiherr von der Heydte', in Kurowski, *Knights of the Wehrmacht*, pp. 95–6.
15. Beevor, *Crete*, p. 342.
16. Bessel, *Nazism and War*, p. 161.
17. Jürgen Witzig to Gilberto Villahermosa 'Rudolf Witzig', 23 August 2005.
18. Villahermosa, 'Interview with Hanna and Jürgen Witzig', 14 May 2005.
19. Bessel, *Nazism and War*, p. 127 77n.
20. Ibid, p. 162.
21. Jürgen Witzig to Gilberto Villahermosa, 'Rudolf Witzig', 23 August 2005.
22. Ibid.
23. Bessel, *Nazism and War*, p. 164.
24. Ibid.
25. Ibid., p. 166.
26. Ibid., pp. 166–7.
27. Witzig, *Das Korps Fallschirm-Pionierbataillon und I./Fallschirm-Pionierregiment 21.*
28. Ibid., pp. 41–2.
29. Villahermosa, 'Meeting with Jürgen Witzig', 23 March 2006.
30. Villahermosa, 'Interview with Jürgen Witzig', 17 August 2005.
31. Ibid.
32. Villahermosa, 'Interview with Hanna and Jürgen Witzig', 14 May 2005.
33. Villahermosa, 'Interview with Jürgen Witzig', 17 August 2005.
34. Villahermosa, 'Interview with Hanna and Jürgen Witzig', 14 May 2005.
35. Forty, *Battle of Crete*, p. 165,
36. Witzig, 'Fallschirmjäger-Denkmal in Chania "außer Deinst gestellt"', *Der Deutsche Fallschirmjäger*, No. 3, 2001, p. 14.
37. Ibid.
38. Ibid.
39. Ibid.
40. *Gespräck mit Rudolf Witzig Am 14 September 2001.*
41. Witzig, 'Fallschirmjäger-Denkmal in Chania "außer Deinst gestellt"', p. 14.
42. Villahermosa, 'Interview with Jürgen Witzig', 17 August 2005.
43. Ibid.
44. Ibid.

BIBLIOGRAPHY

Witzig Family Interviews
'Interview with Colonel Jürgen Witzig, Headquarters CIMIC Group North', Budel,
   The Netherlands, 27 May 2004. Colonel Witzig possesses all his father's wartime
   papers, including planning files and after-action reports, unit and personal
   diaries, maps and photographs, and articles written by and about his father, all
   of which he graciously made available to the author prior to depositing them in
   the Bundesarchiv.
'Interview with Colonel Jürgen Witzig', Budel, 21 July 2004
'Interview with Colonel Jürgen Witzig', Budel, 31 March 2005
'Interview with Hanna and Jürgen Witzig', Mainz, Germany, 14 May 2005
'Interview with Jürgen Witzig', Budel, 17 August 2005
'Meeting with Jürgen Witzig', Brunssum, The Netherlands, 23 March 2006

Other Interviews
'Interview with Siegfried Josef Gerstner', Wallerfangen, Germany, 27 August 2005.
   Gerstner won the Knight's Cross at Brest.
'Interview with Karl-Heinz Hammerschlag', Wallerfangen, Germany, 27 August
   2005. Hammerschlage served in Witzig's battalion in France and Lithuania.
'Interview with Matthias Scheurer', Wallerfangen, Germany, 27 August 2005.
   Scheurer served with Witzig's battalion in North Africa.
'Interview with Rudi Valentine', Wallerfangen, Germany, 27 August 2005. Valentine
   fought as a parachute engineer at Monte Cassino.

Private Correspondence
Jürgen Witzig to Gilberto Villahermosa, 23 August 2005

Rudolf Witzig Collection
*Sturmabteilung Koch der Flieger-Division 7. Enstatehung der Sturmabteilung
   (Versuchsabteilung Friedrichshafen) und Auszug aus dem Kriegstagebuch
   (Hildesheim – Summer 1940) [Geheime Kommandosache!]*
Hauptmann Rudolf Witzig, *Verwendung von Luftlandeeinheiten zur Eninahme von
   Gibraltar* (Berlin, 1 August 1940). Translated by Barbara Seiber.
Major Rudolf Witzig, *F.Pi.11. Am Div. v. Broich E.O.,11 Januar 1943*
Major and Battalion Commander Rudolf Witzig, *F. Pi. 11. Br.B.Nr. 141/43 Betr.:
   Mannschaftsersatz. Am Div. V. Manteuffel, 13 Fev. 1943*
Rudolf Witzig, *Militärisches Leben Rudolf Witzig 1935–1974/Pensionszeit
   1974–1988*
Rudolf Witzig, *Das Korps Fallschirm-Pionierbataillon und I./Fallschirm-
   Pionierregiment 21. Januar 1942–Oktober 1944* (February 1991)
Rudolf Witzig, *Ahnen-tafel Witzig mit Anlagen* (Oberschleißheim 1994)
Rudolf Witzig, *Gespräck mit Rudolf Witzig Am 14 September 2001*

Other Papers
Militärgeschichtliches Forschungsamt, *Eben Emael un die Brücken* (Freiburg im
   Breisgau, undated)

Helmut Wenzel, *Auszug aus dem Kriegstagebuch von Helmut Wenzel Einsatz Tunesien, 16 November 1942 – 23 February 1943* (undated)

World War II Official Histories
Germany
Wilhelm Deist, Manfred Messerschmidt, Hans-Erich Volkmann, Wolfram Wette, *Germany and the Second World War*, Vol. I: *The Build-up of German Aggression* (Clarendon Press, 1990)

Klaus A. Maier, Horst Rohde, Bernd Stegemann, Hans Umbreit, *Germany and the Second World War*, Vol. II: *Germany's Initial Conquests in Europe* (Clarendon Press, 2003)

Gerhard Schrieber, Bernd Stegemann, Detlef Vogel, *Germany and the Second World War*, Vol. III: *The Mediterranean, South-east Europe, and North Africa 1939–1941* (Clarendon Press, 1995)

Horst Boog, Werner Rahn, Reinhard Stumpf, and Bernd Wegner, *Germany and the Second World War*, Vol. VI: *The Global War* (Clarendon Press, 2004)

New Zealand
D. M. Davin, *Official History of New Zealand in the Second World War 1939-45: Crete.* (The Imperial War Museum, 1953)

United Kingdom
Major L. F. Ellis, with Lt-Col A. E. Warhurst, *History of the Second World War. United Kingdom Military Series. Victory in the West*, Vol. II: *The Defeat of Germany* (HMSO 1968)

Maj-Gen I. S. O. Playfair, *History of the Second World War. United Kingdom Military Series. The Mediterranean and Middle East*, Vol. II: *The Germans Come to the Help of Their Ally (1941)* (HMSO 1956)

Maj-Gen I. S. O. Playfair *et al.*, *History of the Second World War. United Kingdom Military Series. The Mediterranean and Middle East*, Vol. IV: *The Destruction of the Axis Forces in North Africa* (HMSO 1966)

United States
Martin Blumenson, *United States Army in World War II. The European Theater of Operations. Breakout and Pursuit* (U.S. Army Center of Military History, 1961)

Hugh M. Cole, *United States Army in World War II. The European Theater of Operations. The Ardennes: Battle of the Bulge* (U.S. Army Center of Military History, 1994)

Gordon A. Harrison, *United States Army in World War II. The European Theater of Operations. Cross Channel Attack* (U.S. Army Center of Military History, 1989)

George F. Howe, *United States Army in World War II. The Mediterranean Theater of Operations. Northwest Africa. Seizing the Initiative in the West* (U.S. Army Center of Military History, 1957)

Soviet Union
D. F. Ustinov *et al.*, *Istoriya Vtoroi Mirovoi Boiny 1939–1945*, Vol. 10: *Osvobozhedenie Territorii SSSR I Evropeiskikh Stran. Voina na Tikhoi Okeane i v Azii* (Voenizdat, 1978)

Official Reports and Publications
Canada
Canadian Army Headquarters, *Report No. 19: Operation 'PLUNDER': The Canadian Participation in the Assault Across the Rhine and the Expansion of the Bridgehead by 2 Canadian Corps 23/24 March – 1 April 45* (General Staff Historical Section, 1948)

Canadian Army Headquarters, *Report No. 32: The Concluding Phase of Operations by the First Canadian Army. Part I: The Operations of First Canadian Army, 2–11 April 1945* (General Staff Historical Section, 1949)

Canadian Army Headquarters, *Report No. 39: Operations of 1 Cdn Corps in North-West Europe, 15 Mar – 5 May 1945* (General Staff Historical Section, 1950)

Canadian Army, Headquarters, *Report No. 56: The German Surrender, May 1945* (General Staff Historical Section, 1958)

Canadian Army Headquarters, *Report No. 77: The Campaign in North-West Europe (Information from German Sources)* (General Staff Historical Section, 1958)

Canadian Army Headquarters, *Report No. 174: The Canadian Army Occupation Force in Germany* (General Staff Historical Section, 1946)

Great Britain

U.K. War Office, *Handbook of the German Army* (War Office, 1940)

U.K. War Office, *Notes on the German Preparation for Invasion of the United Kingdom 2nd Edition* (War Office, 1942).

U.K. War Office, *Pocket Book of the German Army 1943* (War Office, 1943)

Lt-Gen K. A. N. Anderson, Commander-in-Chief, First Army, 'Operations in North West Africa from 8th November 1942 to 13 May 1943', Dispatch dated 7 June 1943, *Supplement to the London Gazette* (War Office, 1946)

Admiral Sir A. B. Cunningham, Commander-in-Chief Mediterranean, 'The Battle of Crete', Dispatch dated 4 August 1941, *Supplement to the London Gazette*, (War Office, 1948)

United States

Department of the Army, *Department of the Army Pamphlet No. 20-261a The German Campaign in Russia – Planning and Operations* (1955)

——, *Department of the Army Pamphlet No. 20-232 Airborne Operations. A German Appraisal* (1951)

——, *Department of the Army Publication No. 20-260 The German Campaign in the Balkans (Spring 1941)* (1953)

——, *Department of the Army Publication No. 20-271 The German Northern Theater of Operations 1940–1945* (1959)

Headquarters U.S. Army Europe, *ETHINT-31 An Interview with Reichsmarshall Hermann Goering. German Military Strategy (1939–1941)* (Historical Division, Foreign Military Studies Branch, 1948), RG 549, National Archives and Records Administration, College Park, Maryland (hereafter NARA).

——, *MS # A-250 Answers to the Questions Concerning Greece, Crete and Russia by General Warlimont, Artillery* (Historical Division, Foreign Military Studies Branch, 1946), U.S. Army Military History Institute, Carlisle, Pennsylvania (hereafter MHI).

——, *MS # A-898 Kampfhandlungen in Nordfrankreich 1944 der 6. Fallschirmjaeger Dviision. II. Teil. Kampf an der Seine und Rueckzugsbewegungen durch Nordfrankreich by Generalleutnant von Heyking* (Historical Division, Foreign Military Studies Branch, 1950), RG 549, NARA.

——, *MS # A-923 II. Teil. Nordfrankreich 25. Juli bis 14. Sept. 1944 by General der Fallschirmtruppe Eugen Meindl Komm. General des II/Fallsch. Korps* (Historical Division, Foreign Military Studies Branch, 1946), RG 549, NARA.

——, *MS # A-956 Kamfhandlungen Nordfrankreich 1944 Der 6. Fallschirmjaeger Division by Generalleutnant von Heyking* (Historical Division, Foreign Military Studies Branch 1946), RG 549, NARA.

——, *MS # A-964, MS # A-965 Report of the Chief of Staff Army Group B (25 January 1945 – 21 March 1945) by General Major Carl Wagener* (Historical Division, Foreign Military Studies Branch, 1946), U.S. Army MHI.

——, *MS # B-034 OKW War Diary (1 April – 18 December 1944) by Major Percy Ernst Schramm* (Historical Division, Foreign Military Studies Branch, undated), RG 549, NARA.

——, *MS # B-084 First Parachute Army (20 November 44 – 21 March 45) by Alfred Schlemm, General of Fallschirmtruppen a. D.* (Historical Division, Foreign Military Studies Branch, 1946), U.S. Army MHI.

——, *MS # B-270 Questions Regarding the General Strategy During the Italian Campaign by Field Marshal Kesselring And General Westphal* (Historical Division, Foreign Military Studies Branch, 1950), RG 549, NARA.

——, *MS # B-349 My Opinions with Regard to Reports 1 (MS # B-238) and 2 (MS # B-348) by General Major Heuser (Chief of General Staff of the First Army)* (Historical Division, Foreign Military Studies Branch, 1951), RG 549, NARA.

——, *MS # B-354 First Parachute Army (28 March – 9 April 45) by Guenther Blumentritt, General der Infanterie a.D.* (Historical Division, Foreign Military Studies Branch, 1947), U.S. Army MHI.

——, *MS # B-368 6th Parachute Division (19 Nov 44 – 10 May 45) by Rudolf Langhaeuser, Generalmajor a.D.* (Historical Division, Foreign Military Studies Branch, 1947), U.S. Army MHI.

——, *MS # B-381 Employment of the 16th Luftwaffen-felddivion in Holland from 1 Nov 1943 till 1 June 1944* (Historical Division, Foreign Military Studies Branch), RG 549, NARA.

——, *MS # B-580 6th Parachute Division (1 April – 10 May 1945) by Rudolf Langhaeuser, Generalmajor a. D.* (Historical Division, Foreign Military Studies Branch, 1947), U.S. Army MHI.

——, *MS # B-641 The Crete Operation by Conrad Seibt, Generalmajor a.D.* (Historical Division, Foreign Military Studies Branch), RG 549, NARA.

——, *MS # B-646 Capture of Crete (May 1941) by Julius Ringel, General der Gebirgstruppen a.D.* (Historical Division, Foreign Military Studies Branch), U.S. Army MHI.

——, *MS # B-701 Summary of Army Group B Engagements From the Middle of Oct 44 Until the Middle of Apr 45* (Historical Division, Foreign Military Studies Branch, 1947), RG 549, NARA.

——, *MS # C-065 Operation Felix by Helmuth Greiner* (Historical Division, Foreign Military Studies Branch, 1945), U.S. Army MHI.

——, *MS # C-098 Recollections of Tunisia by General Hans Jürgen von Arnim* (Historical Division, Foreign Military Studies Branch, 1951), U.S. Army MHI.

——, *MS # C-100 Der Deutsche Feldzug in Griechenland Und Auf Kreta by B. Mueller-Hillebrand Generalmajor a.D.* (Historical Division, Foreign Military Studies Branch, 1951), U.S. Army MHI.

——, *MS # D-066 Situation in OKW (October – December 1942) by Generalmajor Christian Eckhard* (Historical Division, Foreign Military Studies Branch, 3 March 1947), U.S. Army MHI.

——, *MS # D-094 Preparations for the Capture of Malta by Conrad Seibt General Major* (Historical Division, Foreign Military Studies Branch, 1947), U.S. Army MHI.

——, *MS # D-120 The Development of the Situation in North Africa by Walter Nehring, General der Panzer-Truppe* (Historical Division, Foreign Military Studies Branch, 1947), U.S. Army MHI, Carlisle.

——, *MS # D-147 The First Phase of the Battle in Tunisia by Walter Nehring, General der Panzer-Truppe a. D.* (Foreign Military Studies Branch,1947). U.S. Army MHI.

——, *MS # P-105 Evaluation of German Airborne Operations by Hellmuth Reinhardt, Generalmajor a. D.* (Historical Division, Foreign Military Studies Branch, undated), U.S. Army MHI.

——, *Kesselring's Plan for the Invasion of Malta, 31 May 1942*, RG 549, NARA.

——, *The Future of German Paratrooper and Airborne Operations. A Report Addressed to Goering by General Student, 10 November 1942*, RG 549, NARA.

U.S. Army Center of Military History, *Attack on Eben Emael by Oberst a. D. Rudolf Witzig*, Oberschleißheim, West Germany, 10 October 1988, HRC 2, 314.8 Interviews (Office of the Chief of Military History)

U.S. War Department, 'Parachutists (German)', *Intelligence Bulletin*, (U.S. Intelligence Service, 1942)

'Parachute Troops (German)', *Intelligence Bulletin*, (U.S. Military Intelligence Service, 1943)

'Rations as a Factor in Parachute Efficiency', *Intelligence Bulletin*, (U.S. Intellligence Service, 1944)

'German Antitank Weapons', *Intelligence Bulletin*, (U.S. Intelligence Service, 1944)

'What Jerry Thinks of Us . . . and Himself', *Intelligence Bulletin*, (U.S. Intelligence Service, 1944)

'Fortress Battalions . . . and How They Are Used', *Intelligence Bulletin*, (U.S. Intelligence Service, 1945)

'Von Rundstedt Explains', *Intelligence Bulletin*, (U.S. Intelligence Service, 1946)

'German Horse Cavalry and Transport', *Intelligence Bulletin* (U.S. Military Intelligence Service, 1946).

U.S. War Department, 'Junkers 52', *Tactical and Technical Trends*, No. 31, 12 August 1943.

——, 'Construction of a German Battalion Defense Area in North Africa', *Tactical and Technical Trends*, No. 31, 12 August 1943.

——, 'Army Medical Conditions in North Africa', *Tactical and Technical Trends*, No. 33, 9 September 1943.

——, 'German Infantry Division Cut to Meet Manpower Shortage', *Tactical and Technical Trends*, no. 51, October 1944.

——, 'Germany's Replacement Army May be in Last Battle', *Tactical and Technical Trends*, No. 51, October 1944.

——, 'Notes on German Division Artillery', *Tactical and Technical Trends*, No. 6, 27 August, 1942

——, 'West Wall, Springboard of 1940, Assumes Defensive Role', *Tactical and Technical Trends*, No. 51, October 1944.

——, *Technical Manual TM-E 30-451 Handbook on German Military Forces* (War Department, 15 March 1945)

——, *Technical Manual TM 30-430 Handbook on U.S.S.R. Military Forces* (War Department, 15 November 1945)

Books

Peter D. Antill and Howard Gerrard, *Crete 1941: Germany's Lightning Airborne Assault* (Osprey, 2005)

Michael Armitage, *et al.*, *World War II Day by Day* (Dorling Kindersley, 2001)

Rick Atkinson, *An Army at Dawn: The War in North Africa, 1942–1943* (Henry Holt, 2002).

Heintz Austermann, *Von Eben Emael bis Edewechter Damm. Fallschirmjäger Fallschirmpioniere. Berichte und Dokumente über den Einsatz der Fallshirmpioniere* (Verlag der Fallschirmpionier-Gemeinschaft, 1971)

Correlli Barnett, *Hitler's Generals* (Grove Weidenfeld, 1989)

Antony Beevor, *Crete: The Battle and the Resistance* (Westview Press, 1994).

——, *Stalingrad: The Fateful Siege: 1942–1943* (Viking, 1998)

Antony Beevor and Luba Vinogradova, *A Writer at War: Vasily Grossman with the Red Army 1941–1945* (Pantheon, 2005)

Nicolaus von Below, *At Hitler's Side: The Memoirs of Hitler's Luftwaffe Adjutant 1937–1945* (Greenhill, 2001)

Richard Bessel, *Nazism and War* (Weidenfeld & Nicolson, 2004)

Mark M. Boatner, *The Biographical Dictionary of World War II* (Presidio, 1996).

Dermot Bradley, Karl-Friedrich Hildebrand, Markus-Rövekamp, *Deutschlands Generale und Admirale. Die General des Heeres 1921–1945. Die militärischen Werdegänge der Generale, sowie der Ärzte, Veterinäre, Intendanten, Richter und Ministerialbeamten im Generalsrang*, Vols 1–4. (Biblio Verlag 1993–6)

E. H. Brongers, *The Battle for the Hague, 1940* (Aspekt, 2004)

Alex Buchner, *Weapons and Equipment of the German Fallschirmtruppe 1935–1945* (Schiffer, 1996)

John Buckley, *British Armour in the Normandy Campaign* (Frank Cass, 2004)

Charles Burdick and Hans-Adolf Jacobsen, eds., *The Halder War Diary 1939–1942* (Presido, 1988)

Paul Carell, *Scorched Earth: The Russian-German War 1943–1944* (Schiffer, 1994)

Winston S. Churchill, *The Second World War*, Vol. 3: *The Grand Alliance* (Houghton Mifflin, 1950)

——, *The Second World War*, Vol. 4: *The Hinge of Fate* (Houghton Mifflin, 1950),

Le Comité de l'Amicale du Fort D'Eben-Emael, *Ceux du Fort D'Eben Emael* (FLEMAL 1995)

Robert Cowley, ed., *The Cold War: A Military History* (Random House, 2005)

H. P. Dabrowski, *Messerschmitt Me 321/323: Giants of the Luftwaffe* (Schiffer, 1994)

Gregor Dallas, *1945: The War That Never Ended* (Yale UP, 2005)

I. C. B. Dear and M. R. D. Foot, eds., *The Oxford Companion to World War II* (OUP, 1995)

James M. Diehl, *The Thanks of the Fatherland: German Veterans After the Second World War* (University of North Carolina Press, 1993)

Simon Dunstan and Hugh Johnson, *Fort Eben Emael: The Key to Hitler's Victory in the West* (Osprey, 2005)

Luc De Vos, *La Belgique et la Seconde Guerre Mondiale* (Racine, 2004)

T. N. Dupuy and Paul Martell, *Great Battles of the Eastern Front: The Soviet–German War 1941–1945* (Bobbs-Merril, 1982)

Henrik Eberle and Matthias Uhl, eds., *The Hitler Book: The Secret Dossier Prepared for Stalin From the Interrogations of Hitler's Personal Aides* (Public Affairs, 2005)

Chris Ellis, *7th Flieger Division – Student's Fallschirmjäger Elite* (Ian Allan, 2002)

Major Gerhard Engel, *At the Heart of the Reich: The Secret Diary of Hitler's Army Adjutant* (Greenhill, 2005).

Richard Evans, *The Coming of the Third Reich* (2003)

——, *The Third Reich in Power* (2005)

——, *The Third Reich at War* (2008)

Anthony Farrar-Hockley, *Student* (Ballantine, 1973)

Aalther-Peer Fellgiebel, *Elite of the Third Reich: The Recipients of the Knight's Cross of the Iron Cross 1939–45, A Reference* (Helion, 2003)

Peter Fleming, *Operation Sea Lion* (Pan, 2003)

George Forty, *Battle of Crete* (Ian Allan, 2001)

Stephen G. Fritz, *Endkampf: Soldiers, Civilians, and The Death of the Third Reich* (University of Kentucky Press, 2004)

Karl-Heinz Frieser, *The Blitzkrieg Legend: The 1940 Campaign in the West* (Naval Institute Press, 2005)

Klaus Gerbet and David Johnston, eds., *Generalfeldmarschall Fedor von Bock: The War Diary 1939–1945* (Schiffer, 1996)

Martin Gilbert, *The Second World War: A Complete History* (Henry Holt, 1989)

Walter Goerlitz, *History of the German General Staff 1657–1945* (Barnes & Noble, 1995)

Helmuth Greiner and Percy Ernst Schramm, *Kriegstagebuch des Oberkommandos der Wehrmacht (Wehrmachtführungsstab) 1940–1945* (Bernard & Graefe, 1982), Vols. 1–8.

Peter Harclerode, *Para! Fifty Years of the Parachute Regiment* (Arms and Armour, 1992).

——, *Wings of War. Airborne Warfare 1918–1945* (Weidenfeld & Nicolson, 2005)

Stephen A. Hart, *Montgomery and 'Colossal Cracks: The 21st Army Group in Northwest Europe, 1944–45* (Praeger, 2000)

Stephen Hart, Russell Hart and Matthew Hughes, *The German Soldier in World War II* (Spellmount, 2000)

Max Hastings, *Armageddon: The Battle for Germany, 1944–1945* (Alfred A. Knopf, 2004)

Werner Haupt, *Army Group Center: The Wehrmacht in Russia 1941–1945* (Schiffer, 1997)

Holger H. Herwig, *The First World War: Germany and Austria-Hungary 1914–1918* (Arnold, 1997)

Robin Higham and Stephan J. Harris, eds., *Why Air Forces Fail: The Anatomy of Defeat* (University of Kentucky Press, 2006)

Karl Friedrich Hildebrand, *Die Generale der deutschen Luftwaffe 1935–1945*, 3 vols. (Biblio Verlag, 1990–2)

James Holland, *Fortress Malta: An Island Under Siege 1940–1943* (Orion, 2003)

Irmgard A. Hunt, *On Hitler's Mountain: Overcoming the Legacy of a Nazi Childhood* (HarperCollins, 2005)

Michael H. Kater, *The Nazi Party: A Social Profile of Members and Leaders 1919–1945* (OUP, 1983)

——, *Hitler Youth* (Harvard UP, 2004)

David M. Kennedy, ed., *The Library of Congress World War II Companion* (Simon & Schuster, 2007)

Tim Kirk, *Cassell's Dictionary of Modern German History* (Cassell, 2002)

MacGregor Knox, 'The Italian Armed Forces 1940–43', in Allan R. Millet and Williamson Murray, eds., *Military Effectiveness*, Vol. III: *The Second World War* (Unwin Hyman, 1988)

——, *Hitler's Italian Allies. Royal Armed Forces, Fascist Regime, and the War of 1940–1943* (CUP, 2000)

G. F. Krivosheev, *Soviet Casualties and Combat Losses in the Twentieth Century* (Greenhill, 1997)

I. E. Krupchenko, *et al.*, *Sovetskie Tankovye Voiska 1941–1945* (Voenizdat, 1973)

Volkmar Kühn, *Deutsche Fallschirmjäger im Zweiten Weltkrieg. Grüne Teufel im Sprungeinsatz und Erdkamp 1939–1945* (Motorbuch Verlag, 1974)

——, *German Paratroopers in World War II* (Ian Allan, 1978)

Franz Kurowski, *Knights of the Wehrmacht: Knight's Cross Holders of the Fallschirmjäger* (Schiffer, 1995)

——, *Jump into Hell: German Paratroopers in World War II* (Stackpole, 2010)

Jean de Lagarde, *German Soldiers of World War II* (Histoire & Collections, 2005)

Louis P. Lochner, ed. and trans., *The Goebbels Diaries* (Doubleday, 1948)

James Lucas, *Storming Eagles: German Airborne Forces in World War Two* (Arms and Armour, 1988).

Callum MacDonald, *The Lost Battle: Crete 1941* (Macmillan, 1993).

Thomas McGuirl and Uwe Feist, *Fallschirmjäger* (Feist Publications, 1993)

Kenneth Macksey, *Kesselring: German Master Strategist of the Second World War* (Greenhill, 1996)

Chris McNab, *German Paratroopers: The Illustrated History of the Fallschirmjäger in World War II* (MBI, 2000)

John Man, *The D-Day Atlas: The Definitive Account of the Allied Invasion of Normandy* (Facts on File, 1994)

Roger Manvell and Heinrich Fraenkel, *Goering* (Greenhill, 2005)

Evan Mawdsley, *Thunder in the East: The Nazi-Soviet War 1941–1945* (Hodder Arnold, 2005)

Catherine Merridale, *Ivan's War: The Red Army 1939–45* (Faber and Faber, 2005)

Henry Metelmann, *A Hitler Youth: Growing Up in Germany in the 1930s* (Spellmount, 2004)

Allan R. Millet and Williamson Murray, eds., *Military Effectiveness*, Vol. III, *The Second World War* (Unwin Hyman, 1988)

James E. Mrazek, *The Fall of Eben Emael: The Daring Airborne Assault That Sealed the Fate of France, May 1940* (Ballantine, 1970).

Burkhart Müller-Hillebrand, *Das Heer 1933–1945*, (E. S. Mittler, 1954)

Jean-Ives Nasse, *Green Devils! German Paratroopers 1939–45*, (Histoire & Collections, 1997)

——, *Fallschirmjäger in Crete: German Parachutists in Crete 20 May 1941 – June 1941* (Histoire & Collections, 2002)

Jeremy Noakes, *Nazism 1919–1945*, Vol. 4: *The German Home Front in World War II: A Documentary Reader* (University of Exeter Press, 1998).

Heinz J. Nowarra, *German Gliders in World War II: DFS 230, DFS 331, Go 242, Go 345, Ka 430, Me 321, Ju 322* (Schiffer, 1991)

T. B. H. Otway, *The Second World War 1939–1945: Army Airborne Forces* (Imperial War Museum, 1990)

Rüdiger Overmans, *Deutsche militärische Verluste im Zweiten Weltkrieg* (R. Oldenbourg, 2004)

R. J. Overy, *The Penguin Historical Atlas of the Third Reich* (Penguin: 1996)

——, *Interrogations: The Nazi Elite in Allied Hands, 1945* (Viking, 2001)

Matthew Parker, *Monte Cassino: The Story of the Hardest-Fought Battle of World War Two* (Headline, 2003)

Martin Pegg, *Luftwaffe Transport Units 1937–1943. Volume I* (Classic, 2006)

Martin Pöppel, *Heaven & Hell: The War Diary of a German Paratrooper* (Spellmount, 1988)

Bruce Quarrie, *Fallschirmjäger: German Paratroopers 1935–45* (Osprey, 2001)

——, *German Airborne Divisions. Blitzkrieg 1940-1941* (Osprey, 2004)

——, *German Airborne Divisions: Mediterranean Theatre 1942–45* (Osprey, 2005)

Bruce Quarrie and Mike Chappell, *German Airborne Troops 1939–45* (Osprey, 1983)

——, *The Rise and Fall of the German Air Force 1933–1945* (St Martin's, 1983)

Kevin Conley Ruffner, *Luftwaffe Field Divisions 1941–1945* (Osprey, 1990)

Percy Ernst Schramm, *Hitler: The Man and Military Leader* (Quadrangle Books, 1971)

William L. Shirer, *The Rise and Fall of the Third Reich* (Fawcett Crest, 1983)

Dennis Showalter, *Patton and Rommel: Men of War in the Twentieth Century* (Berkley Caliber, 2005)

C. P. Stacey, *The Canadian Army 1939–1945: An Official History* (Edmond Cloutier, 1948)

Hans-Martin Stimpel, *Die deutsche Fallschirmtruppe 1942–1945. Einsätze auf Kriegsschauplätzen im Süden* (E. S. Mittler & Sohn, 1998)

——, *Die deutsche Fallschirmtruppe 1942–1945. Einsätze auf Kriegsschauplätzen im Osten und Westen* (E. S. Mittler & Sohn, 2001)

Fredrick Taylor, *Dresden: Tuesday, February 13, 1945* (HarperCollins, 2004)

Hugh Trevor-Roper, ed., *Final Entries 1945: The Diaries of Joseph Goebbels* (G. P. Putnam's Sons, 1978),

——, ed., *Hitler's War Directives 1939–1945* (Birlinn, 2004)

Gerd R. Ueberschär and Winfried Vogel, *Dienen und Verdienen: Hitlers Geschenke an seine Eliten* (S. Fischer, 2000)

René Vliegen, *Fort Eben Emael* (Maastricht: 1993)

Baron F. A. von der Heydte, *Daedalus Returned* (Hutchinson, 2001)

Walter Warlimont, *Inside Hitler's Headquarters 1939–1945* (Presidio, 1990)

Gerhard L. Weinberg, *A World at Arms: A Global History of World War II* (CUP, 2005)

Peter Wende, *A History of Germany* (Palgrave MacMillan, 2005)

Wolfram Wette, *The Wehrmacht: History, Myth, Reality* (Harvard University Press, 2006)

Charles Whiting, *Hunters from the Sky: The German Parachute Corps, 1940–1945* (Cooper Square Press, 2001)

Gordon Williamson, *Knight's Cross and Oak-Leaves Recipients 1941–1945* (Osprey, 2005)

Martin Windrow and Michael Roffe, *Luftwaffe Airborne and Field Units* (Osprey, 1972)

World War II Day by Day (Dorling Kindersley, 2001)

World War II Decisive Battles of the Soviet Army (Progress Publishers, 1984)

Harry Yeide, *The Longest Battle, September 1944 to February 1945: From Aachen to the Roer and Across* (Zennith Press, 2005)

Niklas Zetterling, *Normandy 1944: German Military Organization, Combat Power and Organizational Effectiveness* (J. J. Fedorowicz, 2000)

Earl F. Ziemke and Magna E. Bauer, *Moscow to Stalingrad: Decision in the East* (Military Heritage Press, 1988)

Mark Zuehlke, *Terrible Victory: First Canadian Army and the Scheldt Estuary Campaign, September 13 – November 6, 1944* (Douglas & McIntyre, 2007)

Magazine Articles

'Eine Insel wird aus der Luft erobert', *Der Deutsche Fallschirmjäger*, No. 5, May 1961, pp. 5–7.

'Bald finden sie die ewige Ruhe. Die toten Kreta-Kämpfer warten in einem kretischen Kloster', *Der Deutsche Fallschirmjäger*, No. 5, May 1961, p. 15.

D. M. Davin, 'Battle of Crete, Phase 1', *History of the Second World War* (Marshall Cavendish, 1972), Part 18, p. 486.

Anthony Farrar-Hockley, 'The Follow-Up to Torch', *History of the Second World War* (Marshall Cavendish, 1974) Vol. 3, No. 41.

Jerry D. Morelock, 'Walk Where They Fought: Teutoburger Wald. Arminius vs. Varus, 9 A.D.', *Armchair General*, November 2005, pp. 80–7.

Richard Rule, 'Göring at Nuremburg', *WWII History*, July 2005, pp 38–45.

F. A. von der Heydte, 'Crete: The German Viewpoint', *History of the Second World War* (Marshall Cavendish, 1972), Part 18, p. 502.

Rudolf Witzig, 'Die Einnahme von Eben-Emael', *Wehrkunde*, May 1945.

——, 'Albert-Kanal und Eben Emael', *Der Deutsche Fallschirmjäger*, No. 9, September 1960, pp. 8–10.

——, 'Albert-Kanal und Eben Emael', *Der Deutsche Fallschirmjäger*, No. 10, October 1960, pp. 8–10.

——, 'Albert-Kanal und Eben-Emael', *Der Deutsche Fallschirmjäger*, No. 1, January 1961, pp. 11–12.

——, 'Coup from the air: the capture of Fort Eben Emael', *History of the Second World War*, Second Edition, Part 4 (Marshall Cavendish, 1973), pp. 106–11.

——, 'Fallschirmjäger-Denkmal in Chania »außer Deinst gestellt«, *Der Deutsche Fallschirmjäger*, No. 3, March 2001, p. 14.

INDEX

Aachen, 40, 53, 58, 179
Abbeville, 70, 166
Abraham, Gen der Inf
  Erich, 184
Ackermann, Lt, 174
Albert, Lt von, 159, 169,
  174
Albert Canal, 36, 38, 39,
  41, 42, 48, 51, 58, 60,
  64, 67, 71, 85, 106,
  178
Algeria, 121, 126, 139,
  140, 153
Algiers, 121, 123, 130
Altman, Lt Gustav, 45,
  57, 64
Anderson, Lt Gen K.,
  120, 130, 131, 133,
  136, 156, 157
Antwerp, 176, 178, 179,
  191
Ardennes, 179, 189, 191,
  192, 198, 203, 223
Arendt, Lt, Ernst, 52
Arnhem, 188, 194, 202
Arnim, GenObst Jürgen
  von, 129, 138–9,
  147–8, 153–4, 156
Athens, 89, 119, 124
Aubin Neufchâteau,
  69–70
Australian Army, 84, 96,
  97

Barenthin, GenMaj
  Walter, 118, 128, 222
Bartels, Dr, 124, 145
Bastogne, 108, 191
Béja, 131, 153, 154
Belgium, vii, xix, 24, 29,
  34–7, 39, 42, 45, 56,
  62, 65–7, 69, 114, 178,
  185, 236
  Army, 65, 66
  Lower Meuse Region,
    38

2nd Grenadier Regt,
  38, 55
7th Inf Div, 38
18th Inf Regt, 38
20th Mot Arty Regt,
  39
105th Arty Btn, 39
Bizerta, xviii, 124–8,
  130–2, 134, 137, 139,
  141, 156
Blaskowitz, GenObst
  Johannes, 183, 204,
  210
Blücher, Rfmn Hans Graf
  von, 99
Blücher, Pvt Leberecht
  Graf von, 99
Blücher, Lt Wolfgang
  Graf von, 98
Blumentritt, Gen der Inf
  Günther, 184, 204,
  205, 206, 210
Bohn, Rfmn, 124, 127,
  135, 136
Bräuer, Bruno Oswald,
  21, 42, 44, 220
Braun, Lt, 124, 159
Braunschweig, 30, 32,
  72, 109
Broich, GenLt Friedrich
  Freiherr von, 126, 127,
  131, 137, 223
Bulgaria, 80, 175
Bulow, Victor von, 13
Bundeswehr, 177, 219,
  224, 227, 228, 229,
  230–2, 237
  7th Engineer Btn, 228
  140th Engineer Btn,
    232
  Engineer School, 231
Busch, FM Ernst, 210

Canada, 158, 190
  First Canadian Army,
    179, 186, 190, 195,

201, 202, 210, 215
  I Can Corps, 192, 202,
    214
  II Can Corps, 190, 195,
    203, 206, 215, 216
  1st Inf Div, 202, 203
  2nd Inf Div, 196, 203
  3rd Inf Div, 196, 203
  4th Armd Div, 190,
    196, 208, 210
  5th Armd Div, 202,
    203, 210, 212
  1st Armd Bde, 202
Canal North, xviii, 42,
  60, 61
Canal South, 62
Canea, 81, 83, 88, 90,
  94, 103, 233
Churchill, Winston, xv,
  102,107
Cleve, 189, 195, 196
Conrad, Lt, 124
Corinth Canal, 81, 166
Corsica, 120, 121
Crerar, Gen Henry, 190,
  198, 202, 215
Crete, vii, xvi, xvii, 24,
  29, 69, 74, 80–9, 93–9,
  101, 102, 104–9, 112,
  114, 116–17, 123, 166,
  183–4, 187, 219–20,
  226, 229, 233–4, 236
Cunningham, Admiral
  Sir Andrew, 84, 85, 96
Cyprus, 101, 102
Czechoslovakia, 31, 47

Deichmann, Gen Paul,
  140
Delica, Lt Egon, 49
Der Deutsche Fallschirm-
  jäger, 233, 236
Dessau, 48, 114, 118,
  119
Djebel Abiod, 128, 131,
  132, 133, 154, 159

Djebel, Azag, 140
Djefna, 134, 135, 141, 152, 153, 160
Dönitz, Adm Karl, 214
Dresden, 7, 19, 143

East Prussia, vii, 31, 138, 163–6, 167, 168, 176, 193, 217
Eastern Front, 107, 110, 112, 157, 161, 164, 165, 174, 175, 213, 219, 223
Eben Emael, vii, xv–xvi, xviii, xix, xx, 34–45, 47–55, 57–8, 60–1, 63, 65–74, 76, 85, 90, 106, 109, 114, 123–4, 136, 154, 219, 229–30, 232, 234–7
Eckhard, GenMaj Christian, 122
Eisenhower, Gen Dwight D., 108, 120, 191, 198
El Alamein, 116, 119, 121, 122, 134, 152, 174
Elbert, Capt, 159
Elson, Capt, 142–3
Emmerich, 177, 196, 200, 203, 232
Engel, Maj Gerhard, 181, 182
Erdmann, GenMaj Hans, 195
Ernst, Lt, 124

Fallschirmschule, 21
Feigl, Corp, 125, 127, 139, 140, 152
Foertsch, Gen der Inf Hermann, 181
Fortress Holland, 67, 214
France, vii, viii, xvi, xvii, xix, 8, 34, 67, 70, 120, 121, 162–4, 166–7, 176, 178, 183, 185, 204, 222, 226
Army, 121
 Corps d'Afrique, 153
 Foreign Legion, 142
 Air Force, 121
French Resistance, 162, 227
Freyberg, Gen Sir Bernard, 85, 97, 226
Friedrich, Lt, 140
Fromme, Lt, 171, 174

Fuchs, Col, 189, 211, 212, 213

Gabès, 127, 131
Gafsa, 131
German Cross in Gold, xvi, 59, 183, 187, 219
German Paratrooper Association, 226, 232–3
Germany, viii, xv, xvi–xviii, xix, 1–3, 6, 8, 9, 11, 13–15, 19–23, 28, 30–3, 37, 41, 47, 58, 67, 72, 78–80, 94, 98, 105, 109–11, 115, 121–3, 131, 143, 145, 149, 151, 152, 156, 158, 160–2, 165, 175, 176, 178–80, 187, 195, 201–3, 204, 209, 215, 216, 218, 219, 221–6, 228–9, 233, 234, 236
Aircraft
 BV-222, 123, 126
 DFS 230, 49, 53–55
 DFS 232, 116
 Do-23, 28
 Go-241, 116
 He-111, 28, 116, 118
 Ju-52, xxi, 26, 27, 34, 44, 49, 53, 58, 69, 77, 79, 83, 88, 89, 90, 91, 96, 100, 101, 116, 117, 123, 125, 126, 147
 Ju-87, 55, 59, 66
 Ju-290, 123
 Me-321/Me-323, 115, 116, 118, 123
Army, 6, 14–15, 17
 OB West, 178, 200, 204; *see also* Bundeswehr, Reichswehr
Army Groups
 B, 177, 178, 180, 206
 G, 183
 H, 183, 204, 206, 210
 Afrika, 156
 Blumentritt, 210
 Centre, 161, 164, 165, 166, 175, 182
 North, 161, 165, 193
 North Ukraine, 165
 South Ukraine, 175
 Student, 206
 Vistula, 214, 221
Armies

First, 179, 181
Second, 164
Third Pz, 164, 166, 223
Fifth Pz, 138, 145, 179, 185, 223
Sixth, 41–2, 151
Seventh, 179, 185
Twelfth, 103
Fifteenth, 179, 195
Nineteenth, 179
Twenty-Fifth, 183, 208
Pz Army Africa, 120
Corps
III Motorized, 18
XLVII Pz, 184, 196, 198, 203, 206
XLIX Inf, 77
LXIII Inf, 206
LXXXI Inf, 185
LXXXVI Inf, 184, 196, 200, 205, 206
LXXXVIII Inf, 178, 188, 208, 209, 212
LXIII Inf, 206
LXV Inf, 184
XC Army, 126
XCI Army, 206
Africa Korps, 119
Divisions
5th Mountain, 81, 83, 93, 95–6
5th Pz, 83
6th Pz, 166
6th Mountain, 83
10th Pz, 153
15th Pzgren, 198, 205
61st Inf, 45
84th Inf, 196, 205
116th Pz, 198
149th Training, 211
180th Inf, 205
190th Inf, 205
245th Inf, 205
340th Volksgren, 169
334th Inf, 147
347th Inf, 178
711th Inf, 188, 191
712th Inf, 189
719th Inf, 178, 189
von Broich, 127, 131, 137
Manteuffel, 137
Regts and brigades
6th Arty, 212
7th Pz, 128
98th Mountain Inf, 77

103rd Pz Bde, 166
151st Inf, 45
162nd Inf, 45
176th Inf, 45
240th Arty, 166
305th Inf, 34
324th Inf, 34
399th Pzgren, 166
501st Heavy Tank
  Bde, 153
1067th Pzgren, 166
Grossdeutschland, 77
Kampfgruppe *Fuchs*,
  189, 211–13
Battalions and below
  7th Engineer Platoon,
    32
  8th Assault Gun Det,
    166
  16th Engineer Btn,
    12, 18, 20
  17th Replacement
    Btn, 128
  18th Replacement
    Btn, 128
  20th Replacement
    Btn, 128
  21st Replacement
    Btn, 128
  30th MG Btn, 188,
    189
  46th MG Btn, 188
  49th MG Btn, 188
  51st Engineer Btn,
    45, 60–3
  190th Pz Btn, 128
  256th Anti-Tank Btn,
    166
  296th Flak Btn, 166
  501st Pz Btn, 128
  510th Heavy Tank
    Btn, 147
  731st Anti-Tank Det,
    166
  800th Russian Btn,
    189
SS units
  II SS Pz Corps, 188
  16th SS Police Regt,
    166
  500th SS Para Btn,
    168
Luftwaffe , vii, xv, 14,
  19–22, 24, 29–30, 32,
  34, 43, 48, 53, 58, 62,
  67, 69, 71–2, 74–6,
  79–80, 83, 85–6, 88,
  96, 99, 101, 102–3,

110–11, 114, 116,
  119, 122–3, 125–8,
  133, 147, 151, 155,
  158, 160, 164, 174,
  183–7, 189, 193–4,
  207, 211, 219–20,
  223
Luftwaffe units
  Second Air Fleet, 68,
    69, 110
  Third Air Fleet, 187
  Fourth Air Fleet, 83
  Condor Legion, 187
  V Fliegerkorps, 187
  VIII Fliegerkorps, 89,
    183, 184
  XI Fliegerkorps, 78,
    83, 93, 115, 119,
    144, 145
  3rd Fliegerdiv, 22
  4th Fliegerdiv, 187
  7th Fliegerdiv, vii,
    21–2, 29, 32, 42, 44,
    45, 74, 78, 79, 83,
    88, 94, 102, 111,
    112
  22nd Air-Landing Div,
    21, 42, 74, 78
  Hermann Göring Div,
    153, 160
  Air-Landing Assault
    Regt, 78, 79, 83, 87,
    90, 102, 112, 117,
    184
  Assault Regt *Meindl*,
    79
  Barenthin Regt, 128
  Combat Unit
    Schlemm, 183
  Gen Hermann Göring
    Regt, 21, 33, 220
  Gen Hermann Göring
    Depot Regt, 178
  Barenthin Glider Regt,
    125, 128, 135–7,
    160
  Hermann Göring
    Depot Regt, 178
  Kampfgruppe
    Heidrich, 87
  Ramcke Bde
  1st Jager Btn, *Gen
    Göring* Regt, 21
Major ground formations
  First Parachute Army,
    160, 178–9, 183–5,
    193, 195, 198–201,
    203–6, 210, 214–15,

222–3
I Para Corps, 158,
  178, 183
II Para Corps, 155,
  164, 178, 183, 196,
  201, 203, 205–6,
  208–9, 214–15, 223
Hermann Göring Para
  Pz Corps, 174
1st Para Div, 157,
  184, 186
2nd Para Div, 157,
  164, 184, 188, 193
3rd Para Div, 164,
  178, 222
4th Para Div, 157,
  186
5th Para Div, 164,
  178, 186
6th Para Div, 174,
  177–8, 184, 185,
  187–92, 194, 196–8,
  202–3, 207–16, 223,
  232
7th Para Div, 184,
  195, 196, 198, 203,
  205, 208, 209
8th Para Div, 184,
  195, 203, 205, 209
9th Para Div, 220
19th Field Div, 187
20th Para Div, 213,
  222
21st Field Div, 184
Hermann Göring Para
  Pz Div, 158, 160
Parachute Training
  Div, 213
Luftwaffe, regts etc
  1st Para, 21, 25, 30,
    33, 34, 42, 44, 98,
    111, 112, 220
  2nd Para, 112, 126,
    166
  3rd Para, 84, 111,
    112
  5th Para, 123, 128,
    153, 164, 166
  16th Para, 166, 167,
    187, 189, 193, 213
  17th Para, 187, 189,
    210, 212, 213
  18th Para, 174,
    177–8, 187–9, 198,
    201–2, 210, 212–13,
    216
  21st Para Engineer,
    162, 167, 169, 173,

174, 194, 234–5
21st Para *Lehr*, 185
31st Para, 210, 213
Ramcke Bde, 119,
　123, 145, 150, 152,
　158
Battalions etc.
1st Para Btn, 25, 27,
　34, 174
1st Para Engineer
　Btn, 145
2nd Para Engineer
　Btn, 174
3rd Para Btn, 79, 84,
　88, 89, 91, 93
6th Para Engineer
　Btn, 174
11th Para Engineer
　Btn, 114, 118, 119,
　124, 126, 128, 131,
　134, 138, 140, 142,
　147, 150, 156, 162,
　234
17th Reserve Sqn, 45
Parachute Inf Btn, 30
Parachute Engineer
　Btn, 111
Assault Gp Concrete,
　45, 58
Assault Gp Granite,
　45, 53, 55, 59
Assault Gp Iron, 45
Assault Gp Steel, 45,
　57, 64
Kampfgruppen
　Frankfurt, 145
　Heidrich, 87–88
　Stoltz, 131
　von der Heydte, 233
　Witzig, 127, 131, 133,
　139, 142, 143, 145
Sturmabteilung *Koch*,
　44, 52
Kriegsmarine, 4, 30, 34,
　75, 76, 126, 155
Volkssturm, 180, 200,
　208
Police units
　3rd Regt, 203, 210,
　211, 212, 213
　Gen Göring Regt, 21
　Zwolle Police School
　Regt, 211
Gerstner, Capt Seigfried,
　174
Gibraltar, 76–8, 80, 81,
　121
Goebbels, Joseph, 151,

156, 157
Göring, Hermann, 20–2,
　30, 32, 71–2, 75–6, 78–
　9, 82–3, 85–6, 88, 101–
　2, 118, 121, 220–1
Greece, 80–1, 84, 89–90,
　100, 104, 166, 175,
　220
Greiner, Helmuth, 76
Guderian, Gen Heinz,
　165, 181, 182

Hammerschlag, Karl-
　Heinz, 163, 174
Hardt, Lt, 124, 152, 159
Harlinghausen, Col
　Martin, 126, 127
Heidrich, GenMaj
　Richard, 30, 112, 220
Heise, Lt 124, 126, 156,
　174
Heraklion, 81, 83, 99,
　166, 233
Heyking, GenLt Rüdiger
　von, 185
Himmler, Heinrich, 182,
　208
Hitler, Adolf, xv–xvii, xix,
　2, 5–6, 8–9, 11, 14–15,
　19–20, 22, 33–4, 36,
　41–2, 49, 51, 55, 63,
　64, 68–72, 74–81, 83,
　86–7, 101–2, 106–11,
　117–18, 120–3, 137–8,
　147–8, 151–2, 154–8,
　160–1, 164–6, 168,
　175–83, 187, 191, 193,
　206, 210, 213–14, 220
Führer Directives, 180;
　No. 6, 34; No. 18, 77;
　No 51, 165
Hitler Youth, xvii–xviii,
　11, 12–14, 24
Holzmeister, Dr Hans,
　194
Höxter, 2, 3, 6, 10, 12,
　18, 20, 71, 72, 112,
　113, 143, 194, 216,
　218, 219, 224
Hünichen, Lt, 124, 133,
　134, 159

Illing, Lt, 124
Iron Cross, 21, 30, 70,
　71, 98, 150, 154, 158,
　219
Italy, 8, 79–81, 108,
　119–21,123–5, 137,

150, 151, 157–9, 179,
　183, 198, 202, 204,
　218, 232, 237
High Command, 116,
　122, 138, 148
Army, 76, 80, 115, 119,
　122, 126, 128, 130–1,
　133–5, 139, 147, 149,
　152–3, 156–8, 161
Superga Div, 128
10th *Bersaglieri* Regt,
　128
Air Force, 96, 116, 126,
　147, 150
1st *Folgore* Para Div,
　133, 134, 136
Navy, 81, 96, 126, 147
San Marco Marine Regt,
　128

Jeschonnek, GenObst
　Hans, 79, 86
Jodl, GenObst Alfred, 78,
　152
Jottrand, Maj Jean Fritz,
　39, 60–62, 65

Kanne, 36–7, 45, 55, 60
Kesselring, FM Albert,
　68, 70, 75, 110, 116,
　119, 120, 123, 126,
　138, 140, 149, 152,
　153, 154, 159, 210
Khania, 81, 83, 93
Kiess, Lt Walter, 44
Knight's Cross, xvi, 64,
　70, 71, 83, 85, 88, 99,
　152, 154, 158, 166,
　169, 183, 187, 219,
　230, 237
Koch, Col Walter, 33,
　42–7, 52, 66, 70–2, 78,
　82, 123, 127, 166
Köln-Butzweilerhof, 46,
　52, 56
Köln-Ostheim, 46, 51–2,
　56–8
Kubillus, Lt, 159, 169,
　171

Langhaüser, GenMaj
　Rudolf, 185, 186, 188,
　196, 197
Leningrad, 111, 122
Leute, Lt, 142
Libya, 118, 119, 144
Lithuania, vii, viii, xix,
　163, 165–7, 174

Löhr, GenObst Alexander, 83, 97, 102
Löhr, Robert Frett, 26
Löwe, Hermann, 5
Lüttwitz, Gen Heinrich Freiherr, 184, 196, 198

Maas River, xxi, 39, 42, 58, 68, 184, 191, 198, 202
Maastricht, 36, 40, 42, 55, 58, 178
Malta, 81, 101,102, 115–117, 121
Maleme, 81, 83, 87–90, 93, 94, 96
Manteuffel, GenMaj Hasso von, 137, 223, 154–155, 223
Mateur, 125, 131–2, 134, 139–40, 156, 159
Medjez el Bab, 131, 153
Megara, 89, 90
Meindl, Eugen, 78–9, 87–8, 93–4, 100, 164, 183–4, 196, 205–6, 208–9, 223
Meuse River, 38, 39, 42, 189, 191
Milch, FM Erhard, 25, 30, 76, 78, 86, 99, 151
Model, FM Walter, 165, 166, 178
Monte Cassino, 108, 178, 218, 232, 237
Montgomery, FM B. L., 119, 120, 156, 191, 202, 210
Morocco, 120–1,124, 140
Müller, Lt, 154
Müller-Hillerbrand, Burkhart E., 99
Mussolini, Benito, 80–1, 101, 120, 122–3

Naples, 119, 125, 139, 150
NATO, vii, 224, 227
Nehring, GenLt Walter, 126, 128, 131, 138
Netherlands, vii, xvi, xvii, xviii, 24, 29, 34, 36, 62, 67–9, 98, 106, 107, 114, 175, 177–9, 185, 186, 189, 196, 202, 203, 210, 212, 214, 215, 232
Army, 68

Princess Irene Bde, 190
New Zealand, xviii
Army, 84, 219, 226
21st Btn, 91–92
23rd Btn, 91
Field Punishment Centre, 92
Niedermeier, Lt, 124, 154
Nijmegen, 188, 191, 195, 203
Normandy, xviii, 107, 108, 112,164, 165, 178, 185, 195
Norway, 24, 34, 35, 75, 79, 107, 122

Panzerfaust, 169, 170, 171, 174, 195
Panzerschreck, 169, 170, 195
Parachutists' Ten Commandments, 86–7, 221
Petersen, GenMaj Erich, 111
Plocher, GenLt Hermann, 186–7, 189–190, 192, 195, 198, 203, 207–14, 223, 237
Poland, 30–1
Air Force, 30
Army, 215
1st Armd Div, 190, 192
6th Armd Div, 190
Polish Campaign, 30–2, 67
Pollman, Rfmn, 140
Pöppel, Martin, 25, 102
Posen Glider School, 128
Prince Albert Canal, 36, 38, 39, 41, 42, 48, 51, 58, 60, 64, 67, 71, 85, 106, 178

Ramcke, Hermann Bernard, 94, 118–19, 123, 145–6, 150, 152, 158, 174, 222, 225
Reichhelm, Col Günther, 180, 181
Reichswald, 184, 189, 195, 196, 209
Reichswehr, 3, 6, 21, 22, 30, 79, 94
Reimann, Lt, 144
Remmers, Gerda, 20, 72, 112

Rethymnon, 81, 83, 90, 233
Richthofen, GenMaj Wolfram von, 32
Ringel, Gen Julius Alfred, 81, 83–4, 89, 94–5, 97, 99, 105, 108
Romania, 80, 151, 175
Rommel, FM Erwin, 110, 116, 118, 119–21, 123, 126, 128, 133, 137, 147, 152, 153, 156, 174
Rotterdam, 62, 68, 189
Ruhr, xix, 3, 34, 202
Rundstedt, FM Gerd von, 183, 201, 227

St-Amand, 163, 225, 227
St-Lô, 164, 178
Salzwedel Parachute School, 115, 167
Sardinia, 120, 121
Schacht, Lt Gerhard, 45, 58
Schächter, Lt Martine, 45
Scherber, Major Otto, 88, 89, 96, 100
Scheurer, Matthias, 131, 134, 158
Schirmer, Lt-Col Gerhard, 166, 174, 220
Schlemm, Alfred, 183–5, 195–6, 198–201, 203–5, 223
Schmidt, Sgt Hans-Ulrich, 172
Schörner, FM Friedrich, 182
Schostack, Lt Dr, 145
Schramm, Maj Percy Ernst, 152, 178
Schumacher, Pionier, 133
Schürmann, Lt, 169
Sedjenane, 127, 153, 160
Sfax, 127, 131
shaped charges, 42, 50–1, 63
Sicily, 107–8, 117, 120, 121, 123, 125–6, 139, 156–7, 161
Sidi Bou Zid, 153
Siegfried Line, 179, 196
Simonds, Lt-Gen Guy, 190, 203, 215
Slovakia, 31, 175
S-mines, 135, 140, 143
Sousse, 127, 131

Soviet Union, xv, xvii, 6, 78, 79, 109, 120, 164, 175, 176, 193
Red Army, xvii, xviii, 110, 122, 161, 164–9, 171–3, 175–6, 182, 193, 214, 217
Third Belorussian Front, 166
1st Polish Army, 175
5th Guards Army, 166
5th Guards Tank Army, 166
35th Tank Bde, 167
Spain, 76–8
Speer, Albert, 106, 193
Stahel, GenMaj Reiner, 166
Stalin, xvii, 110, 161, 164, 175
Stalingrad, 122, 151, 152, 157
Stendal, 15, 16, 21, 22, 24, 26, 27, 30, 31, 33, 100, 101, 111, 115; airfield, 21
Stipschüz, Maj, 174
Stoltz, Lt-Col, 126
Straube, Gen Erich, 184, 200
Student, Gen Kurt, 21–3, 30–1, 33, 35, 41, 42, 44, 58, 62, 67–9, 75, 77, 86–7, 94, 98–9, 103, 105–9, 117–18, 128, 155, 164–5, 183–4, 206, 210, 221–3, 226
Suda Bay, 81, 96
Suez Canal, 116, 122
Süssmann, GenLt Wilhelm , 88, 93, 99

Teutoburger Wald, 205, 206
Tiemens, Lt, 152,174
Tietjen, Lt, 118, 158, 159
Tillman, Lt, 145
Timmermann, Lt, 154
Tolstorff, Col Theodor von, 169
Trapani, 125, 156
Treaty of Versailles, 6, 8, 9, 14, 19
Tunis, xviii, xix, xx, 120, 123, 126, 127, 128, 130, 131, 132, 134, 137, 138, 139, 142,

144, 146, 153, 156
Tunisia, 120–4, 126–31, 133,135, 136, 139, 140, 144, 145, 147, 148, 151, 153, 155, 156, 166, 174, 222, 223

United Kingdom, Army
Twenty-First Army Gp, 191, 202, 206
First Army, 130, 153, 156, 157, 185
Second Army, 179, 202
Eighth Army, 119, 120, 145, 153, 156, 158
I Corps, 190
XXX Corps, 195, 216
3rd Inf Div, 190
4th Indian Div, 156
6th Airborne Div, 164
46th Inf Div, 154
49th Inf Div, 190, 194
51st Highland Div, 190
36th Inf Bde, 134
8th Btn, Argyll and Sutherland Highlanders, 135
8th Hussars, 203
27th Hussars, 203
Commandos, 96
Royal Air Force, xv, 74, 75. 155
Royal Navy, xv, 75, 96, 97, 102
United States, xv–xviii, 19, 107, 109, 120, 136, 158, 229
Twelfth Army Gp, 191
First Army, 179, 191
Ninth Army, 195–6, 202
II Corps, 153, 156
82nd Airborne Div, 164
101st Airborne Div, 164

Vilnius, 166, 167
Vistula River, 31, 32, 193, 214, 221
Volck, Monseigneur, 237
von der Heydte, Lt Col Friedrich August Freiherr, 24, 84, 103, 105, 106, 107, 223

Waal River, 188, 191

Wadehn, GenMaj Walter, 195
Wagener, GenMaj Carl, 177
Walther, Lt, 169
Warlimont, GenLt Walter, 101, 122, 152
Weber, Sgt, 171
Weber, Lt, 146
Wehnart, Officer Candidate, 174
Weimar Republic, 3, 5, 22
Wenzel, Lt Helmut, 59, 124–7, 132–3, 142, 154, 159, 229–30, 237
Wesel River, 199, 201, 203
West Wall, 184, 200
Wittenberg, 118, 119, 147, 154, 155, 162
Wittstock Parachute School, 115, 124, 128
Witzig, Amanda, 1, 4, 5, 219
Witzig, Ernst-Georg, 155
Witzig, Hanna, iv, viii, xviii, 13, 20, 73, 112–13, 143, 194, 216–17, 218, 223–4, 232
Witzig, Col Jürgen, vii, viii, 7, 13, 71–2, 77, 218–19, 233, 224, 227–32, 236–7
Witzig, Rudolf Friedrich, 1, 4

Yugoslavia, 80

Zangen, Gen der Inf Gustav-Adolf von, 184
Ziehn, Amanda, 1